D1518870

1 Originally appeared in: Joachim,
Mitchell. "A Century of Ecological
Innovation," 2050: Designing Our
Tomorrow, Chris Luebkeman (ed.),
AD (Architectural Design), Wiley,
July/Aug. No. 236, pp. 68-73, 135.

Design with Life

**Biotech Architecture
and Resilient Cities**

After the Notre Dame Cathedral devastatingly burst into flames, people immediately reacted. They expressed great dismay for such an enduring artifact. The connection was real and heartfelt. A catastrophe of this magnitude happens every day in the natural world. Our work within this volume seeks to address and stop this constant devastation.

In the challenging environment of accelerating climate dynamics, the core discipline of architectural design is evolving, embracing new forms of action. Terreform ONE, a New York-based nonprofit, through our distinctive design practice, investigates projects through the regenerative use of natural materials and the emergent field of socio-ecological urban design. This approach to design uses actual living matter, not abstracted imitations of nature, to create new functional elements and spaces. These actions are grounded in social justice and are far-reaching in their application of digital manufacturing and maker culture. Terreform ONE tackles urgent urban, environmental, and societal concerns through the integrated use of living materials and organisms.

In this volume, Design with Life, we illustrate our nontraditional practice through various projects and prolific research, which has made a significant impact on what is increasingly recognized as socio-ecological thought. This extensive collection of projects validates these unique experimental methods.

Notable among the works are: Monarch Sanctuary, a new urban building skin type to protect butterflies from extinction; Cricket Shelter and Farm, a series of modular volumes for harvesting alternate forms of insect protein; and Mycoform biodegradable structures, invoking principles of synthetic biology to prototype 100% compostable Gen2Seat furniture.

Design with Life also documents and outlines an original direction for a changing discipline, reviewing concepts at a range of scales for metropolitan areas.

In an age where speed is everything, Terreform ONE reveals how future architecture and urban design practices can cultivate biological processes and create resilient answers to tomorrow's complex problems. Our collection of projects intentionally turns the discipline of architecture upside-down. Furthermore, we curated a selection of essays from esteemed architects, biologists, historians, artists, and educators to reframe the way in which design develops as a practice alongside science.

Design with Life explores the embryonic green-tech solutions that make a direct impact on our altered atmosphere. It's a compilation of advanced inquiry that reviews concepts in the art of biotechnology from insect food sourcing to fungi building components in cities across the globe. The planetary climate crisis has reached a penultimate state. The next impending catastrophe and its implications in design have yet to be determined.

For over a decade the works herein were developed in matchless laboratories such as New Lab, Genspace, MEx, Cooper Union Kanbar Center for Biomedical Engineering, and MIT Media Lab, each of which is filled with specialists from diverse qualifications and methodologies. These pioneering individuals refocused their efforts to discover and expand projects into larger frameworks. Terreform ONE collaborates with these labs to cultivate ideas for sustainability in energy, transportation, infrastructure, buildings, manufacturing, waste treatment, food, air quality, and water.

We have an overriding principle to design against extinction. This volume illustrates our intention by designing with life.

Mitchell Joachim and Maria Aiolova, Co-Founders of Terreform ONE
Brooklyn Navy Yard, May 17th, 2019

Alternative Practice

At this stage, we've deliberately sought to avoid maintaining a traditional architecture office. We did not desire to ceaselessly toil for a private client or affluent developer. To operate as a nonprofit group inside a cluster of other innovative tech companies marks our distinction. Our studio space is similar to a "science garage". The garage has long been the pinnacle of American invention. It's an informal anarchic space where everything can be physically manipulated. There is nothing sacred in a garage. One can also identify them as "hackerspaces". Located in an urban fringe zone, such a variegated space departs drastically from the cherished atelier models of previous centuries. We find this flowing topology the best-suited spatial arrangement for producing projects that react dynamically to undeviating, transient, or long-lasting issues.

As architectural designers confronted with a cumulative assortment of technical, manufactured, formalistic, and speculative alternatives, it becomes a formidable task to find a focus. It becomes simpler to mix one's designs from numerous sources and check their justification to the measurable and physical aspects, be it scientific or economic. This narrow-minded inclination, arguably resulting from a reaction to the utterly expansive nature of the field, from our outlook, has led to a palpable level of indifference that resulted in abundant forms of conflict within the discourse. This anesthetized state within which others function, becomes an involuntary proliferation of the banal, the exceedingly consumptive, the inconsequential, and the haphazard. If the concern is toward extending the influence of good design without surrendering its profound qualities, then it becomes essential that the discipline is infused by architects who are analytically considerate of the ramifications of their work on biological, native, regional, and global standpoints.

Architectural designers need to work within nature. The mixture of hi-tech tuning and formalistic liberties that are available to designers today can be significantly developed only through critical foundational principles in each scheme; a grounding which stresses design to pursue consequence by probing the greater and obscured natural environments of every discrete project. Such expeditions of critical discourse and attentiveness necessitate exactitude but, foregoing that, an inclination, which can be encouraged during the developmental stages of a given aspirants architecture education. Ultimately for architects, and their education, it ought to be almost indistinguishable from lessons in biology. Admittedly, the agency of architecture has yet to achieve this union. Our aim is to push the theoretical nature/design boundary until it becomes permanently fused.

Primary Principles

Our research topics span over twenty years of illuminating environmental issues as an amalgam of anthropocentric and ecologically balanced artifacts, procedures, and spaces. Over this period, it has established works that serve as an interdisciplinary authority in nature intensive design operations at the intersection of art, architecture, and cities. By researching how design intentions are derived and why they are cultivated into tangible site-specific interventions, the work has been fortified in embodied knowledge, or an understanding attained through practice and field deployment. These arts intensive schemes find continuous dissemination for public consumption.

Currently, there is no distinct prevailing set of enduring methodologies or theoretical approaches that define a designer. We are inclined to work within a shifting cohort of creative arts practitioners that channel DIY communities, anti-discipline factions, hacker enclaves, well-intentioned entrepreneurs, makers, crowdsourcing advocates and ample other creative outlets. These are fluid tactical linkages used to decipher boundless design problems. In most cases, our generation is unified at solving a host of fluctuating wicked environmental problems. Concerns in climate dynamics, uncontrolled urbanization, lack of social justice, and deficient housing are the explicit challenges we seek to answer through formidable acts of architectural design.

Architectural design, in and of itself, has astonishing power. It's also simultaneously both perpetual and ethereal, like painting a watercolor in a stream. Design is not art. Contrariwise, the differences between art and design are heavily muddled. Design can juxtapose imperceptible properties and just as equally foreground the obvious general physics of almost any challenge. We see design as an action that blends benevolence with radical intelligence. Virtuous architectural designers work together to invent original contributions towards refining human knowledge. Architectural design today, as we see it, is an open, free, limitless, and an exceptionally self-governing process.

Teaching Elements

The following directives characterize our views that generate the teaching methods in a workshop, seminar, or architecture studio setting. It is the confluence of a spirited equanimity amongst methodological priorities, student inputs, and critical interests that trace the roots of our instruction. We instinctively care about teaching and working with engaging and thought-provoking scholars. For this explicit reason, we are continuing to pursue academia on numerous levels. We passionately believe that teaching and research must balance each other. We've had the privilege of being exposed to diverse pedagogical methods and extraordinary mentors within our own completed degree programs.

These influential academicians from dozens of wide-ranging fields have undeniably tested and shaped our philosophy as university professors and design practitioners.

Predominantly, we think that successful teaching consists of two key components: first, inspiring the students by being impassioned about the topic and second, elevating them to vigorously learn the subject through active participatory group exercises and to invoke solutions by themselves independently outside the classroom. In our educational experience, we have attempted to not merely deliver the material, but to aid students in comprehending the perceptions behind architectural design choices and have them interrelate with other colleagues. For instance, when deliberating the trade-offs of dissimilar design tactics, we involve students by posing step-by-step queries and by soliciting reactions from them. This permits students to transmit the material, embolden themselves to come up with the benefits and constraints of numerous frameworks on their own and, in turn, enables us to evaluate their understanding. We trust that these approaches and methods help scholars develop valuable experiences that open pathways to designing superior techniques themselves. We also believe that hands-on proficiency is essential for students to cognize the tangible experiments of architecture. In parallel, we've continually crafted and improved upon syllabi for the interdisciplinary courses we have taught for years. We've advised students to participate in advanced studio sequences that focus on deep-learning multivalent research endeavors. We believe that wicked problems created by certain adverse activities of society can only be solved by equally as rigorous efforts of humankind buttressed by in-depth edifying measures.

Teaching at the university level is a distinct privilege and an undertaking that can provide immense gratification. We've been teaching in the role of professors in various fields of art, architecture, environment, biology, media and transportation. Our instruction primarily revolves around issues of ecological design thinking. For the most part students we've encountered have been extraordinarily affable, intelligent, prolifically creative And very keen on being challenged. Many of them are focused and dedicated to intellectual purists that will evolve their current worldview. Students, we've found, are seeking to reshape and amplify their individualized filters of reason. They wish to grasp the ideas and methods of architecture education and nurture their own concepts.

Customarily, we have design students in a conservatory-based learning model bent on a single pre-defined concentration. Instead, we encourage them to seek new adaptations to their education as a young newfangled artist, architect, designer or something else entirely. They often wish to include overlapping interests culled from separate fields of knowledge. In short, they are fascinated being taught something that is atypical.

Our courses are deliberately attenuated and tailored to gather a myriad of individualized modes of expression. We've found each, and every student has a skill set they like to communicate in class as answers for assignments. We are delighted to accommodate their method of choice to manifest a unique resolution in their projects.

Design Research

An appetite for innovation and change drives the research work we do. This requires many vantage points to address a given investigation. Therefore, it's important to emphasize on the intrinsically collaborative nature of our research. We almost always work in teams of assorted disciplines and heterodox knowledge sets.

Our hypothetical explorations, in the most fundamental of interpretations, exist within the realm of socio-ecological design and architecture. A nascent term that recognizes science-based design alone is not enough to confront the enormous issues facing humanity with regards to climate dynamics. It is our understanding that no matter how comprehensive the technical solutions are to climate change; the socio-cultural constraints are a considerable factor. The knowledge of ecology combined with various methods of design is necessary to achieve planetary stability, but only in tandem with corresponding societal elements. That is why we describe it specifically as socio-ecological design, and not merely eco-design, sustainability, "green" or biomimicry. Even if the key factors in both science and design are tenable, the capricious public may still have an opposite perspective. We've been making headway in this self-defined interdisciplinary approach for almost two decades.

Research has been our most successful contribution. At Terreform ONE, we've been able to complete numerous projects that bring the elements of socio-ecological design to a greater level of depth, consistency, and refinement. We've explored these issues at three primary scopes of inquiry: mobility, architecture, and urbanization. We've been designing environmentally driven transportation systems, buildings, and urban neighborhoods since 2006. They are all cross-linked and integrated with one another at different scales of operation to mitigate issues of waste, energy, water, materials, sustenance, and air quality. All of them are grounded and manifested in substantially visual items. A few key examples are: Urban Tangle spliced map fragments, Mini-stacking electric cars for China, Mycoform structures grown from strains of fungi, Gen2Seat biopolymer compostable chair, Governor's Hook resilient waterfront infrastructure made of decommissioned military ships, and the Bio City Map of 11 Billion People, using genetically modified E. coli colonies as printed geographies.

Public Outreach

Outside the local spectrum, we're also responsible for enlivening the public in an international dialogue on ecological design, art, and urban culture. In this manner we serve as noted public intellectuals and directors of the research institute, Terreform ONE, presenting arguments that help justify the meaning and power of design in relationship to local communities and planetary metabolism. We are intensely involved in publicly speaking, visualizing, and writing about our discipline and how it relates to the cultural and social world around it. This kind of discourse is extremely crucial, and it involves good, clear, simplified explanations of design that bridge many mindsets. Our projects aim to remove obstacles that distort meaning or fail to connect with the general public. Our objective is to annihilate the effects of climate change through spatial and visual vocabularies that promote ecological design thinking.

Design with Life

This volume chronicles the projects and breakthroughs of a nonprofit research group that is defining salient new directions in socio-ecological design and other vital intersections of architecture, synthetic biology, and urban systems.

ESSAYS

Convergence in Environmental Social Governance Thinking

VIVIAN KUAN

As Environmental Social Governance ("ESG") initiatives have gained momentum globally, Terreform ONE's socio-ecological design approach towards future cities has reached new ears and a wider audience in progressive minded companies seeking to keep pace with their business practices. The private sector – under pressure from their constituents, including their investors, who are demanding corporate social responsibility – has entered a new phase. The longtime accepted metric of corporate success – narrowly defined by shareholder value and short-term profits – has expanded to reflect an acknowledgement that our environmental future is dire if we do not address our current behavior patterns as a society. New studies have shown that socially responsible business practice has been proven to equate to better business, period; no longer is the idea of incorporating an ethical or philanthropic dimension to business goals a necessary sacrifice to the bottom line. The demand for ESG integrated business practices has created opportunities for companies like Terreform ONE to help corporations improve their social responsibility agendas, thereby effecting greater environmental change.

Since Terreform ONE (Open Network Ecology) was founded in 2006, the public consciousness towards sustainability has shifted. Resilience goals – including social, economic, and climate resilience – have broadened and created a new set of parameters, raising the bar higher for the design and construction industry at large. As a non-profit founded on the outskirts of traditional professional practice, Terreform ONE approach to urban design research and our model of a transdisciplinary urban think tank have evolved too. Largely operating on an education platform, Terreform enjoyed the white space and creative license to be able to freely experiment with smart city design and conceptual studies without parameters set by any specific client. Terreform ONE mission has always been to create smart urban innovations that elevate the quality of life in our cities, contribute positively to our ecosystem while reconnecting to nature. Represented as a collection for the first time in this book, Terreform ONE portfolio of design research projects – visualizing future cities through full-scale fabricated models and color – saturated renderings – continues to travel through museums, galleries and conferences. Through our ONE Lab Fellowship Program and other educational initiatives, Terreform ONE continues to push the boundaries between academic urban research and applied design practice.

However, as our society has become more mindful of the environmental choices that affect our global future, Terreform ONE's non-profit mission has converged with the growing need for companies to maximize their social impact. Corporations are re-assessing whether the traditional shareholder value driven by short-term profits is still an effective gauge of success. Multinational corporations have actively embraced and integrated ESG goals, partly driven by their investors and partly because it just makes good business sense. When former Secretary of State John Kerry was appointed to head the Global Advisory Council of a large financial institution, he said "Whether it's climate change…, extreme poverty, or the challenges of 21st-century governance and modernity, our council will be analyzing a range of issues and providing our perspective on helping the bank with the developments that will define the future we share as a worldwide community."

Design with Life

As the focus on ESG has intensified in the private sector, the role that Terreform ONE has been able to play in helping to drive those efforts has grown. Large corporations understand it's the right thing to do, especially if they can make it consistent with business objectives. But they are also being forced to change. A recent Wall Street Journal article cited the extraordinary shift that some so-called "activist" investors were making when they demanded computer giant Apple to adopt more focus on the long term effects smartphones were having on child behavior. The role that corporate America plays on the public health of our society has moved under the spotlight, and investors are using their clout to demand accountability. While Terreform ONE continues to delve into the issues confronting cities, we have been able to apply our research process to advise on corporate ESG programs. One of Terreform's most rewarding initiatives was working with ONE of the largest building products and materials company in the world, BASF.

As part of their 150th anniversary global initiative, BASF engaged Terreform ONE as sustainability thought leaders on their Creators Board to develop the content for their North America conference. One of their primary goals was to build a new platform to engage constituents in a dialogue about ESG. What is the future of urban living and what factors will have the greatest influence on the quality of life in future cities? How can BASF and their stakeholders co-create solutions for the social, economic and climate resilience goals facing our society? Holding monthly workshops with BASF teams from North America and Germany, we reframed the questions around an actual community that was fraught with the complexities of urban, social and climate issues. Hit severely by Hurricane Sandy, Red Hook, Brooklyn, served as a case study for other coastal cities around the globe at high risk of flooding and impacts of climate change. In the end, Terreform ONE was able to successfully support BASF through the 3 phases of the engagement:

1. Summit Co-Creation Conference on the Future of Urban Living
2. White Paper documenting the ESG research, content and solutions,
3. Business Plan outlining how to implement the ESG solutions.

Co-Creation Summit included breakout sessions with various stakeholder groups made up from community residents, politicians, business owners, architects, builders and educators.
The conference, breakout sessions, competitions and events produced a set of co-created solutions which include:

A. Establishing a Network of Green Corridors:
Bioswales, paths, creek beds, and canals, which would be strategically placed to improve transportation, social cohesion, and climate resilience/flood prevention.
B. Create a Coastal Park:
Buffer zones made of soft edges that provide barriers against coastal flooding as an alternative to traditional sea walls.
C. Establish a Center for Job Training and Human Services:
A "Hub for Human Potential" would provide the high percentage of unemployed residents living in one of the largest public housing complexes with access to information, education, and services including job training.
D. Rethink Red Hook's Public Housing:
With 8000 residents in one of the city's largest public housing communities, Red Hook Houses could be redesigned to integrate the complex into the rest of the city instead of walling it off in isolation and include sustainability and renewable energy measures to protect it from the next storm surge. Creative financing and sweat equity could offer the residents participation in home ownership.
E. Inspire with a Model Block:

As the foundational unit of a neighborhood, a city block could be smartly designed to become a model of resilience, utilizing renewable energy sources, providing a framework for live/work that incorporates flood-proofing elements and off-the-grid energy sources to confront the next storm.

"BASF sees tremendous opportunity to create a meaningful and measurable impact in Red Hook through the solutions we've identified," says Michael Fletcher, Commercial Segment Manager for BASF. "Six-hundred million people call coastal cities home. And with recent studies reporting sea levels rose faster in the 20th century than the previous 2,700 years, preparing Red Hook and cities like Miami, Florida; Guangzhou, China; and Mumbai, India, is paramount." These solutions for Red Hook is intended to inform and urge the community at large that there is a critical need for a global model of urbanized habitat, citizenship and resilience in light of global warming and the consequential extremes in the changing environment."[2]

Following our BASF engagement, INTEL Corporation sponsored our urban design research on the future role of technology in sustainable buildings. Our research drilled down into deeper questions about the role of buildings in the larger ecosystem, and what role technology can play in mending the damaged ecosystem while protecting endangered species? We narrowed down our scope to focus on the skin or facade of the building and developed a double-skin solution using drones to monitor and improve the local air quality – an issue which has become intensely problematic in urban areas. To contribute to the ecosystem, our double layered skin also houses a sanctuary for Monarch butterflies, a species vulnerable to extinction partially because its main source of food, milkweed, has been eliminated from many parts of the environment. We developed butterfly drones which would become stewards of the actual butterflies. Our solution also calls for integrated drone ports which do double duty in harboring the

drones and the beginning of a traffic monitoring system for local drone flights in cities. As technology companies such as Intel and Apple are faced with their role in transforming the future of urban living and lifestyle, Terreform has been able to develop innovative solutions that help technology contribute back to the environment in a positive way.

For Terreform ONE, our work with the Red Hook and Monarch Sanctuary Research Projects, confirmed the need for innovative thinking and a solutions-oriented approach to working with large multinational corporations like BASF and INTEL. And why is this important? The ESG efforts of these progressive global corporations have not only presented us with new opportunities, but it enables our cities to effect change at a speed and scale that is critical to confront the overall environmental challenges facing our urbanizing planet. Corporate sustainability initiatives are an essential part of the solution to global resilience. By creating this new platform powered by the ESG initiatives in the private sector, we are now aiming to expand to the public sector through city governments preparing for the next wave in smart cities – from infrastructure to mobility to renewable energy..

Are we futurists? The ancient Japanese Noh theater illustrated a prevailing theme – that only by forcing the confrontation between life and death, can one understand life more clearly. Thus, by envisioning through design research the complex issues facing future cities, can one understand the trajectory that our current lifestyle and decisions play in the future outcome.

Bilbiography

1. Edmans, Alex, "Does the Stock Market Fully Value Intangibles? Employee Satisfaction and Equity Prices" (January 20, 2010). Journal of Financial Economics 101(3), 621-640, September 2011.

The Utopia Question
Interview

DARRAN ANDERSON
MITCHELL JOACHIM

In dark times, cynicism seems a safe bet. There is a strange kind of comfort, even catharsis, in letting go or wallowing in dystopian visions. It lets us off the hook. Utopia gets a bad press, much of it justified; it's impossible, even undesirable. Yet abandoning the utopian impulse is arguably even more naïve and ultimately self-defeating. Last year, for the 500th anniversary of Thomas More's Utopia, I spent a great deal of time giving talks on the theme, beginning with profound skepticism in London and ending with the realization of utopia's necessity months later in Venice.

The problem of our age is not necessarily the unattainable or corruptible nature of utopian ideas so much as their absence. Failing to construct or contribute to a vision of the future merely ensures living in the nightmare that is someone else's dream. It's not naivety that should draw us back to utopian impulses, but skepticism and realpolitik, or as Antonio Gramsci put it in a letter from prison, "pessimism of the intellect, optimism of the will." (great sentence).

Mitchell Joachim is not utopian in the fantasist sense. He is the co-founder of Terreform ONE, whose ambitious and forward-thinking projects delve into real-world problems and solutions, often from unforeseen and startling angles. While it can easily be said that visionary architects and designers clear conceptual space that others then build on, Terreform ONE seem to go further. As experimental and speculative as their concepts appear, they operate in terms of actual technological, sociological and ecological application. Rather than indulging in reveries, their intention is to envisage the future that is coming, following existing threads and historical studies, and to influence and engineer what is to come or, at least, our response to it.

I spoke to Mitchell about their work and urbanism, both speculative and real, in the past, present and future.

DARRAN ANDERSON
The first time I came across your work was your Urbaneering Brooklyn 2110 project. What struck me about that project is that it's incredibly futuristic but also organic. Rather than begin with a blank slate, it incorporates existing infrastructure and architecture. It remembers that the future is older than the present, and that nature is intrinsically part of that. When you're developing a project like Urbaneering Brooklyn, are you aware of influences or does it come as a response to solving problems?

MITCHELL JOACHIM
Recognizing the influences is paramount and it happens early on. It's not only standing on the shoulders of giants but also trying to tease out where they didn't quite explore, identifying the areas they never polished or thought through. When you're doing any project that involves 'future' in its name, there's some level of speculation or even clairvoyance – and we're not clairvoyant. What we do is create very detailed fictive scenarios that don't promise the future will end up this way, but we think about what the inherent issues are and talk in a logical way about how cities might respond. This is nothing new; the entire field of design is this way. Jules Verne is a great example. There's a guy who has written something like eighty books on this little island in Paris a century ago. He never promised we'd get to the moon, but what he did was write a very careful speculative narrative that looks at technologies either readily available or on the cusp of happening, and said, "This is most likely

how it will go down." That, in and of itself, influenced the actuality of those events. Jules Verne talked about a staged booster rocket system, launching from a peninsula, that would escape the atmosphere; the sections would decouple from the central mass; a lunar module would land on the moon. So, when John F. Kennedy said, "We're going to go to the moon," all those folks who ended up doing all the engineering were influenced by the design and speculation that Jules Verne had put forward. That's exactly the napkin sketch they used to get to the moon. When we think about cities, it's the same level of thinking. It's not as difficult to think about cities as it is to create the Apollo mission, because we don't have to invent a lot of the engineering from scratch. When you talk about changing cities, the actual city morphology doesn't shift overnight.

Take, for example, my iPhone. From a napkin sketch to an actual device you can purchase, it's a five year process. So, if I said, "holographic smart phone," which by the way I just pulled out of my ass, someone in Apple will have a prototype of the technology required, but it's five years before you have a pretty shitty but working model. That's the timeline required to change a telecommunications device. Architecture occurs forty years before the paradigm shift is established. You can see all these experimental buildings with unbelievable forms, but that's not the everyday act in architecture. Doors and windows and roofs and boiler heaters take a long time to change. I'm not going to buy a super-sustainable boiler until the current one I have utterly fails or simply costs me too much money. And that's when you see replacements in architecture. With cities it takes a hundred to 150 years before all of this discussion and all of those different scales rationalize themselves and become everyday practice in city design. To be a really good city designer, you need multiple hats, bridging multiple disciplines, looking at all facets of technology and how society evolves at their timescales before you find a new city. Thinking of historical cases that have worked, Ebenezer

Howard's Garden City is a notable one. That worked because it was a meme. It had a great title. Who didn't want to live in a garden city? How do you argue against that?

DA So, it's a PR victory first of all?

MJ Massively so. Right now, everyone's writing about smart cities because no one wants to be in a dumb city. No one knows what a smart city actually is. We've settled a lot of arguments about what future cities may or may not be under these memes that have incredible sticking power with folks.

DA The thing with smart cities that's always got me is the frequent lack of consideration towards repercussions. If there's data about everything, where does privacy fit(yes)? The old "who watches the watchmen?" question keeps springing to mind. And there's an element of the snake oil salesman or shyster politician to it; pitching something conveniently ephemeral. I've no doubt developments are and will be happening in those directions, – Songdo and Masdar, for instance, but much less thought seems to have gone into the side effects, sociological and political, and a lot of thought has instead gone into the future as a sales pitch.

MJ Well, we consider it a polemic. All of our models and projects are meant to question what that city will be like rather than saying, "This is utopia, build it like so." Designing a city is like painting a watercolor in a stream. Once you settle infrastructure, there's going to be an air quality issue, a waste management problem. Some kind of flow is going to shift it. So, you settle on bold colors.

DA When you're designing a project, how important is it to consider how it might go wrong?

MJ That's where we start from. I'm not a severe pessimist, but I am a sceptic. We don't make promises – we just speculate. One of our scenarios is called "drunk on energy". If energy is totally renewable and it's for free, are there any limitations? Why should I ever turn off my air conditioning? I wasn't at home all day, but my plants wanted to feel cool. Or my cat. Or I don't want to wait fifteen minutes when I get home. We run through all sorts of scenarios; it's part of how we build up these dialogues. Urbaneering, which you've mentioned, is almost a ten year project, morphing into different projects. I don't know where it's going to end. I'll probably be dead when it comes to fruition. It'll be a grad student of mine who writes the paper saying, "That's what Mitch meant." I'll be dead, but I'll be like, "Wow, that guy got it. I had to die before they figured that one out." After a certain period of time, we'll try and codify the relationships we created about that area of the city. For instance, the idea of having vertical farms in cities, or riparian corridors replacing streets: automation in farming that's not only there for food or sustenance but also air quality and waste management – every single surface in New York, vertical or horizontal, somehow fitted out with edible groweries. We have 3000 acres of unshaded roof space in New York City: why not grow everything imaginable up there? We'll look at the big metrics and we'll propose what Urbaneering could mean. We're interested in many others coming and taking up that torch.

DA I was reading his book Making recently and he frames it all as if he's solving problems constantly, but I'm not so sure he is. He has a particular aesthetic, quite an impressive and often beautiful one, but, for me, he seems to go with that first and then works back to show how he solved a problem. Speaking of designers or inventors, I get a recurring sense that those who were seen as speculative or visionary -take Buckminster Fuller or Nikola Tesla, were just too far ahead of their time. For a long while, they were regarded as cranks and eventually technology catches up and, as you mentioned with Jules Verne, their ideas have already changed the future.

MJ It's a feedback.

DA Yes, so they get rehabilitated fifty or a hundred years in the future and are retrospectively recast as prophets and we paper over the ridicule they faced. Yet we never seem to learn from the original dismissals and we continue to do it to the next bunch of visionaries who come along. I like to follow the threads back and try to bring people's attention to the fact these people were laughed at, even projects that are popular memes nowadays, but were still critically dismissed like, say, Archigram's predictions of Smart Cities and the internet in the early 60s.

MJ Well, the Archigram projects weren't necessarily something they intended to realize – an appreciation of them will be on paper. Architecture happens when the architects operate in the mind space, or page space where they create a drawing or a physical model. That is the intention. When Frank Gehry is done crumpling the paper, it takes many people to turn that paper into computational modelling, into building science, so that that can be assembled and constructed. That has nothing to do with architecture. All of the thought happened in Gehry's hands. Once it becomes a physical building and has gone through that process, it is architecture again. But the real body of work and the thing we strive to do is actually the paper part. That's what Archigram is, or Claude-Nicolas Ledoux and the whole French Enlightenment – those imaginary structures like Newton's Cenotaph...

DA Boullée's globe.

MJ That was impossible to build at the time, but it's in every single book on the history of architecture because it is an act of architecture.

DA It looks crazy even now. It must have seemed insane at the time, but it's really a logical extension of domes in basilicas.

MJ It doesn't need to be built to be a rational piece of architectural history; the same applies to Archigram or Lebbeus Woods and his work. Those drawings were meant to be occupied by the mind and they have enormous influence and range in terms of who they've inspired.

DA It's interesting you say that. I remember reading a comment by Lebbeus Woods to the effect that "I draw these things and if others want to go build them that's up to them, but I've already created what I intended."

MJ He's a great example. An even deeper one would be John Hejduk who built nothing but a few installations and yet, has influenced probably every single contemporary architect.
I don't know if the public absorbs that. They might think, "It's got to be a building or it's not architecture." Maybe somewhere it's part of the mission of architecture to explain what we do and we're trying, but perhaps we're not doing so well. Considering most structures in the built environment don't go through the hands of an architect, you can see that it's still our fault, in terms of what we consider architecture and what we do not.

DA There's an expectation these days for an architect to be a politician and a philosopher and a sociologist. Part of me, as I continually argue at talks, believes that space is innately political, but then there's a part of me that thinks an architect is really there to design buildings. Zaha Hadid took a lot of critical flak in terms of the political implications of her buildings, and in cases very justifiably so, but even I concede she wasn't a politician and she shouldn't have been expected to be a politician in the conspicuous absence of actual politicians. So maybe, to play devil's advocate for a moment, the public and people like me, expect too much.

MJ Look at Bjarke Ingels. He's taken the philosopher out of architecture. He's taken doubt out of architecture. He's really jumped into the Silicon Valley mentality of believing in making the world a better place, this utopian sense of progress. He's almost infinite in his ability to compromise; he calls it bigamy or polygamy.

Whatever your idea is, he'll morph his concepts to make it happen. In a way, that is his politics. And the dark days of Rem Koolhaas, filled with theory and doubt, not even being sure what he means, like Yoda or Jesus Christ levitating three feet off the ground, importing things from God knows where.

DA The architect as priest. I have to confess to having nestled under that wing, in terms of admiration for Koolhaas, Gropius and others. But there is a sense of the architect as some kind of detached monk performing sacred work. That has me wondering.

MJ They're really great at controlling the story of whatever that topic is, much more so even than many scientists who can sometimes be too myopic in their own research to zoom out and see why it might be interesting to the public and how this will impact different actors and agents.

DA In terms of the ecological side of the equation, the Rapid Refuse project is an interesting one, as it runs somewhat against the common tendency I've seen, where waste is approached as a problem to be simply rid of. Your project begins almost as if it's a strange opportunity.

MJ Early on, there was this thought that the term waste is a problem. Period. Even having two small kids, even telling them there's garbage, "Urgh, what am I doing?", I'm instilling the kind of values that were instilled in me. And garbage is the wrong value. There is no such thing as waste. Waste is supposed to go away but there is no away. We look at a state where waste doesn't exist – a steady-state economy that cycles back and recognizes the limits of the earth's metabolism and what we can take out. Everything is a nutrient whether it's that cup you're drinking from or those eye-glasses you're wearing. Everything is a nutrient and we have to treat design objects as nutrients. What they feed on isn't really clear sometimes. We have to recognize that they are servicing you for a period of time and then they move on to feed on something else. We see the synthetic biology we embed into the projects as really important because it keeps this general theory of 'everything is a nutrient' working really well. In a culture of biology, you don't design something for a single purpose. A cherry tree is servicing thousands of other forms of life. It doesn't produce three cherries so that three new cherry trees start to grow. It produces thousands of cherries that get absorbed into the soil, feed all different types of flora and fauna, over the lifetime of that tree. It's connected into a web of life. We don't throw out an iPhone and expect it to help thousands of other things. We might have that in the software side, in the connectivity, but not in the hardware side, not in the products we make.

DA If you think about the crash in 2008, the West had wholeheartedly opted for a Ponzi scheme (I was working for a bank then, so I saw it in real-time), a delusional and cynical faith in endless growth, much of it funded from shady sources and buoyed by derivatives. When the nerve holding it together wavered, when reality could no longer be kept at bay, it all came crashing down. And really the only reaction or idea in mainstream circles following that was to ensure the collapse occurred in slow motion and then we'll just somehow get the growth and the Ponzi scheme back up and running again.

MJ There's also something more insidious than that. I've been trying for a long time to locate what the real enemy is, and it's called 'predatory delay'. If you're an oil company, you're going to say "Yes, solar panels are great. We have to grow and grow and grow, and we'll invest in that. We think in 2050, we'll be using solar panels." Until then, every single day they are in business there are such enormous profits that the point is to delay. It's only when you get a giant ugly crisis that you have to stop delaying and you need to implement the new technology. After the crisis, which wasn't big enough and was mostly financial, the 'best' thing to do was more predatory delay in every

single part of what we're discussing about cities. It's an extremely effective bridge especially for those in power and those who are profiting.

One example is the issue of fracking. When I saw Barack Obama and Mitt Romney, on the same page for energy in the United States, it was game over. They both said no to coal, but they were totally fine with natural gas and that we'll deal with the environmental consequences later. We're going to delay, yet again, an infrastructure of renewables – geothermal, solar, wind, hydro. Let's not go there.

DA So that delay is a constant drag on progress?

MJ It's built to do that and it's really hard to argue with predatory delay, because they're on your side mostly. "We really love that new [low-energy] car, what a great concept. Here's a little bit of money. And a little bit of press on it. And everything's good, but we're not going to get into it today. Let's do it in 2020-ish."

DA Talking of coming change, let's consider the sea level rise. Most of the world's major cities are on the coast. There was a line that struck me in your future city of Governors Hook where "instead of keeping the water out, the design allows the water in." That was rather refreshing after years of seeing ideas that are built on either ignoring or building siege conditions against the sea.

A Century of Ecological Innovation*

MITCHELL JOACHIM

"We are called to be architects of the future, not its victims."
R. Buckminster Fuller, 1895-1983

"Innovation distinguishes between a leader and a follower."
Steve Jobs, 1955 –2011

As humanity faces its greatest disruption to date – climate change – placing the planet and its long-term survival in jeopardy, the design team at Terreform ONE incites optimism. Rather than being defined by disruption, they predict that the 21st century with be characterized by innovation, which endeavors to solve the global challenges we face.

Looking forward to a future that shines is not a platitude; it's an absolute imperative. All designers, by their very nature, are empowered to speculate about the near future. In fact, that is the objective. The act of invention is the governing rule of remarkable design. To grasp the imperceptible and make it visible is the most powerful instrument a human can wield.

Tomorrow is an unshakable discourse. Everything must draw from its past, connect the dots and venture onward with foresight. Design in its best wide-ranging procedures formulates the stratagem for tomorrow. Without a shadow of a doubt, the art of imagination is a limitless attribution of humankind. Case in point: Walt Disney, Elon Musk, Norman Bel Geddes, society is still enthralled by the futures they

promoted. If used for positive intentions and checked against deleterious effects, it depends on design to innovate our path forward.

What will be the predominant narrative for the 21st century? Each era has a philosophy of progress and decline, of blossoming and withering, of expansion and devastation, otherwise known as an idea of nature. Every age also has a concept about the previous and the current, of what elapsed and what persisted, a view of temporality and a notion of what is defined as historically significant.

Philosophies of historical narratives used to be paranormal: the heavenly governed time; the finger of divinity, an extraordinary sagacity, lay beneath the demise of every species. If the current differed from the historical, it was habitually wicked: mystical concepts of the past leaned towards degeneration, a descent from refinement, the loss of a deity's support, dishonesty. The eighteenth century encompassed a sense of expansive progress; the nineteenth century had evolution; the twentieth century had development and then modernization. The terminology that defines this century is debatably disruption but more accurately, innovation. Innovation promises to solve the global challenges we face and re-orient humanity.

Why innovation and not disruption? Parts of the hyper-mediated landscape of our age have defined this period as the era of disruption which, despite its promise, is crude. It's a notion created on a weighty nervousness verification? Disruption is too often perceived as mischievous or even damaging. Yet, as a society we must seek innovation and not the negative symptoms of disruption. Innovation is the healthier narrative of today and it has many variants. What tomorrow ascendancy is humbling? The 21st century future faces an immense disruption, that of climate breakdown. The future looks like it critically depends on the current innovations.

Design with Life

Innovation is like painting a watercolor in a stream. It changes like our climate. Climate change and associated environmental problems, although disruptive, are best solved through stimulating acts of invention. Copious innovative designers and architects make bold claims about environmental recovery. Unfortunately, others capitulate to economic limits at the expense of the environment. Starchitects are affordable to less than 1% of the population and most pay negligible lip service to eco-system basics. The other 99% of the population demand designers for a salubrious society.

We've had this impression before, that we could be at a crossroads, that we're learning devastating data, that there's a grassroots rebellion for change. The litany of events that led up to it after the second half of the twentieth century is familiar enough to us. In 1946, one year after the bomb was dropped at Hiroshima, John Hersey's shocking account in his book Hiroshima portrayed the vast and continued destruction of a city and almost everything in the surrounding environment. Atomic desolation was the first-time humankind realized that it is entirely within our power to end nature. Soon after, accounts of humans distressing the earth became more commonplace. The early battle calls have been cited over and over. In 1953 the New York Times published its first article on the budding subject of global warming. Rachel Carson's 1962 bestseller Silent Spring etched the issue of environmental degradation, especially the wide use of DDT, into the world mindset. In 1970, gatherings around the world celebrated the first Earth Day – with over one million celebrants New York's Central Park alone.

In 1989 Bill McKibben's thoughtful and urgent call to action in The End of Nature inspired a generation of environmental activists. Today, a veritable cottage industry of manuscripts exists around the topic of sustainability, from Betsy Kolbert's The Sixth Extinction to Timothy Morton's Hyper projects': Philosophy and Ecology after the End of the World to Edward Mazria's 2030 challenge. People have been raising awareness and participating in public debate on environmental matters. How much longer do we need to proclaim the planet is in jeopardy?

As stated earlier, now is the tipping point. Since 1958, the Keeling curve has charted the atmospheric carbon dioxide atop Hawaii's Mauna Loa volcano. Scientific consensus has set the safety threshold at 350 ppm; as of June 2014, it has risen to almost 405, exceeding the treacherous threshold of 400 ppm. In 2014 the UN released another sobering report on climate dynamics decades following the Rio Summit and Kyoto protocols. It bitterly declared that most prior carbon emissions caps placed on the leading developed nations remain ineffective. It also announced that numerous developing countries have increased their carbon output.

From 1991 to 2011, 97 percent of all peer-reviewed published research on climate change affirmed that humans have triggered the precipitating events. Major world scientific institutions concur, Yet only 66 percent of the media supports the concept of anthropogenic global warming and, unfortunately, 55 percent of the American public believes there is scientific disagreement. The gap is closing. At this stage, even the most drastic emissions reductions will take decades to reverse the damage. We are locked in for substantial added global warming from the greenhouse gases already emitted. We must face our failures head-on. It's our duty to correct the course.

We will need to act in accordance with the UN as we already face the sixth mass extinction event ever identified in geological time. The epoch of the Anthropocene, which started with the industrial revolution in the late eighteenth century, will come to an end. China is thrusting forward with a colossal scheme to transfer 250 million rural inhabitants into freshly minted cities by 2025. Mega planning cities from scratch, or rather warehousing, is a forceful action that could set off an upsurge of growth or burden the republic with difficulties for decades. How this is implicated into a world perspective of resource consumption remains an unknown. Design can reveal these impacts to the public. Designers have the capacity and authority to convince us change is coming, and we can do better.

Here is a series of projects that defies apocalyptic climate change scenarios. They are predicated on the near future. Each project ranges from; architecture and transportation to global plans. All are in profound response to contemporary urban design and quotidian city dwelling. Our century is about innovation, and these projects intentionally push forward the upper limits of what is possible. If we can't think and experiment in vast terms, we can't solve vast problems.

* Originally appeared in: Joachim, Mitchell. "A Century of Ecological Innovation," 2050: Designing Our Tomorrow, Chris Luebkeman (ed.), AD

Creating Productive Green Space in Cities

MARIA AIOLOVA

The front lawn has long been the iconic American space. Research shows that North Americans devote 40,000 square miles to lawns, more than wheat, corn, and tobacco land use combined. Americans spend $750 million dollars a year on grass seed alone. Additionally, only 2% of America's food is locally grown, and 12% per dollar of food consumed at home comes from transportation costs. In July 2005, Los Angeles-based architect Fritz Haeg launched a campaign known as "Edible Estates". Haeg says he was drawn to the lawn because it cuts across social, political and economic boundaries. "The lawn really struck me as one of the few places that we all share," he says. "It represents what we're all supposedly working so hard for – the American dream." The concept of tilling one's front yard is not new . In 1942, as the U.S. emerged from the Great Depression and mobilized for World War II, Agriculture Secretary Claude R. Wickard encouraged Americans to plant "Victory Gardens" to boost civic morale and relieve the war's pressure on food supplies – an idea first introduced during The Great War and implemented in Canada, the U.S. and Great Britain. The slogan became "Have Your Garden and Eat It Too." Gardens soon began to pop up not just in American suburban lawns, but virtually everywhere – plots sprouted up at the Chicago County Jail, a downtown parking lot in New Orleans, and a zoo in Portland, Oregon. In 1943, Americans planted 20.5 million Victory Gardens, and the harvest accounted for nearly one-third of all the vegetables consumed in the country that year. Twenty-five million U.S. households planted vegetable and fruit gardens in 2008, according to the National Gardener's Association. First Lady Michelle Obama and Secretary of Agriculture Tom Vilsack have planted organic vegetable gardens this year (Q: what year? Adjust for 2019 publication date). Roof gardens are sprouting nationwide. Community gardens have waiting lists. Seed houses and canning suppliers are oversold. The time for urban farming is NOW.

But is it really? As America emerges from the Great Recession, is urban agriculture going to stay? Once the economy recovers, are we going to continue to grow our own tomatoes or are we are going to go back to imported produce from Florida, Mexico or even China? Can designers provide answers to these questions? ONE Prize is a design and science award to advance the burgeoning environmental movement by encouraging designers to imagine new solutions and give them a platform for their ideas.

For its inaugural year, ONE Prize took as its theme "Mowing to Growing: Creating Productive Green Space in Cities". This award was launched in the context of larger issues concerning the environment, global food production and the imperative to generate a sense of community in our urban and suburban neighborhoods. Mowing to Growing was not meant to transform each lawn into a garden, but to open up the possibilities of self-sustenance, organic growth, and perpetual change. In particular, it sought specific technical, urbanistic, and architectural strategies not simply for the food production required to feed the cities and suburbs, but the possibilities of diets, agricultural methods, and retrofitted facilities that could achieve that level within the constraints of the local climate. Mowing to Growing envisioned ways future-in which proof spaces and systems can explore the larger framework of urban agriculture and its effects on architecture and urban design.

An open call to the international design community asked the following questions:
– How can we break the American love affair with the suburban lawn?
– Can greenhouses be incorporated in skyscrapers?
– What are the urban design strategies for food production in cities?
– Can food grow on rooftops, parking lots, building facades?
– What is required to remove foreclosure signs on lawns and convert them to gardens?

The results were overwhelming. Entries ranged from vertical farms, neighborhood farms to farming on vacant lots and buildings, abandoned infrastructure, front lawns, strip malls, rooftops, river barges and inside trailers. The competition drew 202 teams and 850 team members from more than 20 countries across five continents. Narrowing them down to thirty semifinalists became a daunting challenge, and an even bigger one to select the finalists. In the end, they decided on two winners that represented two general groups of entries: Design Proposals and Community Proposals.

The Design Award went to AGENCY Architecture LLC. Their project proposes a global system of levees, serving also as a new brand of urban farms at the city's edge, preserving local ecologies while protecting cities from emerging dangers. By appropriating and expanding "super levee" construction technology, planning principles and grading strategies, the city is reconnected with the waterfront, and its natural heritage. Each stage of the levee supports the next. Clippings, compost, and surplus crops from farming levels are used as nutrients and food for a series of fish farms, marshes, and restorative dune ecologies. Waste from marine life and nutrients from algal habitats are then used to fertilize farm levels, making the levee a complete ecology. The project expands necessary infrastructural and environmental improvements to propose a more productive urban and personal life.

The Community Award went to the Thread Collective and TheGreenest.Net. Their proposal for Naturally Occurring Retirement Community (NORC) Farms engages the population of aging New Yorkers and utilizes inaccessible lawns in order to "create and cultivate farm plots and social spaces within public housing complexes." NORC Farms will use urban agriculture to transform grass into a socially, ecologically, and economically productive space, activate older New Yorkers, and transform public housing open spaces into local agriculture. The tower in the park now becomes the tower in the farm. A naturally occurring retirement community (NORC) is a unique housing model that allows older adults to live in the community rather than an institutional setting. New York City has over 1.3 million people over the age of 60 – and this population is expected to grow by 50% in the next 25 years. Over 1/3 of the retirement community in NYC lives in public housing projects almost exclusively surrounded by grass enclosed by fences. This inaccessible, inert space reinforces the social segregation that both the elderly and public housing residents experience. NORC Farms transform the swaths of poorly maintained grass by creating active social spaces & new connections to the exterior and providing access to fresh healthy food.

One of the jury's favorite finalists were Michael Arad of Handel Architects with Rachel Kangas and Abbe Futterman. Their project, *Kids Farming in the City* was a simple gesture with profound effects. Located at a public school in Manhattan's East Village/ Lower East Side, the project is retrofitting a green farm-able roof on an existing public school building. The intention is to enable school teachers to weave growing and cultivating plants into the curricula of different classes and areas of inquiry, ranging from science to art. They asked the question: If we were going to grow plants on the roof, why not grow plants we could eat? A program called 'Days of Taste' introduced school children to neighborhood chefs and taught them about food, nutrition and health through hands-on learning about ingredients and preparation, leading to communal feasting at the chefs' restaurants. A permit was granted by the New York State's Department of Agriculture for the harvest of the container garden to be offered as lunch fare in the cafeteria.

Some of these proposals might have been utopian, but they were not revolutionary, and they were not advocating for something novel, but for a return to things that are old and familiar in many ways. As Michael Arad of Handel Architects put it, "they are calling for a return to our roots; it is about rediscovering practices that have historically been an essential part of our lives." If thrifting helped motivate city farmers seventy years ago, we have many compelling reasons to bring small scale urban farming back into our lives. At the same time, what is new and hopefully revolutionary is the fact that the results of the ONE Prize Award are redefining the design profession. Parallel to the calls from Architecture from Humanity and Public Architecture, the call from ONE Prize establishes the emergence of a new breed of designers/activists. Whether it is to combat global warming, childhood obesity, or to build better ties in their communities, these designers have the ability to shift the profession back to making the world a better, safer and healthier place.

Making, Knowing, and the Evolution of Aesthetic Judgment

CHRISTIAN HUBERT

One of the central ironies of the contemporary geological period that has come to be known as the *Anthropocene* is that humans are developing new technologies to alter or even synthesize life, even as they destroy or degrade the global biosphere and bring myriad species to extinction.

What is the relation between the extension of human scientific and technological dominion over life itself and the potential for creative, non-instrumental, and aesthetic design, whose benefits are both social and ecological? How can design protect, enhance, and create all forms of life?

Eighteenth Century discussions of life were constrained by the limits of what humans could *create* at the time. These limits were not only technical, but seemed also conceptual. The nature of life, as well as its origins and development, were thought to be unknowable precisely because life itself exceeded human capacities for making.

It was necessary, therefore, to include stories of divine creation, intention, and design – or at the very least, to posit an intrinsic formative power to the natural world d – a *Bildungstrieb* or *élan vital* – that in-formed the development of life. Prior to the Darwinian revolution, the debates between Mechanism and Vitalism were structured around this paradigmatic state of affairs. But was the mystery of life a philosophical necessity or an only historical and technical phenomenon?

In *The Critique of Pure Reason*, Kant argued that the basic structures of time and space were strictly necessary for causal thinking to be possible at all. But did aesthetic or teleological judgment also have necessary conditions as well? If so, were aesthetic qualities inherent in artworks? Or were they a direct product of human judgment? And was there any basic link between the two?

In his *Critique of Judgment*, Immanuel Kant posited a softer connection between the judging mind and the object of beauty. Unlike the conditions of the Critique of Pure Reason, which spelled out a necessary link between logical concepts and the very possibility of thinking, he considered this latter connection to be more contingent, a looser homology based on the unifying conditions of life. This mode of addressing questions of beauty and was based on a shared experience of nature, and specific concepts of beauty.

For Kant, there was a deep affinity between Aesthetic philosophy and the biological study of life (conceived in pre-Darwinian terms of Teleology). Fortunately for the possibility of aesthetic or teleological judgments, there seemed to be a homological relationship between the conditions of human thinking and the objects of both art and nature, which enabled the correspondence between the inner structure of the objects and the structure of mind and emotion.

The connection between aesthetic judgment and the appraisal of natural purpose – teleology – is not an obvious one today, as the biological thinking of that time was not evolutionary. (In fact, the pre-Darwinian version of evolution considered it only an unfolding of inherent structure, not one which significantly changes over time and is open to chance.)

Today, technological and scientific advances have fundamentally altered the conceptual frameworks for thinking about life. Although the origins and essential features of life may still thought to be self-organizing processes without agency, and subject to random chance, the new-found human capacities for engineering life forms – to consider them as intellectual property recognized by patent law --have displaced aesthetic and teleological issues and led to both aggressively grandiose ambitions (think Silicon Valley or Monsanto) as well as to fears and ethical doubts (about designer babies, automated warfare, and self-driving cars for example).

With the impact of Darwinism still far from exhausted, two other previously metaphysical barriers have also become more permeable: the barriers between humans and other life forms (especially those closer to us, such as the higher primates) and our accelerating transfers of human agency and autonomy to machines.

Darwinism, be it in life forms or in machines, is interpreted as a constant testing process for adaptations that confer advantages for survival. If design is thought of in this manner, its success is primarily a function of adaptive innovation. Yet these ideas do not address any yearning for beauty that also motivates design, or any corresponding evolution of aesthetic judgment or of reverence for life. The capacity for aesthetic judgment is not a high priority for research into artificial intelligence, but as animal minds come to be better understood and appreciated, the beauty of the animal world is increasingly coming to be understood as evolving through the agency of animal minds.

Is aesthetic judgment only the province of humans? In *The Evolution of Beauty*, the ornithologist Richard Prum revives some of Darwin's theories from *The Descent of Man* and argues that beauty (as animals perceive it) is an effective means for understanding mate choice – and that sexual ornaments and courtship rituals co-evolve with the aesthetic preferences of individuals – and of females in particular. This is particularly evident in species of birds whose food is relatively abundant, such that the female can raise a brood pretty much on her

own. In these species, she does not need to pair up with a male on a long term and can choose mates based on her own preferences – not necessarily as a function of their "fitness" for survival, but rather as an echo of Kant's aesthetic criterion of "purposiveness without purpose." For Prum, this co-evolution is a historical process in which changing judgments and changing courtship features reciprocally influence each other – that purely aesthetic mate choice exerts evolutionary pressures that underlie the proliferation of beauty in the animal kingdom. Prum's approach challenges a number of generally accepted interpretations of evolution. In his view, the evolution of beauty is not necessarily adaptive. It is more like an improvisational dance with two partners (or many). Is aesthetic judgment only the province of humans? The idea of birds or other animals making aesthetic judgments seems jarring to scientists who forswear anthropocentrism, and who maintain a rigid separation between human self-consciousness and the mental states of animals. But the study of the human mind has been transformed by evolutionary thinking (see, for instance Jaak Panksepp and Lucy Biven, The Archaeology of Mind, The Neuroevolutionary Origins of Human Emotions), and the idea of a "feminist" evolutionary biology – which focuses on ways females find to free themselves from male sexual aggression – could hardly seem timelier. Nonetheless, the main takeaway from Prum's theory is that changes in "design" co-evolve with aesthetic judgment and preferences in the animal world and that is should come as no surprise that they do as well in humans.

In calling for "Socio-Ecological Design", Terreform ONE claims its own niche in this dynamic interplay between environmental innovation and the social evolution of judgment. The group's provocative images harken to both technological futurism and to transformations of the natural world not only to the benefit of humans, but to other species as well. The importance of the global issues addressed in the work could not be more important.

The Secret to Innovation: Incorporate as a not-for-profit + design for mission = social-impact innovation

JOHN RUDIKOFF

As a young lawyer in 2012 I was faced with an existential question: How do I apply my time and trade to participate in what I understood as the most pressing pursuits of our day – social-impact innovation? The answer I found was to do a 180 and leave my relatively-safe career path (5 years as a state prosecutor followed by a foray into private practice) to join a social-impact design firm as General Counsel. This move was accompanied by some professional skepticism and significant risk: From a normative legal perspective changing horses midstream (particularly to an unfunded startup) ran the risk of representing past professional missteps and/or failures. On a personal level the costs of moving cities and to a nonprofit pay scale brought significant stresses and sacrifices to make this choice remotely feasible.

However, this move proved transformative for me – both professionally and personally – and continues to pay dividends in how I have been privileged to contribute to social-impact innovation through practice. In my years at MASS Design Group we achieved a measure of financial sustainability and impact on the field of design – including receiving the Cooper Hewitt National Design Award - in which I am proud to have played a minor role. When personal circumstances required, I returned to New York (my ancestral home). I was recruited by Brooklyn Law School to run the Center for Urban Business Entrepreneurship (CUBE), a law center focused on providing essential legal services to unfunded startups and training lawyers to better serve this constituency. Whereas new ventures (for-profit and nonprofit) often have a hard time sourcing effective and affordable legal services, CUBE has offered a mandate to reimagine the legal academy and how we as attorneys can engage with underserved markets. As a liaison between Brooklyn Law School and its community I have been provided a unique view of the innovation economy in the borough and beyond.

Which brings me to Terreform ONE and their indelible Cricket Shelter. Terreform ONE invests its capital in designing projects that will improve the human experience of navigating the urban centers of the future. These are design projects that think holistically about not just form and budget, but mission and purpose. In 11 years of practice, they have developed a portfolio of projects that illustrate the essential role of robust research and design creativity in addressing the systemic and environmental challenges facing our world.

The Cricket Shelter is just such an example. It is at once a whimsical yet visionary project that illustrates the dual-potential for delivering a fast-deployable shelter system while providing a healthful and sustainable food source for its denizens.

Its organic form (constructed from decidedly inorganic and readily-available materials) recalls an asymmetrical, weaving passageway emerging from the ground to a human scaled foyer. It is at once a child's play structure crossed with a matrix-habitat-system for breeding and harvesting cricket carcasses for human consumption. As we imagine these modular forms multiplying across a landscape,

Design with Life

a sprawling labyrinth emerges embedding the structural needs of a temporary community inside of a local (i.e., low-calorie *and* low-carbon) food source. Over time, the project's mission evolves from addressing acute disaster relief to chronic food-insecurity, thereby minimizing waste and adding long-term value to the community it serves.

But also embedded in this project is much that does not meet the eye. Researching, designing and building prototypes is a high-tech, high-touch and expensive process. Who pays for their research and design? What actors have a vested interest in innovating the way displaced populations are fed and housed?

Perhaps no decision has been more pivotal to the breadth of Terreform ONE's creativity and success than their decision to incorporate eleven years ago as a nonprofit. Formally prioritizing mission over financial motivation has liberated its designers and academics to focus their intellectual capital on the world's most pressing challenges. Under this structure, Terreform ONE has been funded by a veritable-cocktail of philanthropy, grants and earned-income that has allowed the group and its portfolio to iterate and evolve strategically with an eye towards social-impact innovation, and not simply as a byproduct reflection of the market's demand. The value of this dynamic cannot be overstated.

Terreform ONE pursues projects based on a broad definition of ROI including environmental, social and economic impacts. It is not enough that the sculptural form is beautiful. Insufficient if it only serves a linear function. Terreform ONE understands that every project is a unique opportunity to rethink and multiply the impacts that a building can create. Under this guise, the challenge becomes finding the symbiosis between a building's functions to address near and long-term needs for its inhabitants.
The Cricket Shelter succeeds at bringing Terreform ONE's mission to life. By marrying mission with form,

it demonstrates how holistic solutions can improve the efficiency and empathy of disaster relief efforts. Ignore the naysaying detractors poking holes in their ambitious strategy. The Cricket Shelter is a manifestation of Terreform ONE's design advocacy. Its long-term success can only be measured as its components infiltrate and influence major infrastructural interventions performed by the AECOM's of the world. As the term 'resiliency' is increasingly understood as not an optional luxury, but a necessity and tenet of global security.

Philanthropy & The City: Case Studies in Eco-Urbanism, Education & Economic Justice

HEATHER NEWBERRY LORD

With cities, it is as with dreams: everything imaginable can be dreamed, but even the most unexpected dream is a rebus that conceals a desire or, its reverse, a fear. Cities, like dreams, are made of desires and fears...
-Italo Calvino

Philanthropy and urban planning operate at the swirling intersection of our communal dreams, fears and desires. They each espouse social ideals and rally resources to make those ideals happen in the world. At their best they can embody an applied utopianism that sparks change and helps communities flourish. At their worst they privilege a class of drive-by problem solvers engaging in grandiose social engineering experiments which, if they fail, leave little recourse for those who must suffer the consequences of ineffective social programs or disastrously designed buildings and neighborhoods.

Given these and other pitfalls, knowing where to begin can be overwhelming for those interested in making strategic philanthropic investments on urban and environmental issues. Several thousand (or even several million) dollars here and there will hardly eradicate homelessness or undo the damage that years of industrial waste have had on urban landscapes. However, somewhere between despairingly doing nothing and randomly disseminating funds in a

potentially harmful way, there is a wide range of social investments that might not save the world but that can at least nudge the world in the right direction. The likelihood for success increases when each investment is understood as part of a whole, implemented with room for an honest learning curve, and developed in true partnership at every step of the way with impacted communities.

I serve on the board of a small, private, spend-down family foundation which is a "first mover funder" investing in new ideas focused on changing the status quo. This kind of early stage funding gives innovators and community leaders runway to try new projects they can eventually put in front of other funders once they have some impact metrics under their belts. It is similar to angel funding or startup venture capital, but in this case the return on investment is a social good. To illustrate how we have worked with partners to nudge the world a little, below are case studies from two very different programs addressing the intersection of eco-urbanism, education and economic justice. I've also included a brief comment on some of the rationale for funding these projects.

Program: Cass Tiny Homes

Who & What?
Cass Community Social Services is a Detroit-based agency providing programs for food, health, housing and jobs. They serve a million meals a year and help hundreds of homeless and low-income individuals and families get back on their feet through their programs. In addition to managing temporary-to-permanent housing, running a community garden and a green jobs center turning tire waste into products like doormats and sandals, Cass has just launched a neighborhood of energy efficient "Tiny Homes." The residents in the first 25 homes will include low-income senior citizens, college students who have aged out of foster care, and formerly homeless people who have

an annual income of as little as $9,000. After renting for 7 years, residents will own homes with a projected value of $50,000 which they can sell, leverage for a traditional loan or leave to their children. Additionally, Tiny Homes residents have access to the full Cass network of services including financial mentorship, mental health services and other personal and professional development opportunities.

Why?
The Cass Tiny Homes overall project is attempting a deep intervention in asset building for marginalized populations and offering a powerful example of community-based, community-benefit, green urban development. As Faith Fowler says in her book *Tiny Homes in a Big City*,

"The final yardstick for Cass Tiny Homes will be determined by how many people establish wealth by owning a (tiny) home, if an abandoned and blighted neighborhood starts to be repopulated, and whether the program inspires others to build quality micro housing which will consume fewer resources, utilize less energy and emit substantially less CO2."

Program: Terreform ONE's ONE Lab Fellows

Who & What?
Terreform ONE is an experimental, nonprofit consulting group promoting eco-urban smart design, working on everything from resilient neighborhoods to waste management and transportation. Since 2009, over 200 emerging young designers, architects, artists, inventors, scientists and urban planners have come from around the world to participate in the ONE Lab fellowship program, a hands-on, intensive 12-week immersion on smart cities. The core program is developed around a real-world project, taught by faculty and experts spanning a diverse range of fields. Skill-building workshops designed to augment the core studio work

address urban agriculture, synthetic biology, parametric design and digital fabrication, soft infrastructure and biomaterials.

Why?
Traditional educational institutions and workplaces are generally not geared towards giving emerging designers time to learn, experiment and collaborate on cross-sector teams while inside the framework of a nonprofit organization with a social mission. The ONE Lab program is training the next generation of architects, planners and cultural creatives to bring eco-urban theory and speculative design to practical research and products with immediate applicability for city governments and urban planners. Former fellow Cecil Howell writes,

"As a practicing landscape architect... I still rely on the methods I learned at Terreform ONE for approaching research and design and am dedicated to the Terreform principles of creating smarter cities that support diverse ecologies and societies."

There are many problems to solve in this world, but as philanthropic investors we believe it worthwhile to put resources in the hands of community leaders like those at Cass operating the intersection of urban renewal, economic justice and environmentalism. We also believe it worthwhile to invest in the next generation of city builders like those at ONE Lab operating at the intersection of educational experimentation, design and eco-urbanism. While these programs differ greatly, it is imperative for the future of our species and our planet that such visionaries and their communities have room to breathe, imagine, dream and do.

Will these relatively small-scale programs save all of our cities or solve all of our environmental challenges? No. But if we do not dare to imagine and take the first steps, we will have neither the cities nor the societies of our dreams, and the environment itself may become an imagined dream of the past.

In the Petri Dish

NURHAN GOKTURK

The Bio City Map is a drawing of a microcosmic world created through the magnification of competing strains of bacteria that were grown in a petri dish. They embody the physical collection of microbial life, applied science and observable nature magnified through the imagination. Since life is ephemeral, the lines on the drawings keep a visual hold of a disappearing biological framework, both real and impulsive. This collective representation of physical ephemera and imagined communities are organizational fields for spatial practices rooted in cartography and geography.

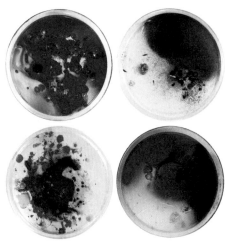

Bio city world map and petri dishes.

Gas and Bees: An Evident Proclamation

ANNA BOKOV
With NINA EDWARDS ANKER,
PEDER ANKER,
and MITCHELL JOACHIM

Based on the recent scholarship on massive environmental shifts explored in books such as Bill McKibben's, Oil and Honey, The End of Nature, and Naomi Klein's This Changes Everything, this proclamation seeks to underscore an architecture for a recovering planet. Gas and Bees is a meta theme that simultaneously addresses the ecological issues grounded in climate dynamics, cultural identities, constructed environments, and political agendas as they impact the ensuing Anthropocene. Gas and Bees is a code for industrial society and nature in furious opposition.

Nature and society must not remain entwined in conflict. The stakes are too high. The effects of climate change and species depletion pose drastic challenges to the architecture and urban design communities. The immediate response has been a turn toward a host of energy-saving technologies or behavior modifications. What has rarely been addressed, however, is how designers can bridge the Gas and Bees divide. By placing human rational, emotional, technological, and social needs at the center of our environmental concerns, we propose a new design initiative. This exploit seeks to collapse the differentiations between these two forces.

Bees play a crucial role in our civilized world. Practiced by humans since 20,000 BC, beekeeping predates the dawn of agriculture. Bees are nature's own architects, highly organized and effective as a collective. In this way, they are a symbol of organization and labor. Practically speaking, bees are essential to all kinds of agricultural production. They are pollinators for more than two-thirds of all plants we eat. The destruction of the bee population will have a cascading effect – known as the colony collapse disorder - entire ecosystems will collapse. The extinction of such species is signal to humanity that we are at a tipping point in our own existence.

Similar to the destruction of bee colonies, industrial society has an internalized self-destruct mechanism. This proclamation is structured in four sections that unpack the various directives towards the redesign of modernism: 1) Climates, 2) Cultures, 3) Constructs, 4) Politics that provide an organizational framework for the architectural, and urban projects from across the globe and engage a variety of stakeholders – from designers to the general public, and a range of scales - from global to local, from nation-wide to site-specific. Temporal dimensions – Past, Present, and Future offer a way to organize and cross-reference the four sections. All of this help categorically understand the basis for a societal redesign.

1. Climates

Climate dynamics, overproduction, heavy farming, pesticides, genetic engineering – these colossal shifts in man's activities – causes bees and other living species to disappear. Climate change is a direct result of mining the fossil fuel and is devastating the environment. This proclamation addresses the effects of the world-wide transformation of a petroleum society within the built environment. What does the end of the petroleum society mean for designers, architects, and planners? We argue for the end of petroleum architecture and instead are driven by geothermal, hydro, wind, solar, and other alternative sources.

Modern architecture has been traditionally closed in, relying on artificially controlled climatized environments. How can architecture rely less on the controlled climate – be less impervious and more porous? This section explores the notion of artificial climates: architecture and Anthropocene – across various climatically challenged environments – from North to South.

Notwithstanding the need for climatized spaces that make it possible for large groups of population to live in weather challenged regions, such as the Arctic Circle or Southern America. Historically designing for extreme conditions in cold climates this has been taken up in the United States, Western Europe, and former Soviet Union. The semi-failed attempts of occupying the Arctic included constructing the Northern Sea Route and cities such as Murmansk or Norilsk. With climate change and the melting of ice caps, the Trans Polar Passage along the northern seas becomes more navigable thus presenting a series of opportunities for inhabiting the territories along the Route. The proclamation explores these new visions as well as histories of settling the Arctic. Instead invites proposals for new types of environmentally friendly architectures, infrastructures, and public spaces using active and passive energy technologies.

Beyond helping raise awareness about climate change (as does the keeling curve) – we demand architects lead the movement rather than react to facts such as these. How can architecture reposition itself as a field and as a body of work to both resist and embrace climate change? What are the steps necessary to contribute to building a green world?

2. Cultures

Bauhaus defined the Modern movement in terms of mass production and functionality. Nearly 100 years later its design achievements are still considered models of excellence. Vkhutemas, a counterpart of the Bauhaus in Russia, and a cradle of Constructivism, pioneered functional design based on the economy of means. It set a standard for a lifestyle "without possessions" – which we now call sustainable. Both schools redefined the everyday objects and developed new standards for how we live.

100 years after the Bauhaus and Vkhutemas – the schools that essentially institutionalized functionalism as a design paradigm – we find ourselves, as architects today, in a world where the new mode of operation is sustainability. As we move from "form as function," we ask ourselves and others – what is the form of green? What is the aesthetics of sustainability?
While we are increasingly aware of the performative aspects of green architecture and urbanism, we have yet to define what it looks like. We believe that it is no longer enough to simply be "green," rather, we have to be mindful of aesthetic dimension of sustainable architecture. We encourage the exploration of the various design solutions and their implications within the framework of sustainability.

Despite the growing interconnectivity brought by the evolving web, telecommunications, and transportation, our contemporary world remains deeply divided. Culture is still a local characteristic. People continue to define themselves within heterotopic perspectives of cultural engagement and variance. The proclamation presents a platform for exploring issues of identity, patterns of migration, and socio-economic issues such as poverty, as they shape the development of our manmade physical domain.

The enormous region of the North is divided between few superpowers, including Scandinavia, Russia, USA & Canada, and Great Britain. Yet it is also populated by the small nations, the indigenous peoples, who struggle to maintain their traditions and national identity. The inherent tension between small and large – local ethnos and enormous states needs to be addressed in how we design with the context and culture in mind. The cultural contexts and sites are still guided by the proverbial yet evasive Genius Loci.

3. Constructs

Constructed man-made environments – i.e. architecture – is one of the largest consumers of energy on the planet. As architects, it is our responsibility to not only be aware of the role that buildings play in climate dynamics overall. What does it mean to create a built environment for a more resilient world? How can we change our relationship to the planet with regards to – food, water, waste, energy, air quality, mobility, equity? We are interested in exploring the most salient design solutions in these categories.

How can architecture be more inclusive not just to humans but also to the different living species? In order to be sustainable, we need to learn to live together, not just with each other but with other species – in a symbiotic way. We are interested in both imaginative and scientifically grounded scenarios for peaceful cohabitation. We propose constructing architecture for non-humans – from butterflies and crickets, to fish and oysters. These projects would offer solutions for the emergent fields of sub-sea, entomological, and aviary architectures, but also offer ways for sustainable farming and ecologically friendly food sources. These are not simply physical structures but also the logistical chains and novel social constructs – reinventing the way we think about nature, as well as the everyday practices and things, such as eating and farming.

4. Politics

The politics of nations and the charged politics of sites – are a complex web of interactions between many stakeholders. Political acts guide and shape our cities. They directly influence the architects, clients, users, and especially the larger pubic. Most leaders follow the capricious desires of their population, endless polling and skewed media. These partisan outcomes are not always aligned with the needs of the planet or the greater good. Politics in many cases limits and

defines areas of effect in order to protect those inside the sphere of influence. This top-down governmental myopia has changed little even after the implanting of global organizations such as the United Nations. Where does design intersect with politics to enforce positive change?

Movement of the people across the globe, prompted by military unrest and ecological disasters effects entire continents. At the same time, migration of entire species prompted by climate change has a major ecological impact, as for example the recent migration of Pacific oysters. These politics of exodus – whether because of extinction, migration, or flows focus on the movements of people, as well as species. It looks at how these are impacting the public domain – from ecological systems to logistical chains.

Steering the future of climates, cultures, and constructs requires political will, manifested as a system of goals and values. Sustainability policies are increasingly taking the form of directives on the national and global scale, balancing the agenda future sustainability with the current economic interests. Many of the large petroleum producers adopt a forward-looking posture to reduce carbon emissions, notwithstanding the legacy of economic issues in collecting oil revenue. How does architecture, as an integral part of creating global infrastructure, play a key role in this transition?

Conversation with Terreform ONE

ZACK SAUNDERS

ZACK SAUNDERS
I hear that more and more... the idea of the signature architect, or figure-head, being a model of the past. And yet, such 'solitary genius' may be necessary to inspire individuals to act, to do something novel and important. Ego, ownership, and innovation all contribute to ones' identity... the relationship between the figure-head architect and their followers might just be analogous to that of the studio or group and its members. Individual signature is the same as group identity in this sense. Except perhaps when the individual dies, the snake is just a headless corpse...

MITCHELL JOACHIM
Archigram, a group that inspired Terreform ONE, was (and still is) quite successful as a league of individuals with various ideas... Peter Cook with his plug-in city, Ron Herron with one that walks... The snake euphemism doesn't hold here. A multi-headed hydra seems more accurate... The signature does exist at the group level, sure, but the hydra doesn't die when it loses a head. In fact, it probably multiplies. The lead designer for Bilbao worked in Gehry's office for two decades, then struck out on his own and opened his own office... sadly, nobody cares. At the same time, Rem is very supportive of his 'children', the signature individual supports a kind of lineage in this way.

ZS I did an internship at Peter Cook's Crab Studio in London a few years ago. It was wholly a good experience for me as a young designer, in fact I was still a student at the time... Peter, and the studio's co-founder Gavin Robotham, are very hands-on and run the place less like an office and more like a studio. Even still, there were numerous times when, mostly in their absence, I sensed that fellow designers were producing not necessarily architecture but their concept of the kind of architecture that Peter and Gavin might do, or want done... in this way, pedagogy becomes style or even fashion in the professional one. With your example of Rem or mine of Peter, the figurehead takes the role of a nurturer, rather than a kind of authoritarian figure, yet a particular pedagogy is still propagated by virtue of the desire to please by those that work for them or associate with them...

MJ We have actually been so interested in pedagogy in schools in particular that we've been working on a 5-year study on the subject. We have also been looking extensively on the ranking systems in architecture schools. What does it mean to receive a high rank? What makes a good school of architecture? Why don't we build a customized ranking system for people that want to study architecture, one that is totally geared towards the students' interests and preferences? A prospective student could fill out a survey that could help narrow the options down which might clarify whether they would do well in a school like Sci-Arc, or Princeton, and so forth. I once watched a TED talk where the speaker illustrated how a researcher revolutionized the tomato sauce industry by not looking for the perfect sauce, singular, but by providing a multitude of options for people to choose from (1).

ZS At the same time, I would hope the 'answer' to such a survey would not be so straight-forward, in the style of Douglas Adams, something like '42' (laughter)... because the college experience is a bit about delving into the unknown, finding yourself, and all that comes with that...

MJ (Laughter) Yes, of course.

Design with Life

zs Speaking of TED talks, variety and choice, I recall one where the speaker uses the plethora of choices available when shopping for jeans, and his own experience with not finding the 'perfect pair', as an example of how too much variety might actually lead to disappointment with one's choice due to the increased expectations one has about how good those options will be (2)... he even argues that a kind of paralysis might ensue whereby a choice is not even made at all due to the overwhelming number of choices.

MJ I can definitely see the correlation between the jeans example and make the right choice when it comes to selecting an architecture school. Gladly, one is a bit more complex than the other! When you go to architecture school, you're trained to be a leader, not just a consumer of goods or a follower of trends. Malcolm Gladwell was his name... the spaghetti sauce guy. The main idea I wanted to illustrate with that example is that customization, rendered possible by a larger selection of distinct and therefore different sauces, for instance, might be a concept that architecture schools could benefit from, rather than all offering basically the same thing.

zs I see mature designers presenting their work in its finished state, I see Mitchell Joachim on TED, for instance, talking about his projects and showing refined drawings, visions, and structures... but I don't see the struggle, the choices, the hours of work and research that went into making, say, the 'meat house', possible... I wonder how much of that is taught, how much of it is 'ego, ownership and innovation' on the part of the designer, and how much is just sheer will not to quit... I think the question is a pressing one because I am not wholly convinced that teaching architecture is even possible...

MJ I strongly believe that there isn't just one way to do or teach architecture. Let me be very clear here, I believe that the educational system should be structured in two tracks. The first should offer an education in Building Science where a student graduates in 4 years and, with at least one year of internship in the field, they get licensed and go out in the world and design buildings. The second is a Ph.D. track, which has its equivalent in the fields of Science, Mathematics, and History, these students would spend 7 years or more going down rabbit-holes, in studios surrounded by other students making things, with the aim of making original contributions to human knowledge. Can you teach someone who should be in one of these realms how to think like someone in the other? Probably not... and that's OK. The hardest thing to do is always to find the question! But yes, the struggle is always there, the research and effort behind the scenes is fundamental to any project that isn't total garbage, but we don't always have to present that part of it to the world. Sheer will to keep going is absolutely a necessity if you're going to do anything creative. And I guess I get ego points as well for breaking off and forming Terreform ONE with Maria Aiolova!

Terreform ONE is thinking not only in terms of new chapters of itself as a group or collective but rather as a part of a larger societal and global exchange. We decided to go outside the bounds of what a design studio normally does: we went non-profit, we created our own school, we run our own competitions, we work with novel materials and conduct intensive research, we work with topics that require extensive expertise... Why? Because, why not? A major driving force behind our initiatives is that we question authority, question the status quo, in order to promote smart design in cities and construct new visions of what the city of the future could be. In fact, we are beginning to grow in unexpected ways because
of this.

zs And yet, for at least the past five years, population growth in America's suburbs has accelerated while slowing in urban centers (3)... it seems the city as a project is dead, or at least on hold until further notice...

MJ We will be launching soon as an extension of Terreform ONE in the form of a private company. We are working on a large-scale concept for an actual city, which we are very excited about. We were approached by a CEO of a major corporation and Preet Bharara, the former New York District Attorney, who wanted to meet and 'chat', literally that's what they said, we had no stated agenda for our meeting. After chatting for a bit, he says 'we are planning to build a city'. Basic premises such as proximity to a body of water hadn't crossed their minds... name one major city that is not either located on the coast or near a river... but we are so disconnected in our thinking toward our relationship to nature that this was not first on the list until we brought it up. Anyway, their idea is that inhabitants will get paid $80,000 or so a year to live there, and people will work because they want to. How will they avoid people moving there to leech off the system I don't know, I'm sure there will need to be some sort of application process... the Tragedy of the Commons is something to keep in mind. But the idea of envisioning a city that can embody the principles of environmentally conscious design with local sustainability in energy, transportation, buildings, waste treatment, how you produce your food, where you get your water... all concepts that we have been working with and studying since Terreform ONE was founded, is very appealing to us.

ZS It almost seems like less of an architectural problem per se and more of a social or even philosophical one... it sounds like you wouldn't just be building a city but would be constructing an entire society, literally from the ground-up...

MJ Exactly. I visited the recent Frank Lloyd Wright exhibit at the MoMA... I'm not sure what came over me at the sight of his drawings for Broadacre City, but there is so much thought in those drawings which were once laughed off as a flight of fancy... towers in the middle of nowhere, surrounded by orchards and farms, drones flying around. It really makes me

think that the Suburbs might be another paradigm to consider in urban morphology that we really aren't looking at seriously today. But yes, you are making a society. And I think most architects, whether advertently or inadvertently, insert their world-view in their architectural works...

We are working on something that I don't believe has ever been done before... like finding a new territory that has yet to be explored. The project spiraled off from of our research into caddisflies and their underwater constructions; they really are a kind of architect of their own habitats, the larvae construct protective cases using detritus bonded together by silk. Could we retrain them to find microplastics and other debris in the environment and use that specific material in their cases? Anyway, we're working on a building facade in New York and this work with insects has trickled into the project. We decided to research an insect that would make sense in such a dense urban environment and we stumbled upon the monarch butterfly, a native species to Canada and New England. Slowly over time, due to human activities namely, the species has slowly declined. The facade we are proposing is not simply a skin to the building but rather a spatial enclosure, consisting of a tempered environment to house and nourish butterflies; a kind of vertical meadow filled with monarchs right in the heart of New York! Designed to be super-attenuated, noise canceling and conducive to the necessary environmental conditions for habitation, the Butterfly House will also act as a kind of ecological and environmental indicator of wellness for the local environs as well; the thinking here is if it's good enough for butterflies to flourish it's good enough for humans.

ZS I was watching 'Jaws' the other day, and most of the movie is concerned not with fighting the shark itself, but rather trying to convince the community that the work of fighting the shark needs to be done in the first place. Thinking of your work at Terreform ONE, I can't help but wonder how much of it is trying to convince the mayor of Amity that there is in fact, a problem?

MJ 'Jaws' is a great example because there is a palpable beast that you can see, in the form of course of the shark... you are able to identify as a threat the moment it begins eating people. I actually just saw the movie 'Piranha', which is a very shitty film compared to 'Jaws', but here fighting one fish becomes less of a task than fighting a swarm... in the film there is massive death, explosions everywhere, it's a mess. We really don't have a Jaws problem; we have a Piranha problem. Paul Kingsworth and Timothy Morton have been talking about it as a kind of Dark Ecology. Kingsworth is saying, in effect, that saving the world is hopeless, it's too late to save it anyway. Morton describes the concept as an ouroboric one, speaking of it in relation to Deckard from 'Bladerunner', who must cope with the realization that he is one and the same with the enemy he is pursuing... in this sense, Chief Brody would have to realize that he is the shark! Morton's ideas, which are influencing architects more and more today, of dark ecology, hyper objects, the end of nature, provide a refreshing new look at notions of ecology and even design, and his writings are very accessible. He speaks of hyper bodies for instance as a kind of embodied presence greater than each individual part. Cities are great examples of this, and architects are starting to learn how to engage these concepts.

ZS It seems where Morton talks about human kind being interconnected with all living and non-living things it has a sense of hopefulness that we might shine a light on the darkness, so to speak, awaken to the truth of the universe, and ultimately rethink our relationship with the world. I see your work as being closely aligned with this philosophy. Kingsworth, on the other hand, writes of a less utopic vision of the future, stating that nothing can stop the impending and ongoing crisis "barring some kind of reset: the kind that we have seen many times before in human history. Some kind of fall back down to a lower level of civilizational complexity. (4)" While this seems dismal and disheartening at first, these moments he is speaking of are responsible for spawning some of the most important moments of human history and carried us from the Dark Ages to the Renaissance, from a medieval world to an enlightened one, and so on.

MJ Major movements, periods where societies emerge from darkness into an age of enlightenment in one form or another, are part of our history for sure. But when you are at the moment, you can't see it for what it is. People are calling this the 'Age of Disruption', perhaps disruption is necessary for change, but it sounds a bit disappointing...

ZS "You recently were involved in a debate for the Seoul Biennale where you talked of the set-backs often faced by environmentally conscious design and the role played by major corporations in this, something about their artificial support..."

MJ Predatory delay, yes. When we first started out, it was impossible to define who we were fighting, particularly when companies like Shell and BP are giving lip-service to renewable energy and even contributing money towards research. Day to day these companies are making incredible profits, so the answer becomes 'sure, 20 years from now we'll change, but today? It's business as usual. Essentially, the Piranha problem isn't just a swarm of identical fish coming at you, but a swarm of individually different kinds of problems...

ZS You have to be quite agile, even...

MJ You have to be resilient!

Design Thinking for a Better World

By DESIGNINTELLIGENCE*

DesignIntelligence talked with Mitchell Joachim, co-founder of Terreform ONE, about living in balance with nature, how the design industry can become more relevant and influential to citizens of the planet, and how design can lead to solutions to the world's problems.

DESIGNINTELLIGENCE

In many ways, Terreform ONE is in the vanguard of experimental design and environmental work, looking at things in a new and different light. What are you seeing from the front?

MITCHELL JOACHIM

We began as an architecture group, but we realized that design itself is even bigger than architecture. The power of the human imagination is a phenomenal instrument. It is an extraordinary tool that we can use in all different sectors and disciplines to come up with solutions to our world's problems. We work on problems that are genuinely difficult and that bleed through many different spheres of interest. We're also restless – we want to do more. As architects, we have this incredible love for the field, and we want to have a broader reach. We want to be more relevant and influential as citizens of this planet and have a conversation that makes sense to ever-increasing numbers of people.

It's not that architects aren't relevant; we are. We just don't expose ourselves as much as we could in a way that shows how powerful design thinking really is. When we make that link, that connection with a broader audience, and we build consensus around relevancy, it has incredible meaning.

DI So, there's a precarious balance to strike when you're doing work that is very experimental, but at the same time having broad relevance and reach with a wider audience. How do you navigate that divide?

MJ Quite simply, it is the issues. For example, climate change is an all-encompassing problem that bleeds through many different industries. What people may not understand about architects is that we are trained at the general physics of almost anything. So, when we tackle an issue like climate change and begin to produce stories or design ideations that people can relate to, then we as architects are actually on the forefront of change on issues like these.

DI But isn't generating ideas and creating solutions only half of the battle? What about communication?

MJ Yes, communication is important. Generating ideas and solutions is just the first step. There is more hard work that has to be done, like moving through regulations and policy, getting political will, obtaining financing and more. But the idea and the possible solutions to a problem is the first principle. If we don't have that first principle in mind, the rest will not fall into place. We don't execute a non-idea. So, the upfront messaging and communication, as well as the clarity around the idea's purpose and intention, is where people get excited and get involved.

DI When we work with firms and organizations, we talk a lot about their ideal state. We use it as an exercise to get them to imagine their best possible future. What is your version of an ideal state for how we can live in balance with the natural world?

Design with Life

MJ I agree with the ideal state model. We deploy the same criteria when we approach a project. We outline the best case and maximal conditions, and then we're able to formally articulate that scenario.

When we talk about dwelling in balance with nature, one of the most intractable problems is our ever-growing, ever-expanding population. The Earth is crowded. It is full. And we are extracting more and more resources from it each year; somehow, we need to stop that. Most of the solutions I've seen have been on some level of mitigation, a slowing down, in our use of and extraction of resources.

I have two viewpoints about the state of our environment today – one is completely pessimistic, and the other is optimistic. The pessimistic viewpoint is that we're waiting for an enormous crisis –something like five times the size of Hurricane Sandy – to hit us. When that happens, people will become very concerned about nature. They will be more willing to change policy, incorporate technology and make lifestyle choices. They will be more interested in a renewable or circular economy. All of this concern and interest will coalesce into a library of ideas to actually make the world a better place. But we don't want to do things like that right now. The crisis factor, I believe, will bring the right amount of energy it takes to move us into Civilization 2.0.

The optimistic viewpoint is that technology will save us. This is the techno-topic version. The idea is that we have a lot of smart people who are working on solutions. Life will continue as we know it as scientists and designers work together to solve all these problems in stealthy fashion. The "logic" goes that all of this is happening behind the scenes, without us really noticing or caring, and suddenly we'll get out of these problems through an immense amount of innovation.

DI How does Terreform ONE set priorities and choose which investigations and projects to focus on?

MJ For us, every year is about finding something that is more meaningful than the previous project or idea. Lately, we've been focused on caring for and saving the lives of other species. In the field of living architecture or living design, we are designing with different forms of biological life. Everything that's in our portfolio now must be or involve a living organism. We're asking the question of how can the millions of living things on our planet help us overcome our problems?

For example, we are working with the caddisfly, training them to clean our freshwater ways of microplastics. They build their larval cases out of the microplastics, making it easier to harvest the plastics before they go into the ocean. That's just one example of how we're using life to solve problems in life.

DI Many of the problems and issues Terreform ONE tackles are massive and complex. What about the scale of application?

MJ In design, scale happens in very succinct increments and measures. It has a known, quantifiable system whether you're working at the scale of nuts and bolts, the scale of furniture, regional scale, atomic scale, whatever. If you've ever seen the movie *Powers of Ten* – which was about scale – the concept was that things flow freely from all points of scale and we have to be accountable for the consequences. For example, if a designer is designing a bicycle, he is accountable for how the bicycle works on the road, how the chain and brake systems are designed, the material choices and how they were created, and more. Every part of that design shifts scale but it happens simultaneously. We can think in just those moments, but they are temporary.

We need to understand scale as a phenomenon, not as a distinct increment. It is much more permeable as many shades of effect, and we must train ourselves to think in all different levels and depths of scale.

DI Let's talk a little about influence and the arena you're in now. The federal government is backing away from agreements and regulations regarding the environment, but mayors are standing up and saying that their cities will still abide by those agreements that were previously held at the national level. So, in this arena where there's a shift away from environmental agreements, have you noticed anything different – either positive or negative – in the support you receive for the kind of work you do?

MJ I think that general hierarchies and more traditional structures of power are becoming flatter. Connectivity is more accessible and available to people. For example, when our president tweets, everyone knows his immediate thoughts in real time. We all have the same access to the same information. This flattening of hierarchies and systems has been valuable for us because now, the work we're doing is more visible. It has a larger presence and a wider reach.

DI What do you see is the potential influence that the architecture and design community could have? Are any barriers to our influence self-imposed?

MJ In general, we can have influence in many different sectors and disciplines, but clients and developers may be pushing us in certain directions. We tend to listen to them. If we unified as an entire body and decided that we wouldn't design or build anything unless certain standards are met – and those standards would get more stringent as time goes on – then our role as influencers would grow.

Today, we have standards as options and possibilities, but they're not necessarily mandatory. It's difficult to pass regulations and legislation sometimes because it becomes associated with a monopoly system. Instead, we can use standards as performance criteria, which may negate the association with direct products and direct industries. If we did more self-regulation internally as an industry, we would also increase our influence.

DI Do you think that individuals from the A/E/C community should become more directly involved in politics and advocacy groups?

MJ There are examples of architects in government; not as many as we should have, though. We are trained in public speaking and communication, and we are trained in the art of representing an idea to a large audience and then defending it. As a part of our field, we do have the capacity to be leaders, but in general we're not necessarily of the politic class.

But we are good at what we do. And by working together both as designers and as citizens of the Earth, we can take our influence and leadership to another level.

*This article first appeared in the 2Q edition of *DesignIntelligence Quarterly*, "Design Thinking for a Better World: Interview with Mitchell Joachim", 2018, pp. 36-39.

Ecological Preservation is the Overlap between Culture and Biodiversity

NICHOLAS GERVASI

Ecological preservation is the joint support of local biodiversity and architecture in order to maintain place. In placemaking, there is a direct link between the culture that was established there, characterized by dialects, styles, and buildings, and the biota that evolved in adaptation to the environmental conditions present. Over time these two strands have woven together to form the locale specific traits that distinguish one place from another. We preserve these places to celebrate the level of differentiation that makes cities innovative and compelling. Productive overlaps of human-made and natural features set in motion sensory elements that compose place. It is the preservation of these processes and continued proliferation of unique characteristics that ecological preservation promotes. For the ecology is inseparable from the meaning of the site.

Vernacular architecture is analogous to local ecology in that it exemplifies a specific location at a point in time. Both reflect the culmination of innumerable forces and the minutiae of small agents acting within a larger framework. Buildings record in materials, such as stone, metal or glass, cultural decisions and trends just as ecosystems analog climatic events and disturbances. Affecting one another, biodiversity helps to ameliorate the human health risks associated with climate change. Pathogens and mutations are stymied by genetically diverse populations because rapid reproductive

and evolution are cut off. Furthermore, building redundancy into the system ensures that crucial ecosystem tasks like pollination are executed.

Ecology is relevant to cities because it brings cognizance to our impact on the environment, protects undiscovered future beneficial breakthroughs, eloquently defends with soft infrastructure against disasters, and philosophically expresses the inherent intrinsic value of the planet. Hence, preserving this ecology pertains not only to our current situation but also to future possibilities.

New York City's allure is attributed to its distinct pockets of culture. These pockets' lasting impact is that they have been allowed to gradually change. As opposed to absolute demolition and tabula rasa construction, the architecture of New York progresses through assimilation. As the wave of new culture descends upon the city, storefronts accommodate through facade alterations. The mercurial turnover of restaurants and bars infuses liveliness into the neighborhoods. Adaptive re-use reinvigorates structures through added or enhanced programming to better resemble our twenty-four-hour lifestyles. Although the concept of preserving a process of change begets difficulties, so does hitting a moving target; this intermixing is crucial to keeping the city operating at its full potential.

New information makes historic architecture relevant to the present discourse by reframing it. Preservation defines objects. In particular, the field assigns objects to a given category based on component parts or grants them a certain type of significance based on their role in shaping a movement. As the recording instruments, such as the camera or laser scanning, become more sophisticated our ability to edit the definition grows radically. Technology adjusts our lens of the world; new ways of seeing lead to new ways of understanding. Thus, an important feature of safeguarding historic objects and architecture is to allow them to be seen through these new lenses.

This repeated exposure spawns multiple and more advanced interpretations.

Objects in the built environment undergo inevitable change. Through time, forces of nature, economics, and politics ultimately metamorphose the original building with its initial design intent into a different object, with varying degrees of resemblance to the original. As an architectural palimpsest, the city becomes layered with restorations, rehabilitations, and replacements. Past narratives are torn down and new stories built upon their ruins. In a similar manner, ecosystems transform as nutrient cycles are modified and subsequently certain species rise and fall.

Imbuing new knowledge into our perception of extant structures has only begun. Scan Pyramids revealed through cosmic ray technology voids and cavities within Khufu's Pyramid including a large one above the Grand Gallery. Technology has expanded our idea of this pyramid and the narrative of how it was built. Additionally, an international research team analyzed protein residues in ceramics from Çatalhöyük to determine that their diet consisted of cereals, legumes, dairy products, and meat. While bones from these animals have been found across the area and previous lipid analyses have identified milk fats in vessels, this is the first time researchers have been able to specifically identify which animals were used for their milk. This novel finding would not have been discovered if the pots had been discarded after what was deemed a full interpretation of them. Further examples can be found in building scanning procedures relating to textures and colors found in walls, floors, and frescos.

Preservation acts as a reading comprehension guide of the built environment. A living library or three-dimensional dictionary of tectonics and style, it catalogs various movements and innovations in architecture. Preservation parallels ecosystems in that both benefit from greater diversity. Just as ecosystems with higher biodiversity have higher stability which includes increased resistance and resilience in the wake of disturbances, cities with designated buildings have increased cultural content and more opportunities for creative crossover. Preserving urban biodiversity ensures these productive overlaps are maintained in conjunction with protecting our heritage for future speculation.

INTERVIEWS

ECOGRAM A
+ Nature
+ Urban Ecology
+ Synthetic Biology

SRDJAN JOVANOVIC WEISS
Who can speak for what you do in terms of philosophy or theory?
I want this conversation to stay raw. I want to keep the softhearted emotion and conceptual flow of this dialogue for posterity. Please be candid, as I am a perspicacious interviewer.

MITCHELL JOACHIM
There are people who have deep philosophies to which we subscribe, such as Timothy Morton, who is at this Yale conference. I've been reading Tim Morton since his first book, at least eight years ago. He made a lot of sense to me when he -used the word "ecology" rather than "nature" because the problem in the prescription of nature was so fraught with different layers of meaning - it was an absolutely useless term in environmental studies -, and the term ecology was actually far more appropriate. Since then he's done "Hyperobjects" and many other texts and is a philosopher who's also interested in dark ecology, deep ecology. This is something we embrace in our work. Do Tim and I really engage in anything on a day-to-day basis? No, but in terms of the philosophical underpinnings, absolutely. He's coming from Arne Naess in Oslo; he's coming from Bill McDonough in some of his arguments. He's going back to Henry David Thoreau, to the environmental intelligentsia and their super leftist perspectives.

SJW What makes it leftist?

MJ Leftist in the political sense in the United States is like being Noam Chomsky. Being on the extreme left means supporting climate change and climate science and wanting to enact policy and think of new regulations and carbon caps. This is a highly leftist proposition because it definitely runs against conservative ideals about business, the interruption of business, free economies and openness, and free trade. Climate totally puts that to a stop. It's at loggerheads. You can't do both. You can't make tons of money and do the Trump thing and at the same time recognize that resources are finite and that the activities we do are damaging the planet. So, our theoretical underpinning goes from Thoreau, Emerson, and Alcott all the way up to more recent philosophers, even Bill McKibben and things like The End of Nature. These are not things that are necessarily in the traditional mainstream architectural dialogue, but if Tim Morton is heading a conference at Yale next week, they're there. So good for Tim and his friends over there.

MARIA AIOLOVA So, was the question more about the people, the theorists who know about our work and talk about our work? Is that what you were asking?

MJ I've seen a couple of texts like that. Even Jared Diamond makes the argument that it's the activities of the natural world that influence the way in which societies and civilizations rise and fall. By now it's kind of a classic thesis. I wrote a recent piece on ten archetypes of nature, simply as a term.

SJW What was the piece?

MJ Ten archetypes of nature and ten meanings of nature that you can easily find. At the end of the day it is kind of confusing. Perhaps we should specify what we're really talking about, which is ecology. At the same time, however, those ten archetypes are one. There's the notion of nature in a primordial state, that is, before man – the geological state of the earth billions of years ago, which also kind of describes the nature of the universe itself. That's what some people think when you say "nature." But not all designers do – certainly not any of those you might ask. Then there's the Edenic of the Bible and all the biblical takes on absolute harmony – the version of nature in which one can walk around naked, everyone's naked, one can talk to the animals. Anything and everything is ok. There's no desire, no presumption.

SJW I have a very funny story. We were in Europe in July and I was explaining German nudist camps to my son and how funny a thing it was to transmit culture through one's own body.

MJ Well, the nudist camp is a state of nature to which some people think we should return. There's also the noble savage – Rousseau – a similar version of the original state of man as being close to the land, in which man can do no wrong. There's no need to own property, there are no boundaries, everything is shared. There's no tragedy.

SJW It's a kind of anarchy?

MJ No, it's native. It's total respect for nature and the understanding that it controls everything. We talk about Design for Life. It's something to which we probably want to return, but something that is totally lost in the modern era. We all have instincts that we constantly ignore. I do as well. They're somewhere in our past but we don't recall them. The noble savage is someone we'd have to go to New Guinea to find. Genuine noble savages in the middle of the Amazon are the people who haven't seen modern man for three centuries. That's a different nature. There's also the pastoral sublime, nature that is very beautiful but managed by man, the nature of Louis XIV. That nature is a part of human culture. Man has the ability to shape and control nature, but it can go spiraling out of control. Some people look at Versailles and think that's nature.

SJW I really do not see your work as dystopian at all, but many textbooks lead other people to think so, to see it as a postcondition. I see your work as humanistic and as involving nature or ecology, so I want you to speak more about this.

MA I've been thinking recently about what it means to design with life and I've been trying to formulate how we define life. In part, it's an ability to reproduce, to multiply. It's living because it is completely self-sufficient, it is contained within itself – it can multiply and reproduce. This comes from information that is in the DNA that doesn't exist in something which is inert. I am troubled by this term '"nature" because typically we think nature stops at the edge of the city – the idea that there is the natural world and then there is the city. In these terms, if you think of ecology then you have to think of urban ecology which is not just about the watershed but also the sewage shed. This is part of something we need to understand. So, it's the way we approach and study nature as being outside the city while thinking about ecology and how ecology is studied as an experiment. The idea is to use this thinking for an urban approach. I see our work as thinking about the urban ecology. Projects like "24 Hour Refuse" are studies of these principles.

MJ What's important about ecology is its replicability. If you make a statement about an ecosystem in a specific area with a set of behaviors that statement works elsewhere. Anything that moves off that pattern of thinking would be an anomaly and would need to be studied and incorporated back into its rule base. Ecology has replicability; it has a reliance on counting and facts that establish patterns that affect cities, affect the landscape. It's not a perfect science but there's an absolute attitude that these are things that are known, and their behaviors are known, and it can be translated to other areas. That's what makes a great point of departure for any project. Water is going to behave this way, corridors around the water are going to behave this way. When you start thinking about human intervention or settlements alongside those things they're going to have certain effects and we want to avoid the impact of those effects being negative. The impacts should absolutely be positive, acting on those existing ecological places.

SJW Who were you influenced by?

MJ Bernard Tschumi who is a real hero both as an educator, theoretician, and a practitioner. Tschumi certainly believed, or promoted the idea of deconstruction, and he did a great job executing it in the buildings he's built. Ecology was not something he was involved in at all, at least for most of the 70's, the entire 80's and the 90's. He's been more recently involved in it at the level of material and building performance, but it was not really his domain. That does not mean his forms, his methodology, his approach to breaking down his ideas on disjunctive architecture are not enormously important, and they don't go away just because we have a new system on top of it. Tschumi, who was a huge hero when I was a student, is still a huge hero of mine but in some ways we had to discard him just a bit because some of his rhetoric is not really relevant to the problems we're facing both as a society and as a body of architects and planners. Some of things we represent are not best represented by some of Tschumi's theories, they're just too specific, too insular to the field itself, too much about the music, not so much about the message.

SJW I really don't see you guys as an offshoot of anything, that's why I'm so curious. I want to know, if you're not an offshoot from architecture, I'm curious from where?

MJ I would argue that we do have architectural offshoots.

MA Science. Synthetic biology was something that was very influential.

MJ Synthetic biology definitely was, but if it wasn't for groups like Archigram or even some things that Greg Lynn has proposed, and some of – geez half the Austrians back in the day, Haus-Rucker-Co and Hans Hollein, were these experimentalists who, in a formal way, were thinking about new natures that weren't achievable in their time. We were lucky enough that the tools of synthetic biology have given us the ability to actually animate them, to move them out of abstraction into real things. But Archigram had the electric tomato; they were all about the propaganda. They were about this explosion of the new age, plus they worked as a group, so they didn't privilege one individual. It wasn't in service of an individual ego, so they weren't a starchitecture team. They were a team.

ECOGRAM B
+ Craft
+ Organic Architecture
+ Phenomenology

SRDJAN JOVANOVIC WEISS
You mentioned something about craft. The person who speaks about craft most is Kenneth Frampton, the nemesis of Charles Jencks.

MITCHELL JOACHIM
Yes? I never picked up on that, I guess.

SJW Well anyway, they are the heavy hitters. I was curious about craft; let's talk about craft.

MJ I think Frampton is pretty much the most sagacious individual in architecture. There's no one alive who's wiser today. He is literally my favorite theoretician, period. And he is real. Even our concept of socio-ecological design came about through a conversation with him. I was talking to him (2006) we were running a conference called Ecogram at Columbia. We were discussing environment and architecture, for which Frampton has always been an advocate even at the time he was working for Richard Meier. He gave him a job and he worked in his firm for about six months until he quit, realizing that he couldn't do it. But Richard Meier was opposed to solar panels, against environment – he's not interested to this day – while Frampton has always been interested in the environment, climate change, in aesthetics and in how the environment influences buildings. He is one of the strongest advocates of this kind of architecture. He fought Wigley pretty much all the time. Wigley refused even to recognize it; he effectively called it climate control in buildings. He wouldn't call it environmental.

SJW How does this affect you?

MJ Well, on a pedagogical level, Frampton's notion of craft should absolutely be the way in which every architecture student explores the matter: build a large-scale model of a section of a major project or work – an example of recent modernism – and learn the systems, connections, the scale, and the assembly of all its components. Do it in drawing, do it in a model, do it in computational form, and then try to write a description. That's architecture. Basically, he's right about that. And then there's his idea about critical regionalism – building with consideration for the influence and the context, in which he promotes Alvar Aalto even more than he does Le Corbusier and others, though he promotes them as well. In architecture, the regional effect had an incredible influence on materials, the impact of Westernization, and the ability to assemble with the craft of local labor and its skill sets. Frampton really captures this kind of architecture and is quick to understand what computers are doing, how they're creating a more universal language and losing that sense of regionalism.

SJW So, is Alvar Aalto one of your heroes in organic architecture?

MJ Absolutely. Alvar's a big hero. We actually have the same birthday.

SJW No kidding. What is it?

MJ February 3rd. It's a good day to be born an architect. But yes...Frank Lloyd Wright was too over the top; Corbusier for the most part was too stripped bare; and Aalto was just the perfect blend of those two.

SJW In terms of not being religious but doing Design With Life, in which many references come from craft, from organic architecture, from people who have been infused with nature and who have then reproduced what they call organic architecture almost as if it were a religion, and have gotten into phenomenology, feelings about being in space, of connection – I don't see you being phenomenological at all, which is something I like. I see Aalto, organic architecture. Perhaps Frampton has the best explanation of Aalto.

MJ Frampton? Well, he's been a major advocate, but it's not as though Aalto lacked people who could communicate and interpret his work. He is a legitimate master. Baker, the dormitory at MIT, was a phenomenal project for its time, even for today and beyond. It is simply fantastic to see. No one gets staircases as Aalto did; no one did brickwork like that. His brickwork is stunning.

MARIA AIOLOVA
Phenomenology is definitely a part. I was really influenced by Gaston Bachelard's Poetics of Space, and I think we apply this to our work. While it's not merely about experience, it is in a way trying to create meaning in the same way that religion does. We create a project with a layer of propaganda. We convince people that we can grow a whole house out of living materials, plants, mycelium, pig cells. It's the idea of doing it, because we're not trying to justify why. We are really focusing on how we're going to do it. That's where the craft comes in. We're solving things on every level, perfecting every detail...

SJW And that's how you bypass the religious belief.

MA Right. Because we're not focusing on why. But we're telling people you how you're going to do it.

MJ I find it so hard to comment on religion. Or even spirituality. I'm a non-practicing atheist, I think the stuff is fairytales. And I even have trouble allowing my kids to understand it because I want them to come to terms with their spirituality and their religious beliefs in their own way. My parents let me do that. One being Jewish, one being Catholic, so I really had to figure out my own religion. Which is basically guilt, from both sides.

SJW What you do is something very close to feelings, but it's not religious, it's not immersion.

MJ For us, the phenomenological part of it is that through the mind's eye we can occupy what it would be like for a group of crickets. We can occupy moments in space that the body can't travel into, but we can visualize, interpret, even feel.

ECOGRAM C
+ Apocalypse
+ Science Fiction
+ Robotics

SRDJAN JOVANOVIC WEISS

OK, let me just show you my cards. I really want to converse with you as with someone who designs the brief and not only delivers the goods of practice – not only in theory, but also in spatial practice, and as opposed to many who don't do that kind of thing.

MARIA AIOLOVA

I think the best way to frame our practice is... the ability to speculate. We speculate about the future; that's become our brief. If we think about the Sci-Fi films we have discussed – humans have always had that yearning to envision the future, almost as a way of controlling, but also justifying it. That's why religions exist – to offer that level of meaning. As for us, we took a different approach. It was the idea that when it's a scientific endeavor it's still speculative, but its goal is not merely to create aesthetic images, which, of course, are so beautiful in films. We began with that but then added a layer of science. In a scientific endeavor, one projects, one experiments. It takes many, many years and the involvement of many people, so it's not simply up to one designer to solve the problem.

SJW Right, but, you do have an aesthetic drive as well. We spoke about this, which is why I want to focus on science, art. Maybe we can talk about the movies; Brazil is one of the movies I too admire most because it's post-apocalyptic. Is the future that bleak? Or will architecture be changed or advanced in the process of advancing humanity.

MITCHELL JOACHIM

That's the problem I have with Blade Runner, and also Brazil, which is my favorite movie of all time. Popular Science asked a bunch of people about the best Sci Fi films of all time. We also had to pick the worst moments in Sci Fi – so the best and the worst moments. As the worst moment I proposed the Midi-chlorian, in Star Wars Episode 1, in which the Force had some idea of control over these little atoms in the air. That was the worst thing they could have done. It actually took first place in Sci-fi history as the worst thing that they could have done – the Midi-chlorians – because as soon as one tries to explain the Force with any rational kind of theory of physics, it totally falls apart. The whole point is to let it be mystical because we've always believed that technology looks like magic to a lesser or a less advanced society. And there's no point in explaining this because Star Wars is supposed to lie a century or two in the future. The idea that we have some way of cognizing what the Force is, is simply pointless. The point is, just leave it as The Force. Although we don't see it as a religious thing, it is a higher power. This also is the best thing to do with clients: let them fill in their own narrative, their own kind of creative arc to whatever it is that is being speculated. That's why the Force works. People can discuss it, we can argue about it all day long, but no one, including George Lucas, will ever tell us what it is. As soon as it's revealed, it becomes a problem. The Brazil-Bladerunner thing, the apocalypse as future, really sucks. It's simply not something anyone wants. I've got kids; no one wants an apocalypse.

SJW Why do you like these movies?

MJ There is a difference between Blade Runner and Brazil. Brazil may have this kind of apocalyptic edge, but much of it has come true. In fact, as a speculative narrative, it is one of the few movies that can lay claim to the kind of philosophy that Google did not even exist as a shadow of an idea at the time. Yet the whole movie was about information retrieval and the layers of power associated with information and a giant corporation that did nothing but command information. That's exactly what Google is. And what was profound as hell to me – and still is – is that terrorism is rampant in the film, to the point that when acts of terrorism occur during dinner, people just put up a little screen and don't stop the table service.

MA I saw Brazil when I was a young teenager growing up in Bulgaria. The Communists kind of got it wrong because they thought it was an anti-capitalist movie, so they released it. That was in '85 or '86, when I was going to the movies every day of the week. I saw it seven times the very first week it opened because I couldn't get enough. Obviously, the narrative is really powerful, but the aesthetic and the design were crucial to telling the story. I don't think it would have had that impact without the aesthetics.

SJW But what you saw and what I saw in 84' was not the director's cut but the producer's. So, it stops at the certain point...

MJ Where did you see it again?

SJW In Yugoslavia. I went to see it every night. First, I went to a club dancing to The Clash, then I went to see the film.

MA Yeah, it became like a cult.

MJ I didn't understand it.

MA The aesthetics of the film are very heavy handed. I think that's what we do in a way. These projects all have ideas behind them, but they're highly formal. And that's hard to defend. The question comes up all the time. We are designers, you know, and though we're speculating and bringing in all these questions, we are still making decisions about aesthetics.

MJ "Heavy Handed" would be a great title for a book, now that I think about it. As in the world of design, where there's a division between those who want fabulous, exotic and gorgeous kinds of lush design, and the sensitive minimal structuralists. There's some negativity associated with the heavy-handed thing, but...

SJW What is the negativity?

MJ Lebbeus Woods is a paper architect. He's a heavy-handed paper architect who belongs to a kind of Pantheon of dreamers that are perfect for the inner sanctum of places like Cooper Union but in many cases really have no business in the built world.

SJW He was seen as visionary and a formalist.

MA He's a formalist, but he's gorgeous – or was. His work is inspiring beyond comprehension. Inspiration is part of what we should do. Brazil is also based around inspiration. The whole point is that the protagonist was dreaming about this other world, chasing this mysterious woman, who in real life was something very different from the one in his dream world. And the things in his dreams were so complex and difficult to make out – like the giant Samurai warrior trying to take him on. But then he had the designs of his own body transformed; he was able to fly and wore armor... I still remember it all vividly, and I keep trying to revisit it. And everytime I see it again, I think, this is just spectacular in every possible way. There were autonomous vehicles in that movie, all of that...

MJ Yeah, it is something like that. The apartment, the guts and the pipes come out of this beautiful clean wall that need Robert De Niro eventually to fix it illegally, which is what's happening now with Bit Torrent to all kinds of ways that we hack systems. The hacker has become dominant. The maker was Robert De Niro, the rogue engineer. I mean the rogue engineer is an awesome statement. Dirty Realism certainly, but I don't know if it was an apocalypse. too didn't really recognize, I don't remember if there was an apocalypse in Blade Runner either; an actual end of the world scenario. But there was definitely a poisoning of the atmosphere in Bladerunner. It was even more apparent in Brazil, it just didn't tell you what the context of the world was, except that everything was dark. And that was probably a combination of things. Blade Runner was very much about, something that happened to the atmosphere that eliminated sunlight and caused constant rainfall, and cities have gone to such a mega scale that the poor have a whole new low. Their bottom is busted out. And that massive corporations are dominating everything in society. And the bigger notion of biotech was explosive in that film. Which is still this kind of long arc, I would say man's desire in this case. Of the replication of people. Mostly women, probably, for sexual objects, then eventually reproducing men for warfare. And this is no different than Westworld that's resurfaced again on HBO. Have you guys seen that? So, same theme. Here's a bunch of robots you can have sex with, rape them, and then kill them. And then go out and kill a bunch of other ones for sheer joy and pleasure, and they're all 3D printed in some kind of bio-printer.

SJW Isn't that apocalyptic?

MJ Well, it is if you think it's the end of the world, but I think the thing about Sci-fi that works is that if the narrative is popular, and continues through many different threads, through many different novels, through many different movies, and it's always constant with subtle variations, you can expect one day it's going to come true. Who does not want to have a FemBot, even as some kind of a joke? Some guy, some sicko, is going to produce the first version of a robotic female, I mean that's Metropolis. So, I don't think it's the apocalypse if it's just a trajectory that we can recognize and speculate about.

ECOGRAM D
+ Memory
+ Manufacturing
+ Genetics

MITCHELL JOACHIM
One of my favorite examples of the phenomenological nostalgia we were discussing goes back to Columbia – Stan Allen, when he was a part of this conversion process. He didn't do the library extension in Schermerhorn over Avery, but when they ripped out all those buildings underground, they decided to leave residual evidence of the old building that used to be there. If you look in the cafe in Avery, there are doors that go nowhere way up in the ceiling. Stan alwyas pointed this out –that, to me, is fantastic.

SRDJAN JOVANOVIC WEISS
Why is it fantastic?

MJ Because it provides evidence that something happened. It preserves that moment in time forever. It's structural, it's logical, it doesn't need more. It's justified by its preexistence and did not need to be ripped out and covered up in sheetrock. It's kind of a wonderful moment. Plus, you get this sensation, the feeling that at one point you were 15 feet taller and able to walk and open up that door and pass through it. And so, it builds in desire – a desire to move through that door, as if you could fly, or float, or pass through it. And that is mythical.

SJW I'm not saying that you're nostalgic, but I see your interest in the memory of something happening in the future.

MJ But it's the translation of the memory, the metamorphosis of the memory, the movement. It's a baseline. We're definitely not nostalgic. We work on a palimpsest; there are always erased histories.

SJW Is it like a matrix?

MJ No, it's tablet on which you write; the impression of what you once wrote there is all but gone, but then you write again and add something totally fresh. It's layers of traces, but the original stuff is simply washed away. So, there is a nostalgia element to that. But in reality we focus on the new piece of paper. It's not that we design from – we do design from scratch, the tabula rasa – but the palimpsest is important because everything needs a context. I think that's what separates design from art.

SJW Tell me more about that.

MJ Our project "Superdocking", about the future of the Brooklyn Navy Yard, as well as others, recognize the fact that the Navy Yard had dry docks. They're from the history of a great industrial military movement and complex, but we translated them into phyto-remediation systems to clean the sewage of people today by using plants and their natural properties to filter out the poisons in the water before it hits the East River. This is a nostalgia that uses an industrial-scaled element in our city – these dry docks – but then repurposes and up-cycles them into a system that's really smart when it comes to biotech. So, to destroy the dry dock and make it something totally new wouldn't work for us because it's so heavy, it's such a charged void.

SJW Heavy handed.

MJ Yes, heavy handed. It was a heavy-handed design before we got there.

Design with Life

MARIA AIOLOVA

We spoke about how we write our briefs. We start by thinking about the future of manufacturing and industrial ecology, then identify a site. But then we get very specific in working within the context of that site. It's that kind of grand propaganda piece that we wanted to push forward. Then came the very granular understanding of the specific case of the Navy Yard, the projecting and determination of what would be possible right here in this complex.

SJW Have you seen the work in the US pavilion at the Venice Biennale?

MJ The Detroit one?

SJW I had a feeling you were really pioneers in that kind of work.

MJ Yeah, I don't know what happened, what's up with that, why they picked it...

SJW I know you were in Detroit. How did that go?

MJ It was fun, thanks for that. We produced an entire book, designing a kind of biological Detroit. We had them thinking about what would happen if one were to combine spider processes, robotics and infrastructure – one of forty threads we have running. They really had to relearn design. We produced unbelievable amounts of products.
I think the students were incredibly receptive, as was the teaching staff, who went nuts. We produced this gargantuan model, as we always do, that was too big to be real, but they went ahead and did it. I think they didn't realize what a seven-by-seven-foot model was going to be, but they did it. They started off making small maquettes, building and building and building. I don't even know what to say because ultimately it was too SciFi – not for me but maybe for some of the others. Many of them didn't realize that they could actually design animals, that they didn't have to think about architecture, but could design insects. They

didn't really get it. I would ask, "Why are you trying to come up with a mechanical solution for a sewage system? Give me a manatee, those giant floating fish. Give it an asshole for a face that sucks in sewage and an asshole that pushes it out, then give it an intestinal tract in between that basically processes most forms of sewage.

SJW I see, like an interface?

MJ Like an interface. And they're like "I can't do that." So I showed them this cartoon about different kinds of designers, artists, and scientists, and what happens when each one of them works on a project. With the artist you get something that looks crazy; with the architect you get something that allegedly functions save some stupid column or something weird; and from the bio-designer – a synthetic biologist, or biological engineer – you get something that should never have existed in nature. And that was the end. There was actually a bunch more, but the bottom line was that no one could do something more insidious than the bio-designer working at the genetic level and giving butterflies six wings and the natural impetus to eat some kind of mosquito that's poisonous for other people. We're not there yet, but CRISPR and this kind of desktop genetic splicing that CRISPR offers, is ripe for architects. Why are we still making stuff out of concrete, glass, and steel? Let's start thinking about taking bits of nature that are out there and clipping parts together at the genetic level. Maybe science doesn't allow us to do the whole thing just yet, but the propositions are well within the realm of architecture. Architects are best suited to take existing systems that occur in nature all the time and think about what properties combined together would service what particular design task. One of the greatest architects who has done that is Daisy Ginsberg. She's a bit crazy but I think she's AA or RCA. She and an architecture student proposed growing a series of plants that would eventually produce mechanical components for weeding out their enemy, an insecticide. One plant would grow a gourd that's hollow, another would grow a straw-like stem – a shaft, another would grow a spring, another would grow a trigger, and another would grow a kind of pressure device. You would combine all of these things together and get a spray gun. Another plant would grow an insecticide that could kill a Japanese beetle or whatever harms that kind of plant. Literally these plants would grow systems that humans would use and deploy directly. None of this was Science Fiction; cobbling this stuff together was all quite possible, though it did come from Cronenberg's Existenz. Do you remember when they were putting together genetic parts and making guns? It's the same thing expect that Ginsberg actually looked at real species of plants that could do that at full scale.

SJW How does the work of Buckminster Fuller get into your system? Or doesn't it?

MJ He's great. He was underappreciated in his day, had a difficult point. We feel like that too. No one got him at the time, not really. Now he's dead and everyone is saying, "Wow, wasn't he an ahead-of-his-time kind of guy?"

SJW He wasn't about nature at all, was he?

MJ He was about nature and math – the math deriving from nature, the optimization coming out of nature. He was about universality. Spaceship Earth is one of the best books in the field. He was also constantly making points that I think fell far outside his expertise, writing entire books about politics that no one in politics ever read – endless blathering. There was a lot of that. He was also an amazing salesman. He would get people to come to his lectures by charging $50,000. That was crazy. And he would up the price all the time because he realized that when the host holding his lecture paid a lot of money to have him there, everyone was more energized to drive the traffic and population to see and discuss him, which granted greater credence and weight to the arguments that he was proposing. He

realized that this was a feedback system. The more he charged, the greater his success. Peder Anker writes about Buckminster Fuller in his Eco-House book – about him and spacesuits. The idea that modernization allows us to control the entire ecology, that closed loop systems are totally knowable, and that we have that power, the spacesuit, the Apollo missions – all of that is Fuller.

MA In a way we also relate to him in terms of practice. You can design a city, you can design a car; if you apply the rigor and the craft, it's interchangeable. There's also the idea of interconnectedness.

MJ A month or two ago, Sanford Kwinter said that we are not known as architects. I know what he was saying. He used Buckminster Fuller as an example. Fuller was not called an architect by his peers at the time. He was simply an inventor or something else. Later on, we tried to co-opt him back into the field, but many other fields are laying claim to what he did. I can see the same kind of argument for what we're doing. We're heterodox in nature; we don't fit into a particular box. We definitely don't do just architecture and architecture alone. I think it's fair to think that more practices should be activated in the manner of Buckminster Fuller and take on invention and different scales of operation and design more often, but we don't. We teach it in schools, we recognize Charles and Ray Eames, but when we get into the field, we do staircase details and want to get published in Architectural Record or Digest, so we show an interesting living room. I flip through gargantuan books of architecture that are total garbage. It seems as though not a single original thought is even being developed – just endless white walls and facades. It's 2016 and they're still doing this, as if anyone cares. It was monumental in the 30s, but if you're still doing it today, I think you'll be judged by history as an utter non-factor.

ECOGRAM E
+ Narratives
+ Intellectual Property
+ Fantasy

an argument and if they had made them into a transportation system then you would've stood to make a bunch of money like Lebbeus Woods did when he sued Terry Gilliam. They were taken from our desk, there's no doubt about it, but they were smart enough to know to change its program. We don't seek this out but when you get to a certain point of exposure, you need it for protection because anytime you engage a lawyer full on, it can be a nasty downward spiral.

MARIA AIOLOVA
But they can be helpful. We've engaged with lawyers in many different ways. Sometimes they're helpful, sometimes we are learning from them.

SRDJAN JOVANOVIC WEISS
Do you work with lawyers?

MITCHELL JOACHIM
We have a lawyer on our board.

SJW What does your lawyer do?

MJ Contracts, whether it's looking at an NDA to help us figure out a lease or looking at larger contracts with a sponsor.

SJW Has that involved the work at the navy yards?

MJ The work at the navy yards is involved work with BASF. We have lawyers who specialize in intellectual property – I mean, I've seen movies come out where there's something exactly like our blimp project. I didn't notice it until 15 or 20 people on Facebook were telling me "have you seen the latest Men in Black with the giant silver blimps with the tentacles".

SJW How did you come up with that project?

MJ I'll get into that in a minute, but if we didn't have our IP lawyer basically say that because those blimps are aliens and your blimps are a transportation system, there's no legal leg to stand on as far as

MJ Only legitimate practices work with lawyers. It's just not smart to ignore lawyers. You should engage them at any phase of any project with almost everything you do. Sometimes the cost can be a problem. Finding lawyers for the arts is a solution for that, through pro bono work. But if you think things happen in a vacuum, that's a joke. Lawyers have a very distinct function and we need to engage them in the business side of our practice. We had a great professor at the GSD, Jerold Kayden, who was a lawyer and taught us everything there is to know about public and private development.

SJW I didn't know he was a lawyer.

MJ Oh yeah, he's definitely a lawyer, one hell of a lawyer. He studied at Harvard law school with Jay Wickersham who is the head of the EPA in Massachusetts and does environmental law. It's a whole different perspective but their tools are a very strong asset, especially when you want to do socio-ecological work. They have a different way of prescribing solutions, a much different way than the field of design. It's not an overwhelmingly big part of what we do, but I'd say it's a fraction of what's on the day to day thought structure, but our emails are always cross checked with some kind of lawyer intervention.

SJW So, we mentioned sci-fi.

MJ Yes. I love sci-fi. That's another thing between Peter Eisenman and us, our generation. Peter Eisenman never mentioned Sci-fi, and as far as I can tell certainly squelched it in many of the references to what was happening in deconstructivism. I could not mention it at school in the 90's at any point, but it was just the drive of so many of my colleagues. Who didn't see star wars in the 70's and think, whoa what is this going to do to our mindset, especially when it comes to the formal and technological aspects of architecture? Those fantasies of the near technology and the speculation of that near technology acting on buildings and the built environment are awesome and best communicated through sci-fi. Neal Stephenson was also an awesome influence on how we think about architecture. Bruce Sterling, different, and yes absolutely a little crazier, more of a magazine guy, but absolutely he's cool, he's done some amazing stuff about brains in your armpit. We actually owe a lot to early sci-fi and Jules Verne.

Jules Verne really created design in his narrative, and his unpacking of how we might get to the moon as a race later on becoming part of the Apollo missions, that's an awesome thought. This is actually how we design. To not think about Jules Verne when you design is absolutely crazy to us. Or H.P. Lovecraft, worlds of upside down cities filled with demons. I don't know if Italo Calvino would fit into sci-fi per se, but it is sci-fi if you think of invisible cities as mirrors of possible worlds that architects can dream of. They're so beautiful.

ECOGRAM F
+ Mapping
+ Fluxus
+ Socioecological

SRDJAN JOVANOVIC WEISS

When Archigram came to New York they talked about themselves as artists and their audience was an artistic, not architectural, audience. Do you feel like that? Like you mean more to non-architects than to architects?

MITCHELL JOACHIM

Yes. Architecture and the voice of architecture is wonderful, and we're in that a bit, but our fingers are in different pockets. The art universe is wonderful, but we don't call ourselves artists because I don't know what the hell that is. I also think that pretty much all artists are selfish in the way that their work explores what they choose to explore, and it tends to be autobiographical, driven by the artist's needs. I don't think that same thing drives us. One word: group. And there are art groups but even those have a selfish drive there. Also, expression, we're not dying to express. Well maybe there is a desire to express but...

MARIA AIOLOVA

The questions that we tackle come from a certain set of beliefs. From the outside they're kind of practical questions: the way we think about cities and the way we think about introducing these processes into cities and how people live and interact with the processes we set in place.

MJ And in that sense they're highly political. Because we have an agenda that's shared, communal. At least we try to build it up communally with folks in the neighborhood to create designs that speak democratically, that provide a better place. That's not an internal act of design, that is the opposite. It is a political act because we are somehow executing or rendering an idea of how people should live in the near future.

SJW I was thinking about it last night, especially about this last project of yours, the Urban Tangle. Tell me more about the algorithmic element of it. And there is this whole tradition of Fluxus art from the 60's, (MJ: Yoko Ono) exactly: Yoko Ono and others creating computer protocols and allowing for chance. Are you following that, or?

MJ That's also Duchamp and the happy accident. This is embedded in our thinking and this is not political thinking, it's not scientific thinking either, it's art based thinking. And it's absolutely beautiful. There's no way that the Fluxus art / Duchampian practice is something we would ignore. This particular piece (Urban Tangle) is kind of a play for or against Patrick Schumacher. I'm not really sure where I stand with him on parametricism. Anyway, we took city maps, from twenty something different places across the globe that related to the place where I teach, NYU, and we parameterized those maps. Then we computer milled them out of plywood, the bamboo material, and made all of these different slats on them, or slots, you can see the piles over there.

SJW So, this is a map?

MJ Yes, individual fragments of a map that the public assembles based on what they desire a future map might be. Or maybe a map that they find more engaging or maybe out of sheer ignorance they're doing it based on physics and how it interacts with the world. The idea though is that the parametric model that was in the computer that produced the millwork is still parametric as there is no single way to accept one assembly. It's quantum; It can be assembled, unassembled, reassembled again. And that's not a new thing. We're not making any claims. There are many kinds of processes that say that this is meant to be infinitely rearranged, it's recursion, but it's exciting to us because it's not the final product it's the engagement. How people engage with it is the intention of this project.

MA But on a kind of very basic experiential level, what we added by letting the public interact was an exercise in judgment because there is an algorithm and there are 21 distinct pieces and we described these optimal arrangements and connections but yet, of course, things didn't happen in quite the prescribed way.

SJW So, you showed people what would be the optimum configuration?

MJ No.

MA We had our crew start by setting up some examples, so in a way we primed them. There were stacks of pieces for them to choose from and they saw some of the possibilities.

MJ There was a little sign that said, "Make it Yourself" and beyond that there wasn't exactly that much instruction except for the team members who were able to do a little bit of an assembly. But there are engineering limits to it. It's based on the body's physical size, so without any ladders you can't get much higher and that's pretty important since it probably would collapse after around 15 feet. I'm glad it didn't have ladders and people weren't trying to make 20 foot tall structures.

MJ You see. That has me thinking. You really do have this very Sci-fi ecological future image, but still in every project that I see there is always a human scale. Do you think about that?

MA There is a lot of human scale, even in our urban

design projects of course, although it's harder to see it when you're doing 300 acres of urban space as opposed to this one that is for a physical, tactile thing with gripping points for the hand. But we have no problem switching between industrial design to regional planning in one smooth stroke, though I don't actually give a damn that there's a disciplinarian difference between the two. There is not any industrial designer that limits themselves to...

SJW It's undisciplined, or indisciplined. I'm very curious about this humanistic approach.

MA We coined a phrase, the socioecological.

SJW Can you explain?

MA The understanding of ecology cannot come about in a vacuum without ever bringing the human into the equation. So, when we think about new materials all the way to the scale of cities it's always about the human. I remember one of the first lectures by Michelle Addington that I saw where she famously said that buildings are never hot or cold, people are.

MJ It's also socio-ecological because the term sustainable is too weak, too status quo. It doesn't promote evolution, change. At its best possible case, it means just get us through it, it means survival. Sustainability is almost synonymous with survival. Will your marriage be sustainable? That's a terrible marriage, you want something to be nurturing, evolving, growing. Socio-ecological unfortunately is a mouthful, it's not as, I guess, useful of a term as sustainability, which has latched on to the public and has become part of politics, part of regulations, part of business, and is associated with LEED and other things and because it's a little bit more acceptable it has worked. We just don't think it's strong enough. And I think I'm right about that and only time will tell. It's certainly a term that's not disappearing, but we like to use socio-ecological design which brings in the human character.

ECOGRAM G
+ Biohacking
+ DIY
+ Adhocism

MARIA AIOLOVA

What is important to realize is that all this was happening at the exact moment when access to bioscience was suddenly being democratized. We had $10,000 to invest in 3D printers, which were very expensive at the time. At the same time, we were going to build an entire bio lab by sourcing things on eBay, Craigslist. For around $800 dollars we built what would have cost $20,000 in a catalogue. And it was fully functional.

SRDJAN JOVANOVIC WEISS

Kind of like DIY.

MITCHELL JOACHIM

It was the DIY movement in full force, but this time, in biohacking.

SJW I'm very curious about that.

MJ All these things that have come up in the past ten years define a number of practices, with DIY, biohacking, the maker movement, nanotech, robotics as some of major themes. DIY has been a pretty big theme; it's been around for a very long time. Victor Papanek was its god; he's written books on DIY furniture, DIY architecture, etc. It got kind of lost,

but now it's blossoming. The Maker Faire, which commands the White House once a year, is a serious endeavor. People are really interested in doing stuff because they see it as light manufacturing, and so many of us in the United States have lost craft. My kids and the generation of architects coming up now are born with this shit [lifts iPhone] and are doing stuff in Minecraft. Why at least don't you play with some Legos – not that that's craft, but Legos are physical. And then, in an amazing kind of turnaround, Minecraft made its own Legos. How's that for confusing? Something that steals from Legos, becomes an all-digital format, a computational universe of brick systems, then re-influences the original object.

SJW How is that not apocalyptic?

MJ Well, I don't think it's negative. I think it's complex, but I wouldn't say it's negative. But DIY makes a lot of sense to us. I think architects have always been doing it, but simply didn't recognize it. When Harry Cobb specs out a certain type of glass for a skyscraper, he's picking an office shelf product from Gardner or another one of these major glazing companies. That's DIY, in my opinion. He's picking out a product that's already there and putting it together in a unique attachment system.

SJW I'm very curious about how you think when you work. We spoke about digital, biological, coding, and the fact that what you do is not religious. But that there is something of a higher order... I want to disentangle it, maybe through Papanek, whom you mentioned. How does one practice it?

MJ Papanek was impossible to discuss in the '90s, even though he wrote the first books on design and ecology. These books were enormously important but have been put aside. They influenced people like Bill McDonough and others who didn't attain any kind of recognition until the turn of the millennium. Papanek is still relevant to us. He wasn't a formalist. In fact, there's really no recognition of that in his work, which is probably where we depart from his idea of design. I don't know whether we can say formalism in DIY exists or doesn't; it can be both. There's also adhocism – Jencks and Venturi. Venturi supported adhocism as its ability to recognize it, Jencks said it was actually a movement. Papanek said it's always been around. Duchamp and others – the Michael Jordan of art – made the greatest possible points. The bicycle wheel and the stool, the urinal, these were clearly, unbelievably recognized as a massive movement in art and all aesthetic procedures. But look at our cricket shelter house, this magazine did an interview with me yesterday. They were obsessive beyond belief. I guess that's fine; we entered the competition and made it to the final rounds.

SJW What were the questions?

MJ Did we custom make the bio-unit plastic components, or were they off the shelf and modified later? They wanted to know the whole story behind them. And I said there was no reason to make a five-gallon container, when one thinks one needs a five-gallon container – the perfect size for our client, -the client being crickets – when there are catalogs on top of catalogs. Everyone in China is making five-gallon containers; there are all kinds of containers. There was no point in our custom fabricating 569 five-gallon containers, when we could buy them for $3.00 per piece, build a computer-driven jig that cuts out ports for ventilation and locking gate mechanisms, areas to lay sacks in, areas for hanging the louvers. We really thought about the jug – even about the screw connection for putting the cap on; we designed our louvers to fit that screw connection. We got a perfect solid seal; no water could get in. Why would we spend all this time designing it from scratch and then fabricating it? I think that was upsetting to them.

SJW Why do you think so?

MJ The obsessiveness with detail and the craft behind it.

MA The uniqueness, right. That's what the designer is educated to do. It has to be new. You cannot merely take something that exists.

MJ It does have to be new and it does have to be well crafted. I absolutely agree with their sensibility. What they don't realize is that the shit's already out there in the world. While I was doing this project, Mark Gage produced a work for the Guggenheim in Helsinki that I really like. I thought it one of his best projects. He took a bunch of models that he had found on the web and splashed them together in a computer model. He took rabbits, Jeff Koons stuff, strange cars, toilets – all of these 3D objects that had been modeled, then stuck them together, created an axial symmetry moment, mirrored it, and instantly made something "beautiful". He turned its entire surface into a museum. We had been doing the DIY modeling thing forever. When I was teaching students in Toronto I used to tell them to stop giving me models created from scratch. Google offers an entire database of 3D models in its Sketchup software. I'd say: "Type in what you want. I want you to take the Hagia Sophia and mash it with a rabbit. Repeat that, scale, shift, change these things infinitely. There are no consequences. You can make phenomenal projects because it's already all out there to be found, like Duchamp." That's adhocism.

SJW Adhocism is something that always infuses more energy into something that already exists?

MJ Sure. It's like taking a chair and adding a scooter to it. It's technically an office chair, but now it's also a scooter chair.

MA The DIY movement that Papanek spoke about so many years ago became possible with the internet, eBay, Google. but we also witnessed that it started breaking down the silos. Suddenly we can work together with scientists and have a conversation. Our contribution is valid, but the scientist can also be part of the design thinking.

Design with Life

SJW It's a kind of connector to a wider audience, right?

MA Yes, democratization of the material, the way in which we can source it and order things from China, get it cheaply, and build a bio lab in our design studio, only happened at this point in history. It wasn't possible before. That's the kind of tension – between predicting the future and living it – I was talking about earlier. It has to happen at the right time.

MJ The truth is, we were doing some early models, but the scientists were better designers than the designers, and in some ways we were better scientists than the scientists.

SJW Can you expand on that?

MJ Yes, we were doing a project for the History Channel, and Oliver Medvedik was making models on a giant city map. What he was making out of foam was mind-blowing. The bridges, museums, even office towers, were quick instant strokes and shocking. Unbelievably, amazingly cool. And I think he didn't even know what he was doing. He just didn't care; he was having fun, thinking, "of course I can do it," because there's no consequence. Just as we say: "Let's rethink this in science, we can build a bio lab, blah, blah, blah," because there's no consequence for us. No designer is going to come and laugh at us and say: "You're not doing legitimate work." We're not worried about interfering in the realm of the scientists, in their kind of sanctimonious/precious line of thought. We can break it at any moment, create a new paradigm, and ask stupid questions that lead to brand new rabbit holes, without worrying too much, in much the same way that a scientist looking at design can ask: "Why did you do that? Why does it look like this?" We can just sit there and say: "You know, your kind of right." It doesn't always happen, and it's not always the case, but I just think that when you switch hats, or wear multiple hats at the same time, your projects definitely become more innovative. When we were at MIT, the practice of giving a car design project to everyone but a car designer was really smart. The idea of giving a city designer a city to design is ridiculous. Give it to an ecologist. Better yet, give the car design to the ecologist, and give the car designer a city to design. Then the world will be totally upside down and the filter or reasoning will be switched around. Foucault spoke about this with regard to the medical lens of various medical specialists; if you present them with a case, a bone doctor will see a bone problem, a psychiatrist will see a mental issue.

SJW Papanek and Jencks – I was going to go on to Jencks. I'm sure you're aware of his 1971 book, Predictions and Methods. It's the one in which he used a diagram for the first time, which he later said was totally wrong.

MJ Of course, but it was influential because he put that out and so many people have used it as a reference. When you start working in some of those future scenarios, it's almost like it's been pre-vetted. It's pre-accepted because someone of his caliber and voice and someone of a constant kind of, person who's registering the successes of various movements and -isms, then predicting these are some new ones coming up. When you decide to do that as a student, or as a young practitioner, it's almost as if it's okay because we read it before, Jencks and others sort of confirmed this would be an interesting area to study. It literally becomes like a gateway, it wasn't a perfect prediction, but it opened up the doors. It gave some people the permission they needed to do stuff that was outside of the norm and break with previous tradition. So, I think it's a self-fulfilling prophecy. And I think we do that too to a certain extent.

SJW Charles Jencks was very influential on me, on my thinking when I was a student. Much like Carpenter, who did Dark Star.

MJ You're one of the few people I know who has seen Dark Star. Dark Star is out there.

PROJECTS

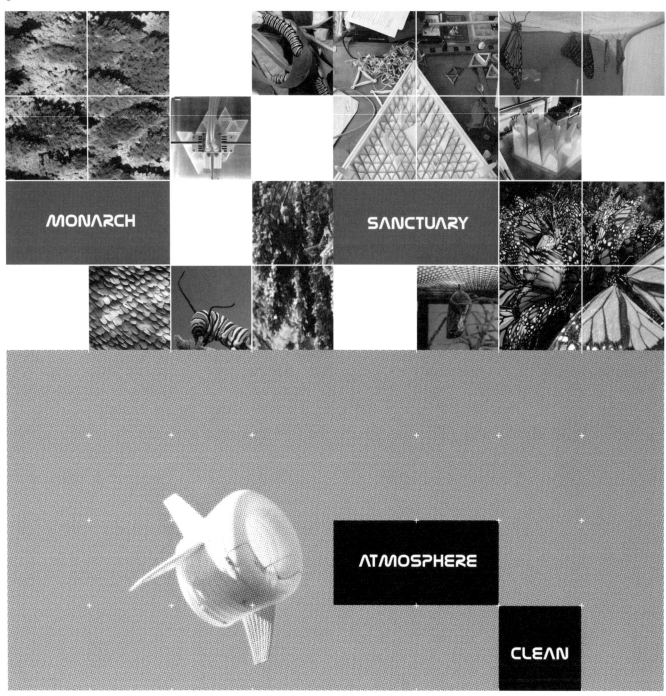

MONARCH

SANCTUARY

ATMOSPHERE

CLEAN

Monarch Sanctuary

Our mission is to design against extinction. The monarch butterfly of North America is a species at risk. The U.S. Fish & Wildlife Service is currently assessing whether the monarch needs to be granted "endangered species" status, while the monarch population erodes due to the combined forces of agricultural pesticides and habitat loss. Monarchs are a delicate presence in New York City.

Monarch Sanctuary will be eight stories of new commercial construction in Nolita, NYC. Yet central to its purpose is a semi-porous breeding ground, waystation, and sanctuary for the monarch butterfly (Danaus plexippus). It aims to be socio-ecologically robust, weaving butterfly conservation strategies into its design through the integration of monarch habitat in its façade, roof, and atrium. Not just a building envelope, the edifice is a new biome of coexistence for people, flora, and butterflies.

The double-skin street façade, with a diagrid structure infilled glass at the outer layer and with "pillows" of ETFE foil at the inner layer, encloses a careful climate - controlled space, 3' deep. This "vertical meadow," the terrarium proper, serves as an incubator and safe haven for Monarchs in all seasons. It contains suspended milkweed vines and flowering plants to nourish the butterflies at each stage of their life cycle. Hydrogel bubbles maintain optimal humidity levels, and sacs of algae purify the air and wastewater. LED screens at the street level provide magnified live views of the caterpillars and butterflies in the vertical meadow, which also connects to a multi-story atrium.

The building will present a striking public face and a powerful argument in favor of a diversity of life forms in the city. The façade of the Monarch Sanctuary building will add a lush vertical meadow for butterflies.

The building is intended to serve as an object lesson in enhancing the urban environment with green technologies, including plant life and other creatures, in designing for other species, and in conveying images of new possibilities for the urban environment. This project alone will not save the Monarch, but it will crucially raise awareness about our much-loved insect residents.

The innovation of this project is to serve as a large-scale Lepidoptera terrarium. This type of façade has never been constructed before in any known context. It will bolster the monarch's presence in the city through two strategies: open plantings of milkweed and nectar flowers on the roof, rear façade, and terrace will provide breeding ground and habitat for wild monarchs, while semi-enclosed colonies in the atrium and street side double-skin facade will grow monarch population. The insects will have fluid open access to join the wild population, enhancing overall species population numbers.

Key features of the project are equally in service of the insects are meant to captivate people. Giant LED screens on the surface of the building provide a spectacle of caterpillars, chrysalis, and butterflies. Interior partitions are constructed from mycelium, and additional planting at the ceiling enhances the interior atmosphere and building biome. The entire project is meant to make ecological systems visible to the public in as many scales as possible.

Close-up view of cable suspended nectar hubs for butterflies and enclosed milkweed growing chambers for caterpillars.

Design with Life

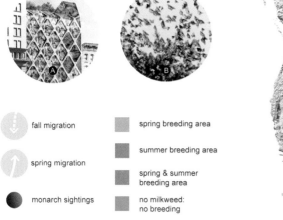

fall migration

spring migration

monarch sightings

spring breeding area

summer breeding area

spring & summer breeding area

no milkweed: no breeding

Above: Annual migration pattern of monarch butterflies from the United States to Mexico.

Right: Building section perspective mapping the trajectory of butterflies from across the street Petrosino Park through the double-skin facade vertical meadow finally up to the pollinator rooftop garden.

Previous page: An architecture that aims to be ecologically generous, weaving butterfly conservation strategies into its design through the integration of monarch habitat in its façades, roof, and atrium. Not just a building envelope, the edifice is a new biome of coexistence for people, plants, and butterflies.

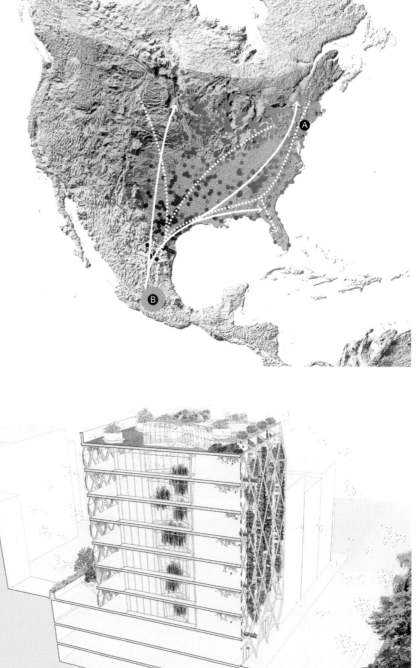

Design with Life

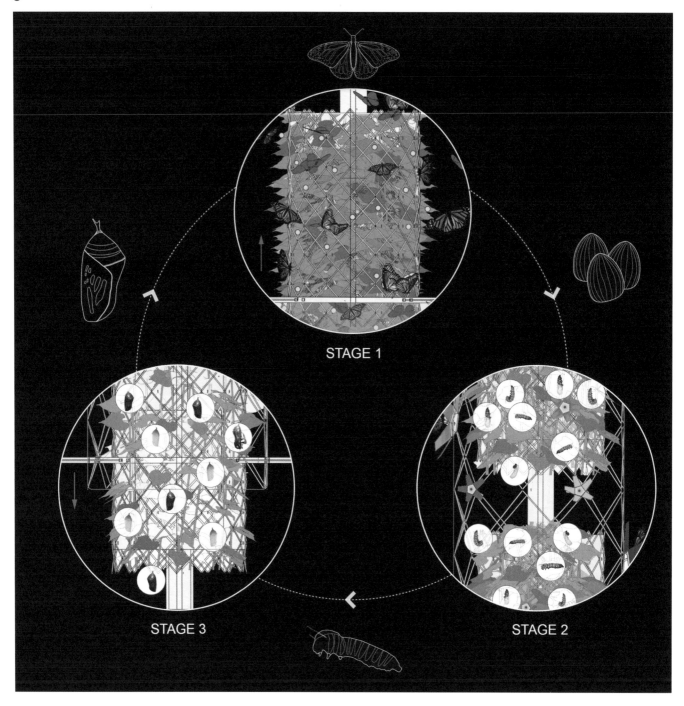

STAGE 1

STAGE 3

STAGE 2

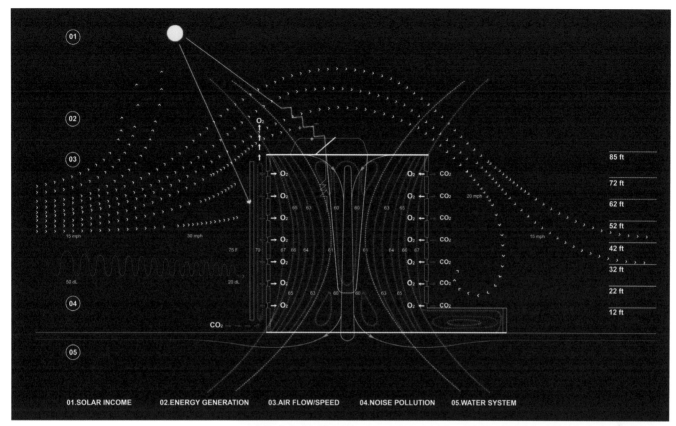

01.SOLAR INCOME   02.ENERGY GENERATION   03.AIR FLOW/SPEED   04.NOISE POLLUTION   05.WATER SYSTEM

Previous Page:
Linked stages of milkweed columns and butterfly life cycle.
Stage 1. Milkweed column rises from glass casing. Fresh milkweed exposed to butterflies allowing them to lay eggs
Stage 2. Milkweed column fully contained within glass casing. Caterpillar development isolated from butterflies. Leaf count slowly diminishes.
Stage 3. Milkweed column lowers from glass casing. Chrysali and hatching butterflies exposed to inner facade. Little leaf structure remains on column.

Above:
Section diagram of the manipulation and regulation of building inputs and outputs.
Right:
Biodiversity wall section components.

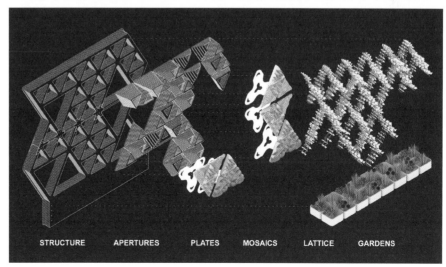

STRUCTURE   APERTURES   PLATES   MOSAICS   LATTICE   GARDENS

Design with Life

Cleveland Place elevation featuring multi-storey screen with magnified butterfly activity and green wall.

Following page:
Full scale building section of double skin façade with integrated biodiversity.

Design with Life

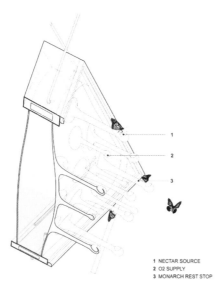

1 NECTAR SOURCE
2 O2 SUPPLY
3 MONARCH REST STOP

3D Printed prototype featuring
elongated spoons as vessels of
nectar dispersion.

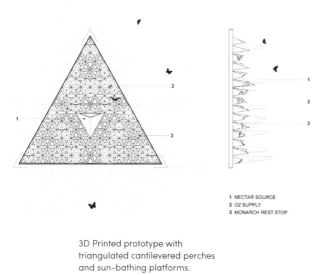

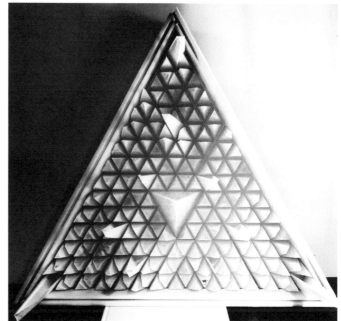

1 NECTAR SOURCE
2 O2 SUPPLY
3 MONARCH REST STOP

3D Printed prototype with
triangulated cantilevered perches
and sun-bathing platforms.

Previous pages: Simulated
renderings of double skin façade
system with concrete cast panels.

Detailed section of the multitude
of living systems and their support
components.

Design with Life

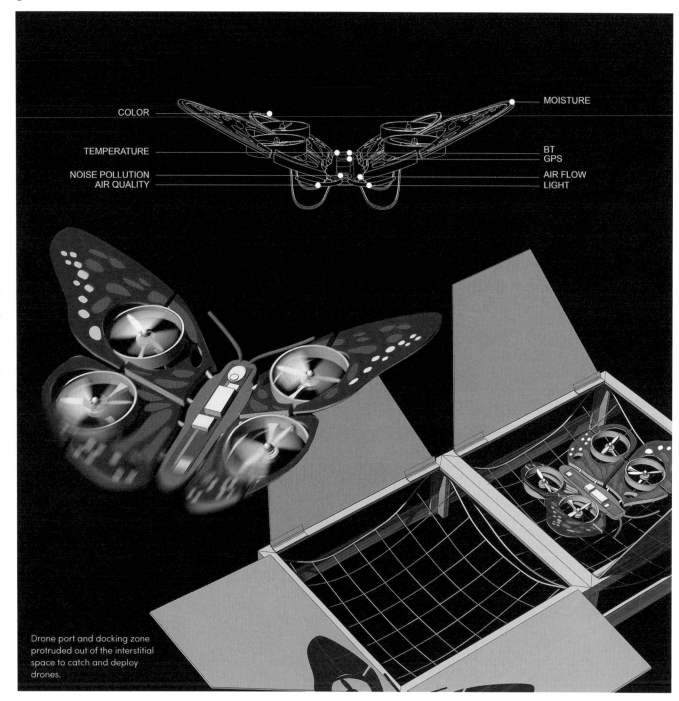

COLOR

MOISTURE

TEMPERATURE

BT
GPS

NOISE POLLUTION
AIR QUALITY

AIR FLOW
LIGHT

Drone port and docking zone
protruded out of the interstitial
space to catch and deploy
drones.

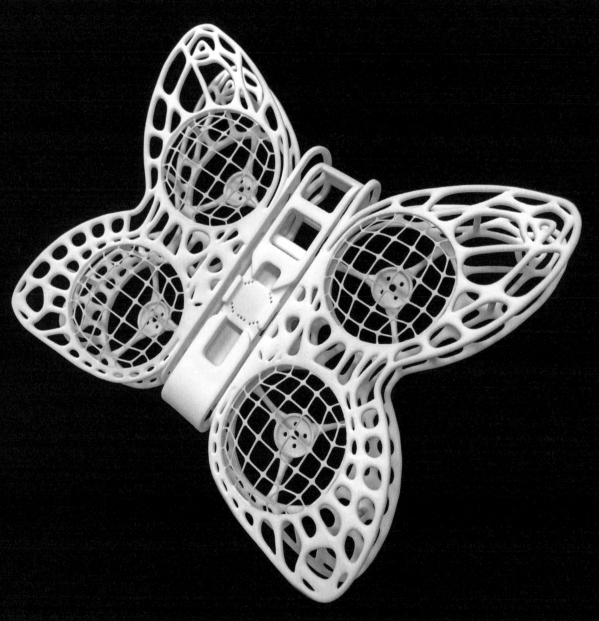

Lightweight 3D printed drone
chassis for butterfly quadcopter.

Design with Life

Previous page:
3D printed suspended and mounted fruit and nectar feeders for butterflies.

Enlarged view of 3D printed nectar feeder including peripheral landing dock, center nectar tray, and perforated sponge cover.

Design with Life

Previous page:
Photo-sensitive 4D flower
activated by butterfly flight
proximity.

Capacitive touch sensors
embedded in plants that
illuminate upon engagement.

Design with Life

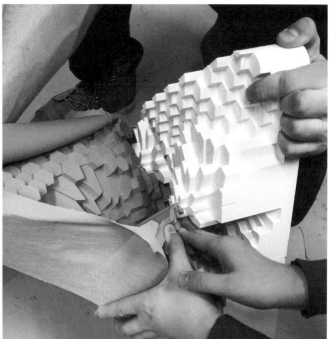

Previous page:
Butterfly feeder design variations
and formal experiments based
on live testing.
Above: 3D printed formwork and
silicone molds.

Design with Life

Lobby interior with lush butterfly
atrium ascending through the
building and mycelium and moss
planted wall.

Wall section perspective emphasizing rising milkweed growing cylinders located between outer glass and inner ETFE foil panels.

Following pages:
Upper left: Air quality moss garden.
Lower left: Interstitial space for biodiversity.
Right and adjacent page:
Fly-ash impregnated concrete vertical landscape mosaic.

Design with Life

Design with Life

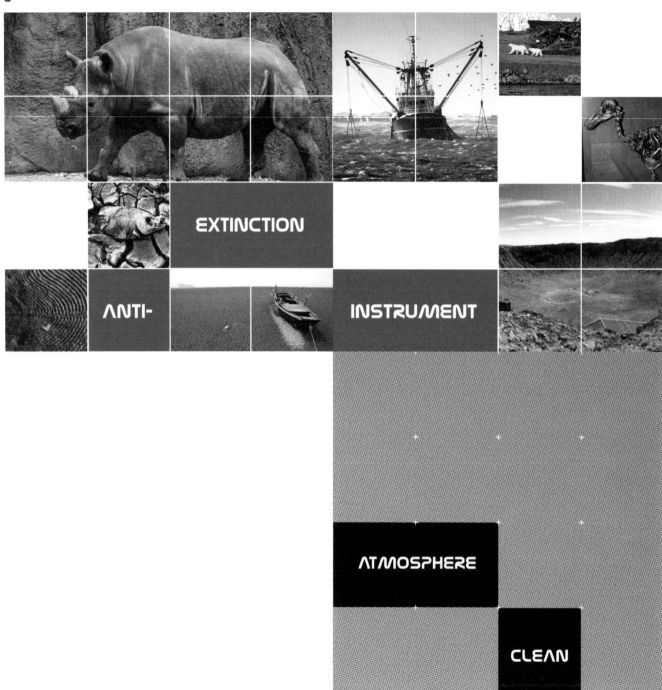

Anti-Extintion Instrument

Approximately every seven minutes our world is suffering the loss of an entire species. This far exceeds the natural rate of extinction associated with evolution. Although species loss is a biological phenomenon, it occurs at an organic background frequency of about one to five species in a given year. Scientific researchers think we are now losing species at 1,000 to 10,000 times the natural background level, with objectively dozens going extinct every day. According to the WWF since the 1970s over 50% of known organisms on this planet have disappeared permanently. Contrasting the mass extinction occurrences of geological time, the present-day extinction difficulty is one for which a singular species - humankind - appears to be almost entirely accountable.

Modern causes of extinction are arguably well known and can be reversed. Although reversal of this extinction event requires new leadership, stringent government regulations, global sustainable practices, and equitable businesses models to move society forward. Some of the primary causes of species loss are habitat fragmentation, industrial agriculture, human over-population, rampant deforestation, and poaching.

Our Anti-Extinction Instrument is an enormously sized architectural provocation to ward off these festering problems. The sheer scope of the instrument reflects the colossal scale of the problem. The design is roughly like ten or more NASA Kennedy Space Center crawler-transporters/ rocket launch pads. The tracked pads are daisy chained together in sections and move as one composite unit. Each one of these ten pad sections is 130 ft. in length, 114 ft. in width and weighs over 6,000,000 lbs. It gradually moves across landfills (or similar devastated territory) and regenerates the land underneath into productive green elements.

Think of it as a kind of goliath self-sufficient iRobot Roomba vacuum. Instead of just extracting waste it upcycles and processes the unearthed resources onboard. After the various material nutrients are successfully filtered and restored the instrument continually replants them in its wake. It leaves behind a complex trail of transformed waste components such as; wind turbines, solar panels, algae farms, geothermal wells,reconstituted wetlands, fresh waterways, forested ribbons, woodland patches, wildlife corridors,

permaculture zones and more. On top of the whole deployable device is a literal village of green manufacturing facilities. We imagined the Anti-Extinction Instrument to be an ultra-healthy land printer powered by a matrix of natural resources. The conclusive step of the land printing process is the celebrated finishing/ rewilding phase. After the land is regenerated it is populated with all kinds of locally adapted living creatures. Remote controlled stewards carefully place insects, fish, reptiles, birds, and various mammals etc. into the freshly primed territory.

NASA crawler-transporter

Design with Life

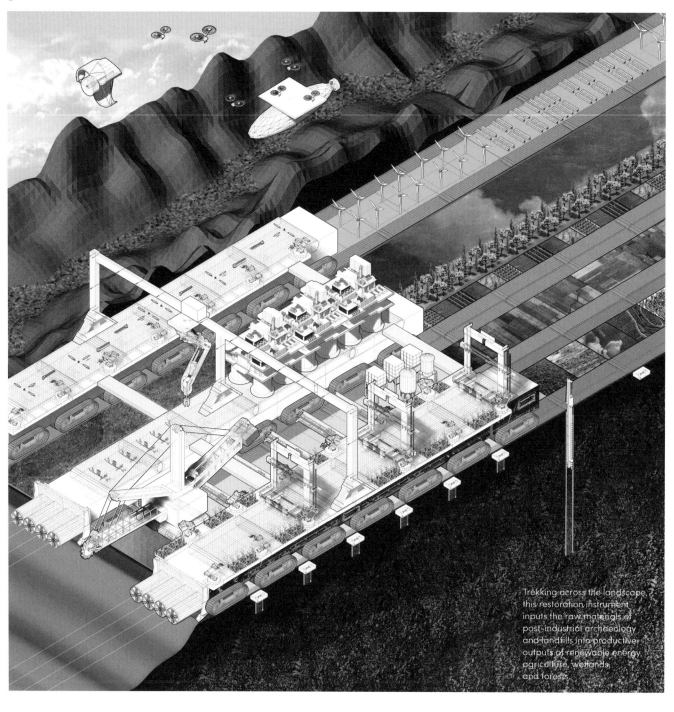

Trekking across the landscape, this restoration instrument inputs the raw materials of post-industrial archaeology and landfills into productive outputs of renewable energy, agriculture, wetlands, and forests.

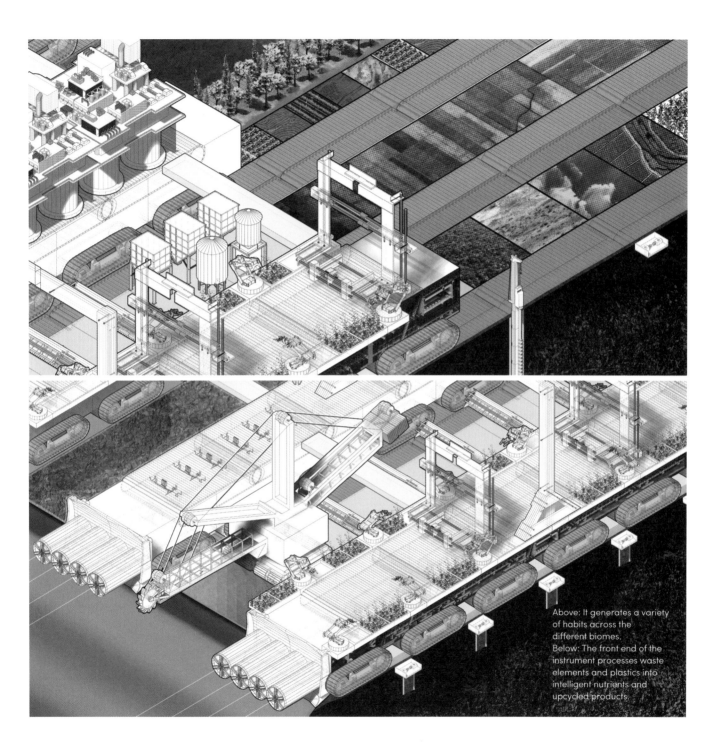

Above: It generates a variety of habits across the different biomes.
Below: The front end of the instrument processes waste elements and plastics into intelligent nutrients and upcycled products.

Design with Life

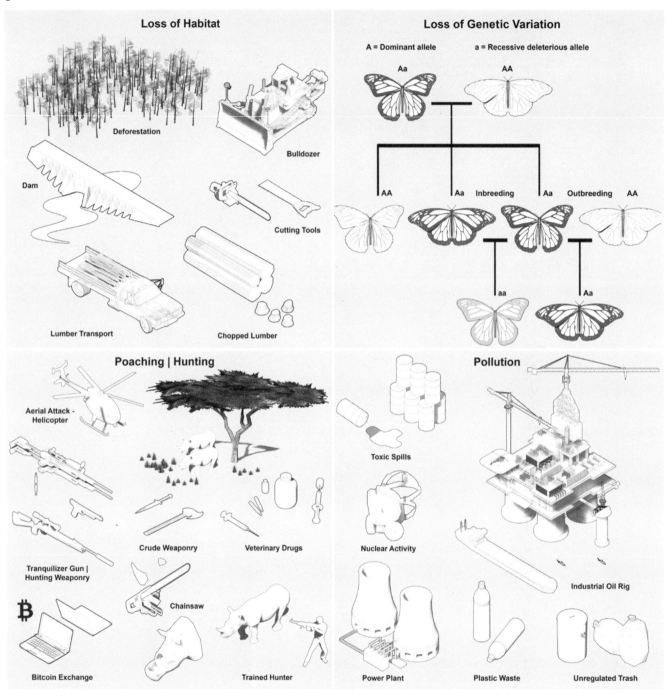

Loss of Habitat

Deforestation

Bulldozer

Dam

Cutting Tools

Lumber Transport

Chopped Lumber

Loss of Genetic Variation

A = Dominant allele   a = Recessive deleterious allele

Aa

AA

AA   Aa   Inbreeding   Aa   Outbreeding   AA

aa   Aa

Poaching | Hunting

Aerial Attack -
Helicopter

Tranquilizer Gun |
Hunting Weaponry

Crude Weaponry

Veterinary Drugs

Chainsaw

Bitcoin Exchange

Trained Hunter

Pollution

Toxic Spills

Nuclear Activity

Industrial Oil Rig

Power Plant

Plastic Waste

Unregulated Trash

96

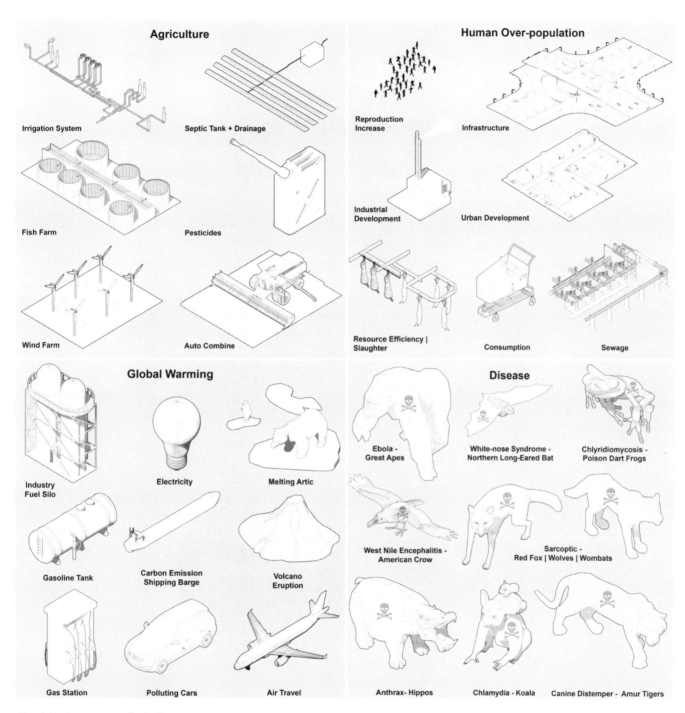

Agriculture

Irrigation System

Septic Tank + Drainage

Fish Farm

Pesticides

Wind Farm

Auto Combine

Human Over-population

Reproduction Increase

Infrastructure

Industrial Development

Urban Development

Resource Efficiency | Slaughter

Consumption

Sewage

Global Warming

Industry Fuel Silo

Electricity

Melting Artic

Gasoline Tank

Carbon Emission Shipping Barge

Volcano Eruption

Gas Station

Polluting Cars

Air Travel

Disease

Ebola - Great Apes

White-nose Syndrome - Northern Long-Eared Bat

Chlyridiomycosis - Poison Dart Frogs

West Nile Encephalitis - American Crow

Sarcoptic - Red Fox | Wolves | Wombats

Anthrax- Hippos

Chlamydia - Koala

Canine Distemper - Amur Tigers

The eight primary causes of extinction

Design with Life

FUTURE

NORTH

ATMOSPHERE

CLEAN

Future North

The Future North Ecotarium project is based on the premise
that within the next hundred years our climate will be
irreversibly altered. Massive migrations of urban populations
will move north to escape severe flooding and increased
temperatures. The area inside the Arctic regions will warm
up significantly, making their occupation newly desirable.
Real estate values will shift to privilege northern climates that
formerly had almost no human inhabitants. To underscore
the intensity of such a global shift, we have moved entire
cities. The reality of hundreds of millions of people relocating
their respective centers of culture, business, and life is almost
incomprehensible. We anticipate this polemical representation
will impact our perception of tomorrow. The movie installation
premiered at: MASS MoCA Badlands: New Horizons
in Landscape.

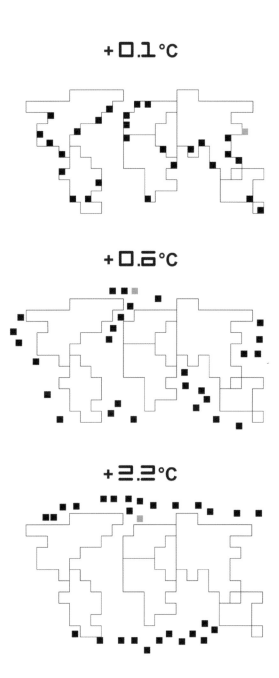

Right:
Temperature increase with
corresponding relocation.

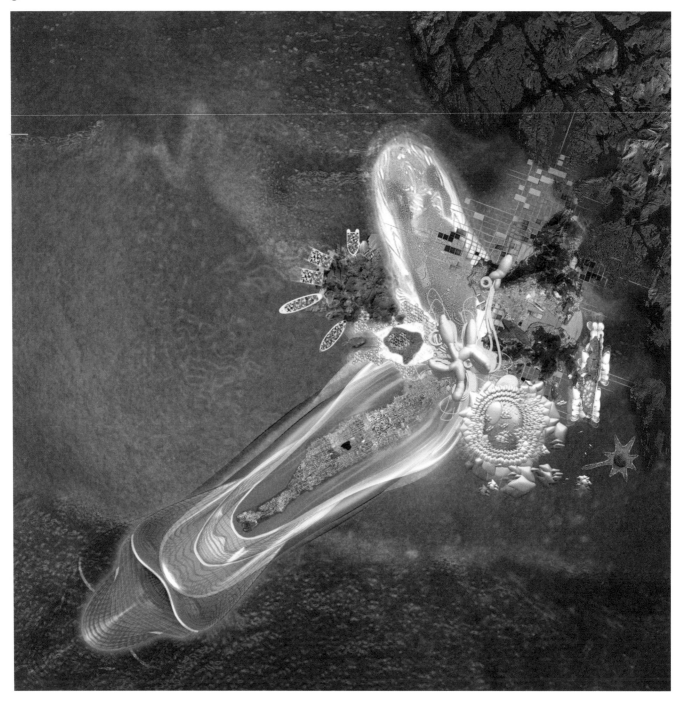

9.6ha pp

ECOLOGICAL FOOTPRINT :: global hectares per capita

1x

UNITED STATES OF AMERICA :: 982 663 000 ha

1x

NEW YORK CITY :: 121 440 ha

1x

CENTRAL PARK NEW YORK CITY :: 340 ha

1American

POPULATION USA :: 304 087 000 Americans

1/3 Population

POPULATION USA :: 304 087 000 Americans

0. 15%

POPULATION NYC :: 8 214 429 New Yorkers

36 New Yorkers

POPULATION NYC :: 8 214 429 New Yorkers

Above: Ecological footprint and population density.
Left: The cities of Miami, Hong Kong, Casablanca and Tokyo.

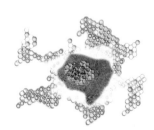

Previous page: Migration of global cultural and economic capitals to the north.

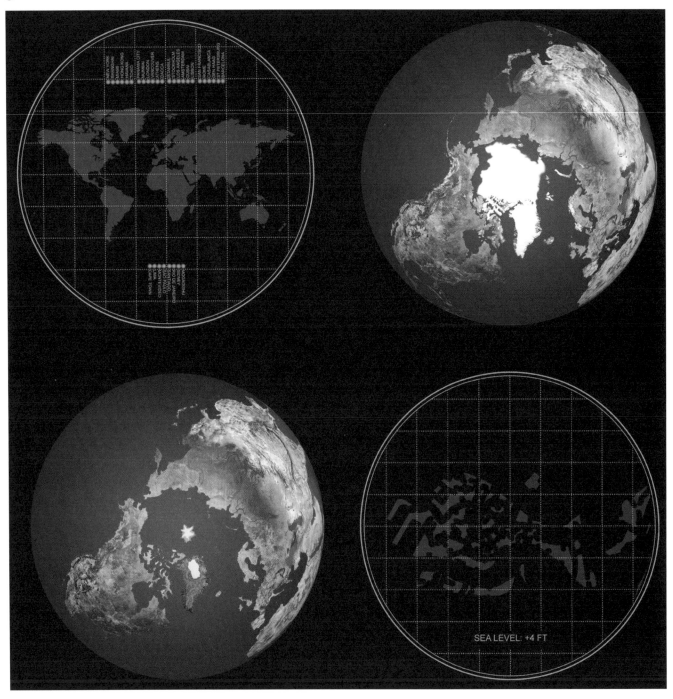

SEA LEVEL: +4 FT

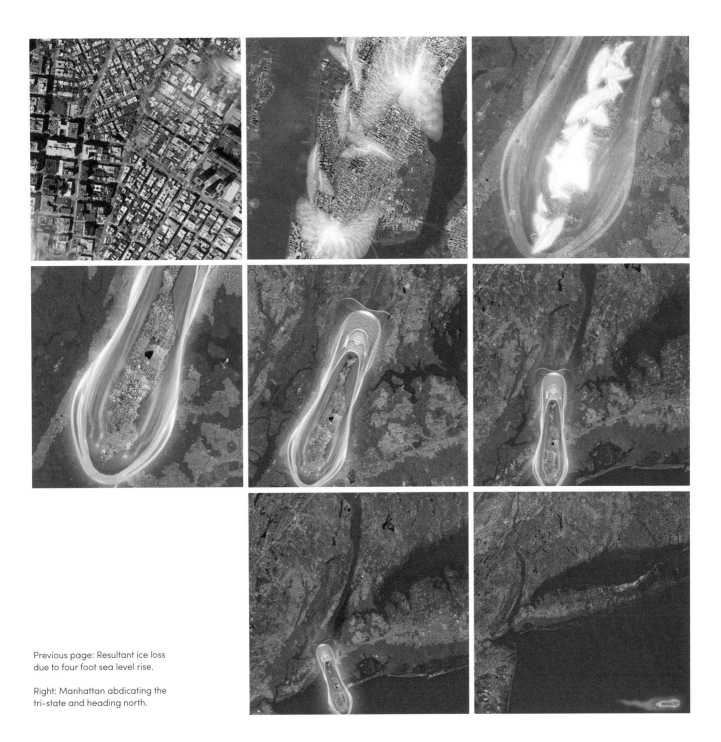

Previous page: Resultant ice loss due to four foot sea level rise.

Right: Manhattan abdicating the tri-state and heading north.

Design with Life

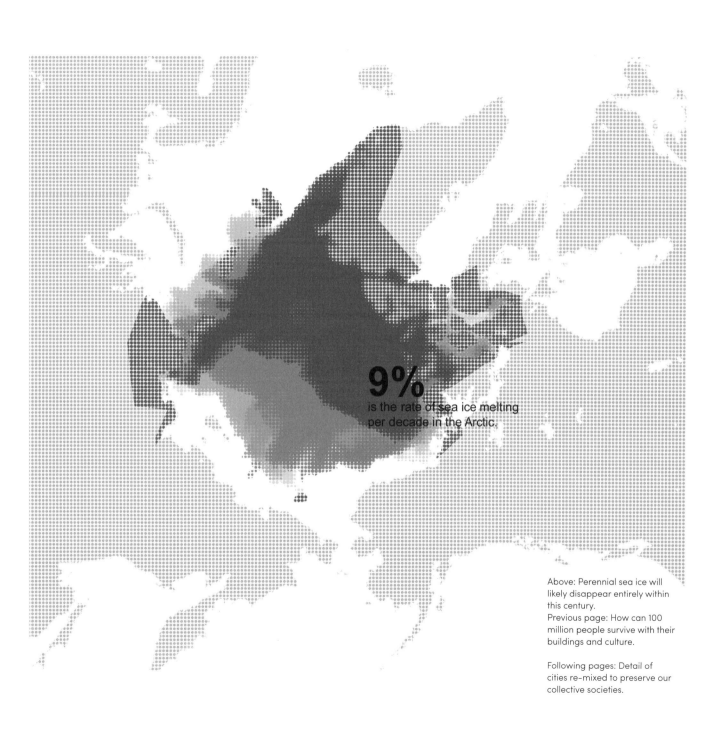

9%
is the rate of sea ice melting
per decade in the Arctic.

Above: Perennial sea ice will
likely disappear entirely within
this century.
Previous page: How can 100
million people survive with their
buildings and culture.

Following pages: Detail of
cities re-mixed to preserve our
collective societies.

Design with Life

Design with Life

BIO-CITY

WORLD MAP

BIO

TECH

Bio City World Map

Bio City World Map is a cartographic installation based on the Dymaxion grid to communicate an all-encompassing view of population density in cities based on probabilistic census data. The map visualizes the earth as one entire urbanized place, instead of unconnected settlements, municipalities, and disparate regions. If we are anticipating growth at this rate almost everything in human society will be comprehensively stressed. This systemic pressure includes: water scarcity, food shortages, overcrowding, air quality depletion, and traffic congestion. The public must be made aware of the consequences related to uncontrolled growth. It is the first step in recognizing a universal challenge in this century. If we cannot foresee the impending difficulty, the potential solutions are hard to justify.

Our Bio City Map displays population density as a parametric graph on the front and the back is made with living biosynthetic transgenic matter. These living elements focus on twenty-five mega-cities, genetically designed and grown inside petri dishes. Our novel approach experimented with living populations that consisted of billions of bacterial cells. We chose colonies of E. coli as a method of demonstrating exponential population growth using synthetic biology. Population density was represented in two different forms of fluorescent transgenic E. coli under UV light. Glowing red E. coli represented future census projections. While green E. coli represented existing demographic conditions, you would find in today's cities. Micro-stencils derived from CAD files shaped the E. coli strains into specific geometries that display the current geopolitical boundaries of cities. Genetic modifications of benign strains of E. coli were carried out at Genspace, the world's first community based biotech laboratory and at Terreform ONE. Genes cloned from bioluminescent oceanic life, such as jellyfish and coral, were introduced into bacteria by transformation. These genes encoded information that would enable our transformed microbes to synthesize either GFP or RFP, two brightly fluorescent proteins.

The transformed E. coli were then incubated overnight on Petri plates containing agar based media with antibiotics, to select our genetically modified strains. Individual bacteria divided through repeated population doublings to produce colonies containing millions of cells. Each selected cell now

expressed our cloned proteins. We then used high-speed centrifugation to concentrate our colonies of transgenic E. coli. A novel method was used to produce stencil-derived bacteria prints for the long-term archival quality gallery display and to underscore the highest zones of growth. Ultimately, the bacterial shapes grow to reveal variant patterns of transformation in urban regions. By using bio-synthetic materials, we expect to narrow the gap between idealized mathematical interpretations and observable events in nature. The Bio City Map is an interdisciplinary project that involved cartographers, urban planners, biologists, and architects to complete a manifestation of future population density. We argue that most nations cannot view the effects of planetary population density through the lens of just one city or region. Instead we aimed to reveal the long-range effects of immense human growth in areas of present and speculative urban intensity.

Design with Life

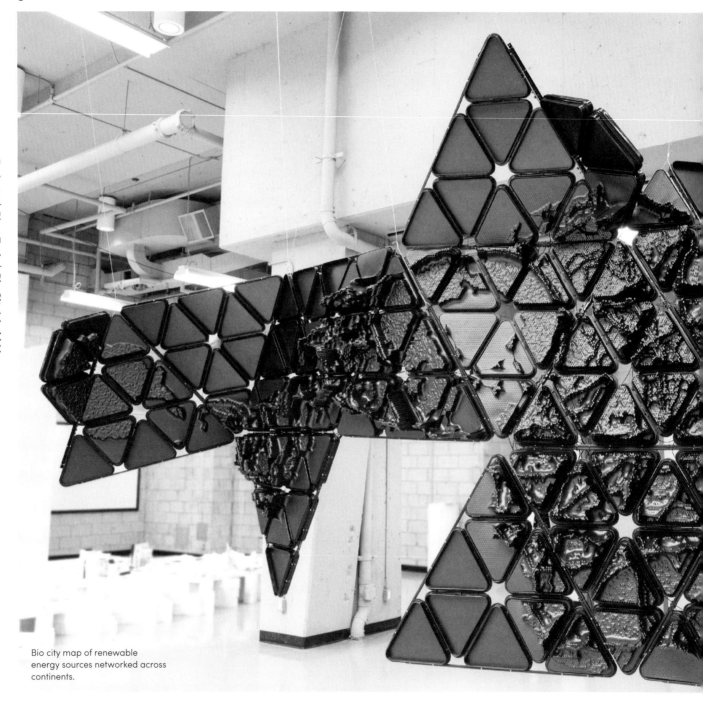

Bio city map of renewable
energy sources networked across
continents.

Above: Detail view of population projection in India.
Right: Detail of illuminated thermo-formed map pieces.

Design with Life

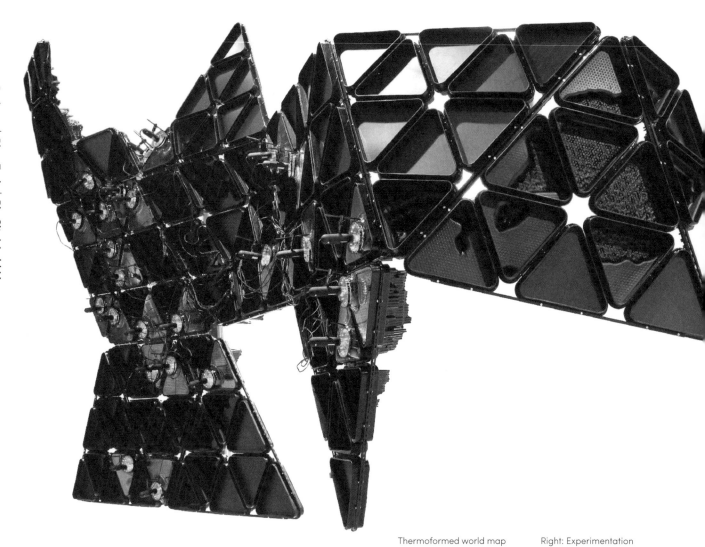

Thermoformed world map based on the Dymaxion grid to communicate an all-encompassing view of population density in cities based on probabilistic census data.

Right: Experimentation with living populations that consist of billions of billions of bacterial cells as a method of demonstrating exponential growth in cities.

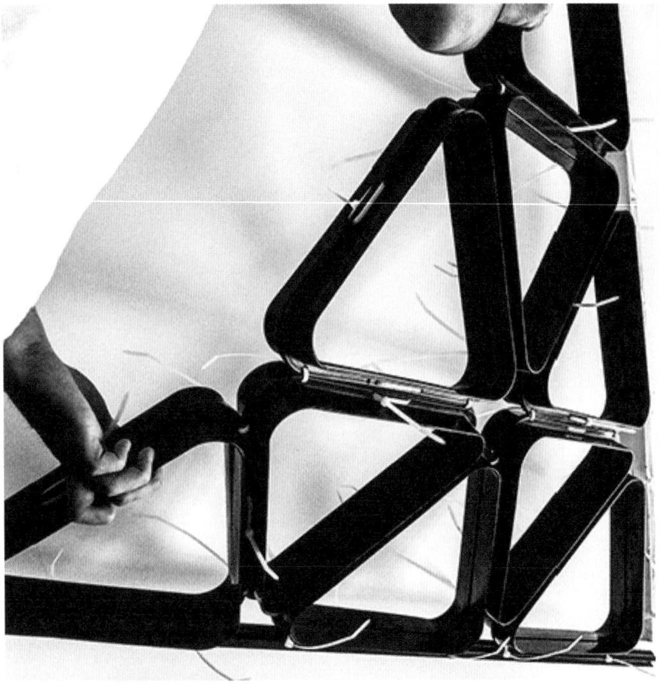

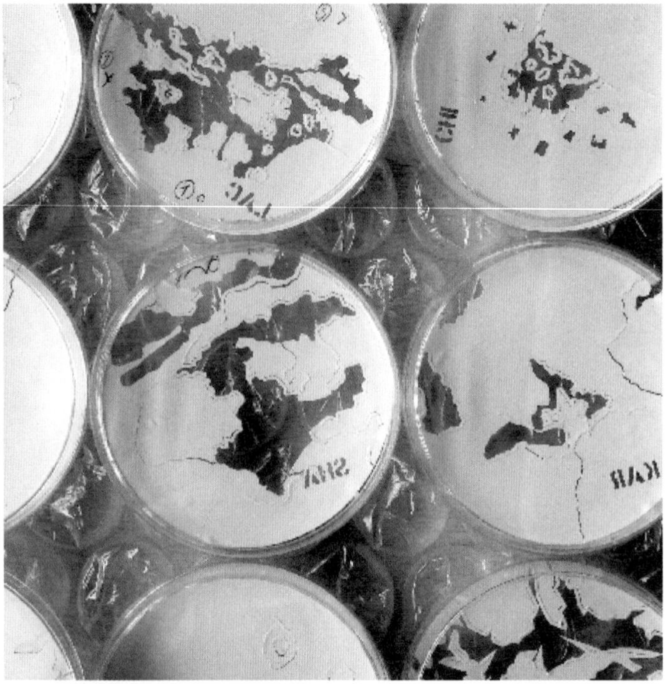

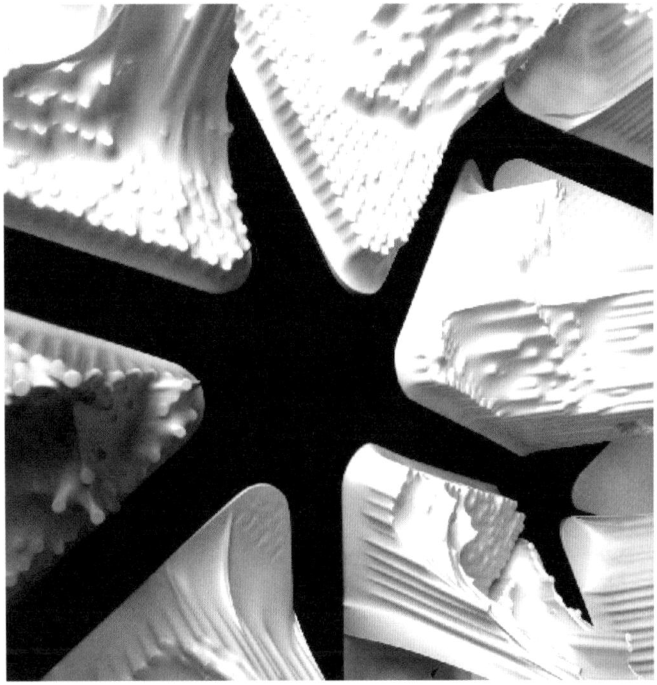

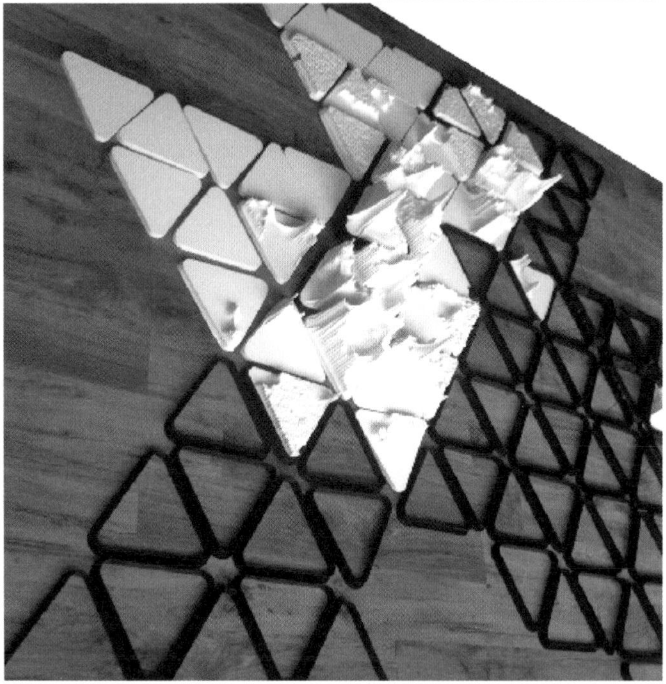

TEH	10.328
KAR	1.924
MOS	4.581
BUE	14.000
RIO	4.781
SHA	7.090
LAO	3.176
IST	2.593
JAK	15.342
DEL	5.855
VAN	18.567
KIN	0.450
LIM	2.846
CHI	8.470
TOK	6.000
NYC	10.630
LON	5.206
DHA	23.029
LAG	7.941
SEO	17.000
MEX	6.000
BOG	4.800
SAO	7.216
BEI	1.200

**POPULATION DENSITY
[PEOPLE PER 50 KM²]**

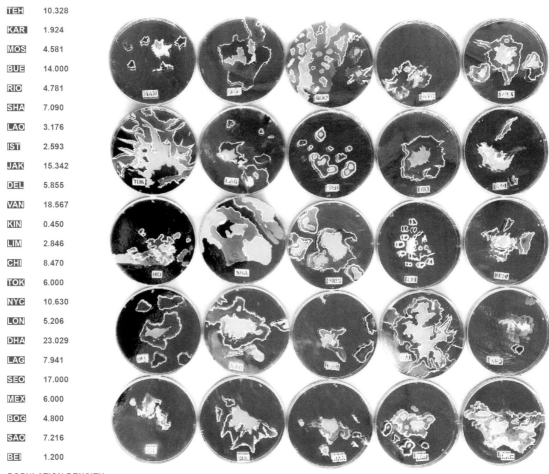

Previous page: Method of
thermoforming the pieces of
the world map and aligning the
Dymaxion grid.

Above: World cities with the
highest population in petri dishes
with red and green E. coli.

Design with Life

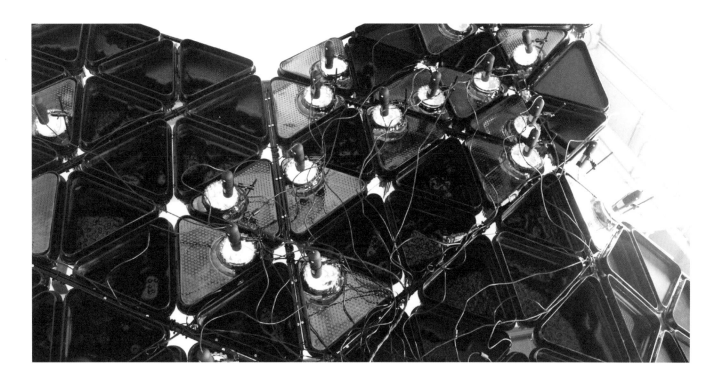

Previous page
Above: Laboratory benchwork with densities of E. coli.
Below: Double sided mapping system.
Side A: 100 petri dishes of bacteria with digital stencil and microscopes. Side B: Extruded population graphs.

Above: Experimentation with living populations that consist of billions of billions of bacterial cells as a method of demonstrating exponential growth in cities.
Right: Buckminster Fuller energy map.

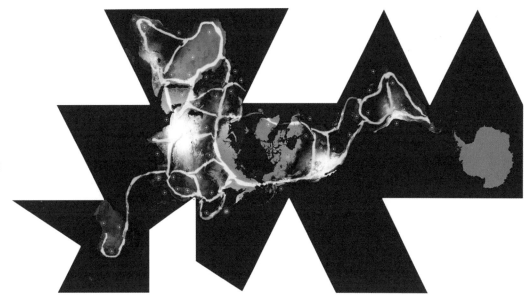

Design with Life

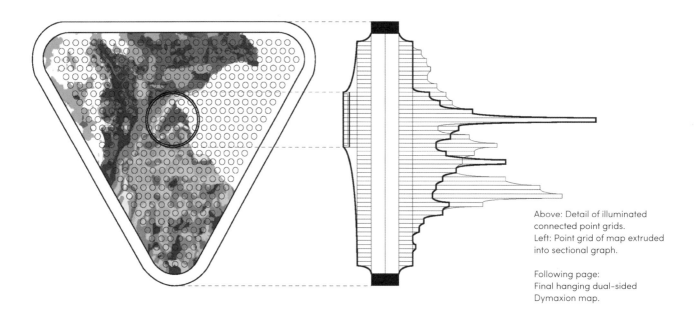

Above: Detail of illuminated connected point grids.
Left: Point grid of map extruded into sectional graph.

Following page:
Final hanging dual-sided Dymaxion map.

Design with Life

BIO CITY MAP OF 11 BILLION
WORLD POPULATION IN 2110

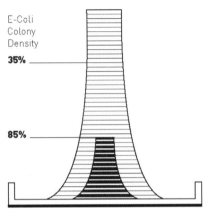

E-Coli
Colony
Density

35%

85%

SCALE: Petri Dish 3.5mm = City 35km

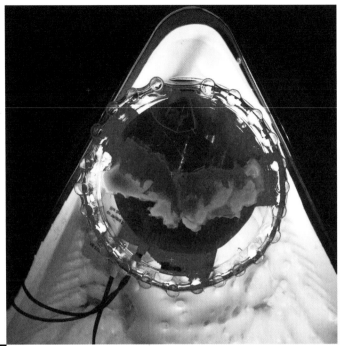

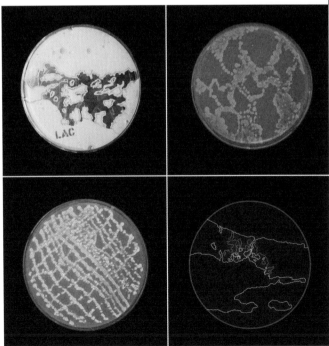

POPULATION DENSITY EXPRESSED IN
E-COLI BACTERIA.

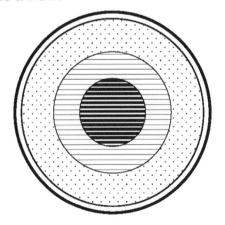

Above, Right: Existing population expressed in green. Projected population expressed in red.
Left:City Plan Studies: genetically modified bioluminescence in Escherichia Coli with UV light.

Graphics: Density expressed in layers of E-Coli.

Following Page: Detail of vacuum formed population graph grid elements.

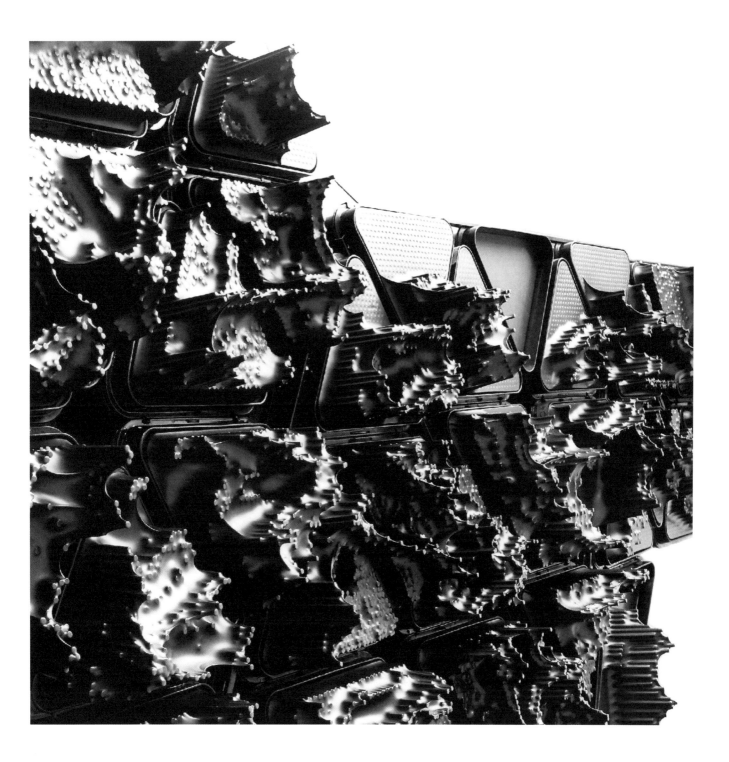

Design with Life

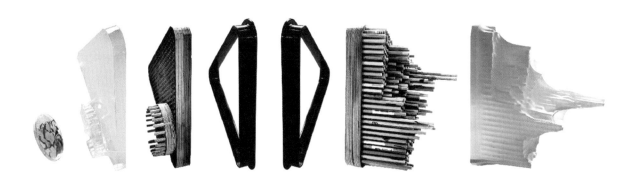

Above: Dymaxion map of global population density in 100 years. Below: Assembly of thermoformed plates inside articulated grid.

Following page: Method of thermoforming the pieces of the world map and aligning the dymaxion grid.

Design with Life

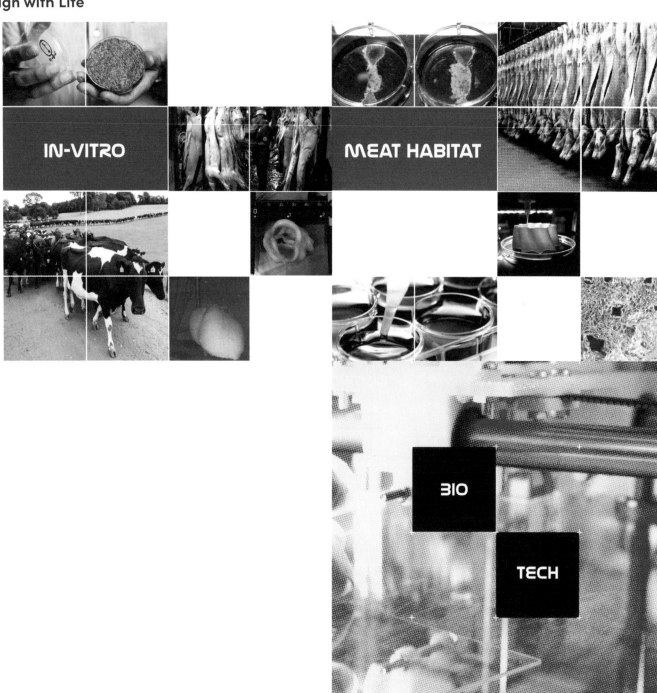

IN-VITRO

MEAT HABITAT

BIO

TECH

In-Vitro Meat Habitat

This is an architectural proposal for the fabrication of 3D printed extruded pig cells to form real organic dwellings. It is intended to be a "victimless shelter", because no sentient being was harmed in the laboratory growth of the skin. We used sodium benzoate as a preservative to kill yeasts, bacteria and fungi. Other materials in the model matrix are; collagen powder, xanthan gum, mannitol, cochineal, sodium pyrophosphate, and recycled PET plastic scaffold. As of now, the concept model consists of essentially very expensive fitted cured pork or articulated swine leather with an extended shelf life. The actual scale of the non-perishable prototype is 11 in. x 3 in. x 7 in..

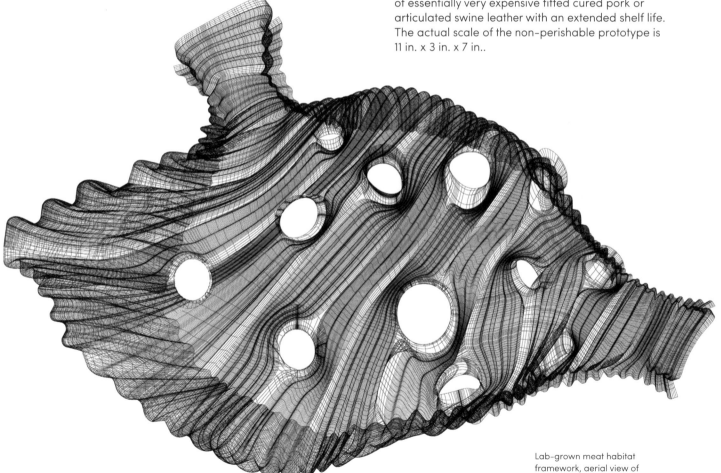

Lab-grown meat habitat framework, aerial view of overall form.

Design with Life

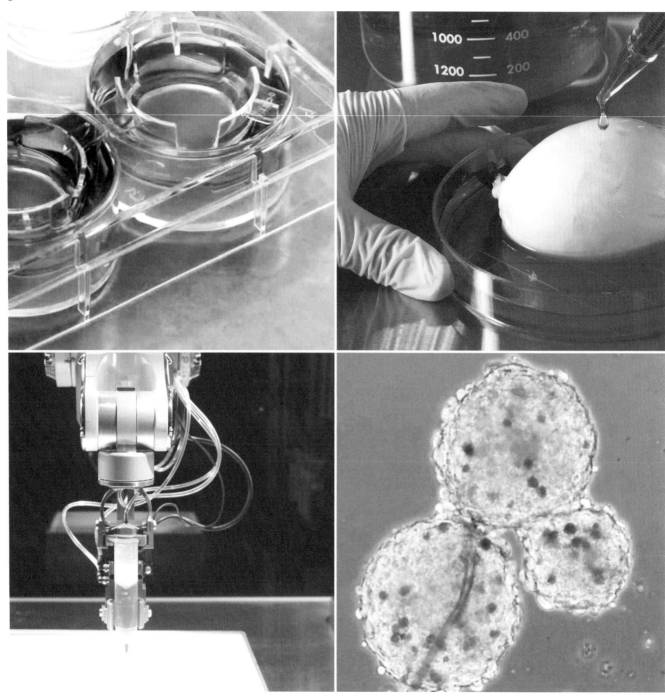

Previous page:
Muscle cell culture. Artificial bladder framework.
3D-printed heart cells under microscope. 3D-bioprinter.

Left: Concept model, 'victimless shelter'.
Below: Shelter in urban context.

Design with Life

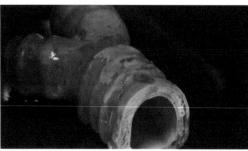

Left: Modified inkjet printer with live cells. 3D printed organ scaffolding.
Below: Meat tectonics, section detail.

Following page
Above: Meat House perspective render.
Below: Concept model aerial view.

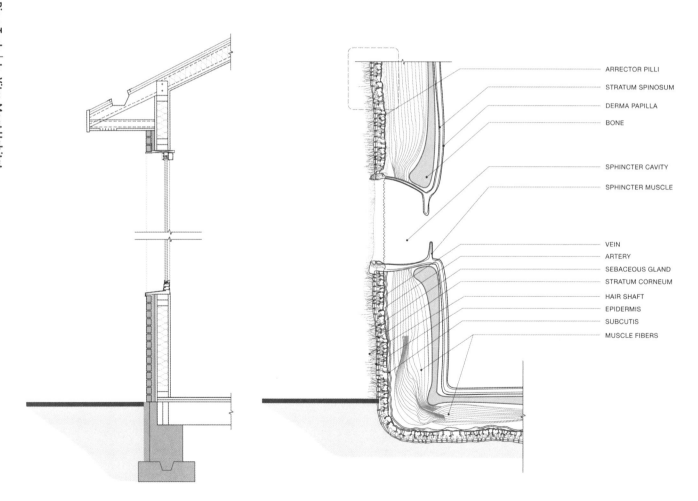

ARRECTOR PILLI

STRATUM SPINOSUM

DERMA PAPILLA

BONE

SPHINCTER CAVITY

SPHINCTER MUSCLE

VEIN

ARTERY

SEBACEOUS GLAND

STRATUM CORNEUM

HAIR SHAFT

EPIDERMIS

SUBCUTIS

MUSCLE FIBERS

Design with Life

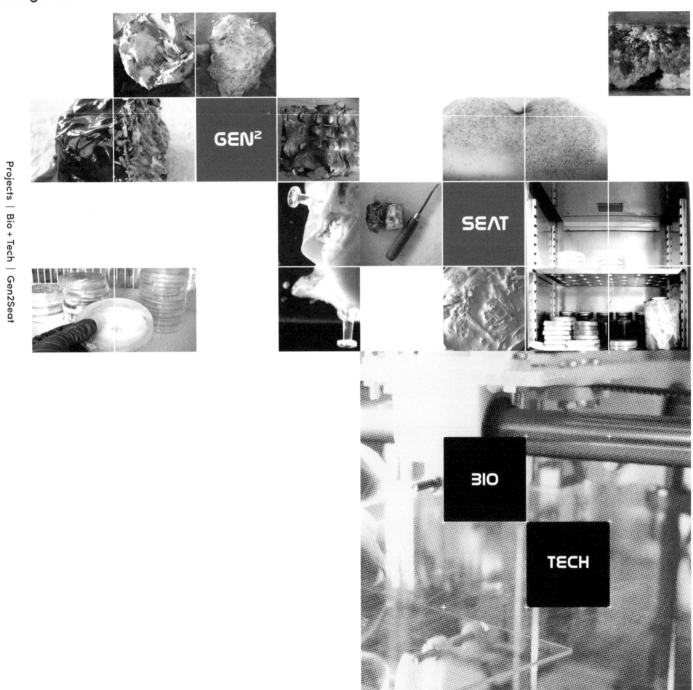

Gen2Seat

For almost ten years our group has been prototyping with living materials made from the dendritic microstructures commonly found in mushrooms. Many have appropriated our work in various forms. This research characterizes seminal explorations for the use of live mycelium in architectural and industrial design applications. The current iterations focus on known limitations of this material applied to complex parametrically driven formwork. Located throughout this research are studies that introduce new methods of growth control of mycelium in combination with other biomaterials such as acetobacter bacteria. We are not making simple bricks, but compound geometries mixed with novel biopolymers. The computational systems deployed in the process govern and predict the formal behavior and shape of mycelium. The ultimate intention of this biomaterial research is to potentially replace petroleum-based plastics with a metabolic and ecological substance. The internal filler is made up of mycelia substrate, a combination of discarded wood chips, gypsum, oat bran, which is consumed by mycelia and then hardened into a tough, durable functional material. The external skin is bacteria cellulose. The mycelia substrate and bacterial cellulose integrate to become a hard biopolymer that is suitable for architectural applications and the Mycoform module.

This platform is defined by various operations we can pre-form with mycelium, the primarily underground fungi threads or hyphae that shape the vegetative part of fungi. We grew the fungus Ganoderma lucidum (or Reishi) into various molds derived from computational output. In many cases architects mimic biological systems, but do not operate in actual wet laboratory conditions. This effort required a close collaboration between biologists and architects to produce synthetic bio design artifacts in conjunction with current digital fabrication techniques.

Mycoform structure grown from strains of fungi into a specific 3D fabricated geometry. The main objective of Mycoform is to establish a smart, self-sufficient, perpetual motion construction technology. By combining fungal mycelia with varying types of organic substrates and carefully controlling their expansion within prefabricated molds, we will create the literal growth of structural materials. The Mycoform is grown from biological materials.

The process is pollution free and has the potential to contain a low embodied energy as part of a local ecosystem. The polypore fungal species Ganoderma lucidum (Reishi), possesses enzymes that readily digest a wide variety of cellulose based organic by-products. The rapid growth of branching mycelia results on a dense matrix capable of structural support. The fungal substance is combined with a strong and durable outer later shield of compacted material such as recycled aluminum. The Mycoform Building Block production is a low-tech, low energy process. Few inexpensive readily available tools, free refuse and agricultural by-products, 80°F and humidity is all that is needed to compact and grow a mycelium building block. The technology is easily transferable to the developing world where building materials are scarce and expensive.

Design with Life

Gen2Seat with 2 year old Mia.

19TH c.

20TH c.

21ST c.

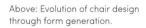

Above: Evolution of chair design through form generation.

Right: Plan view Gen2Seat: Transformative components.

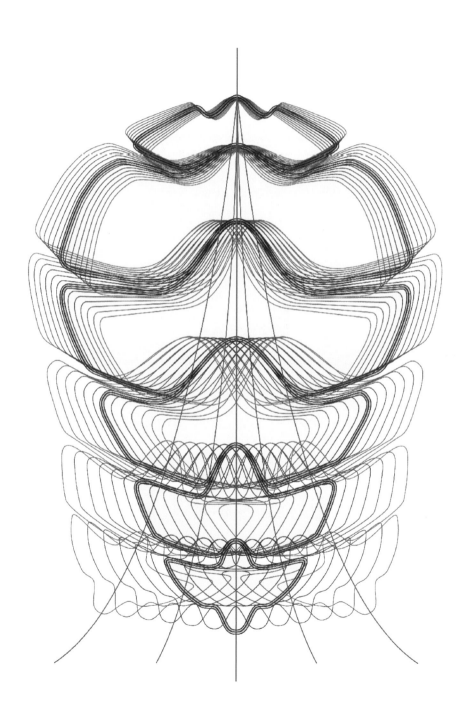

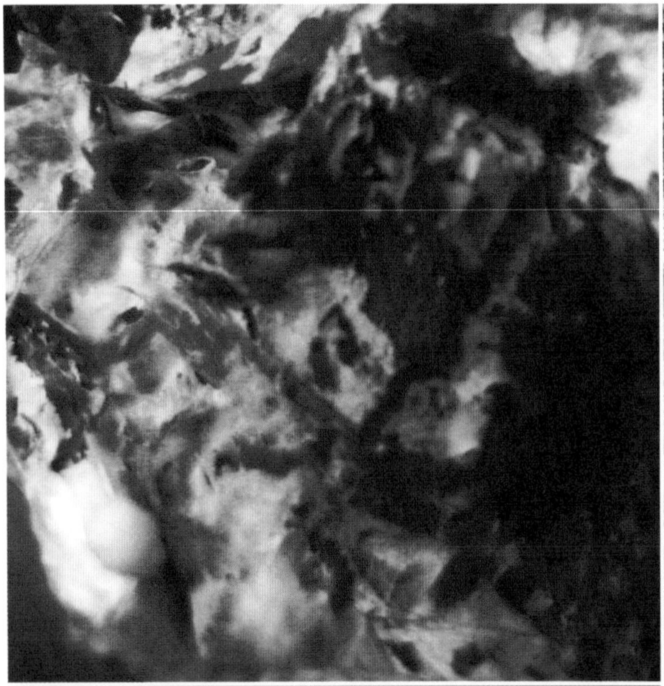

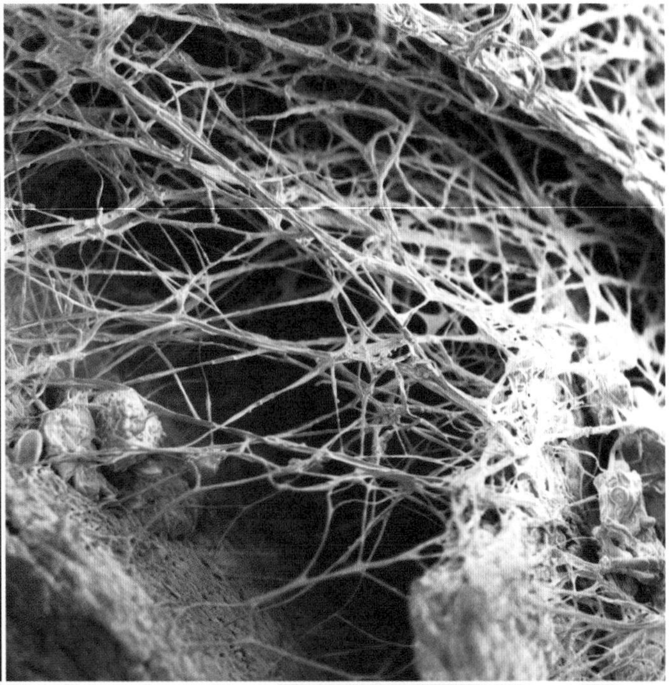

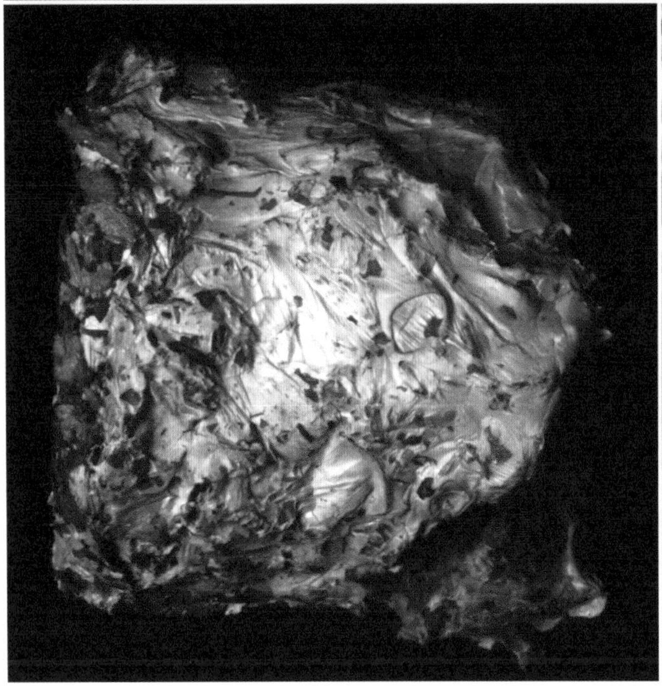

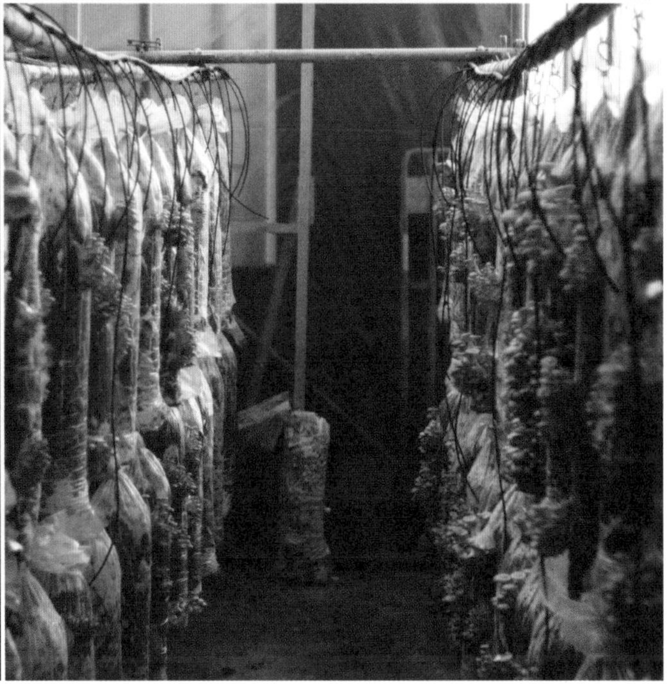

Previous Page:
Mycelium growth on recycled
substrate.

Right: Material assembly sequence.

 01

| 02 | Mycoform Assembly | 03 | Acetobacter Cover | 04 | Gelatin Chitin Layer |

Design with Life

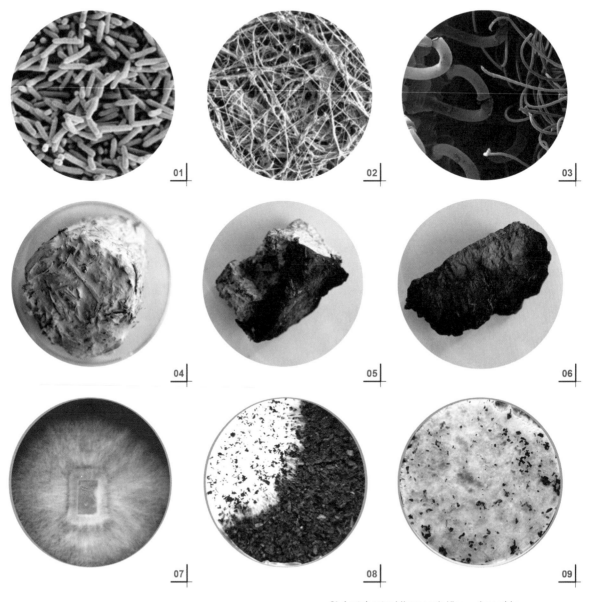

01. Acetobacter Microscopic View   Assembly
02. Mycelia Microscopic View   06. Cellulose Biocomposite
03. Cellulose Biocomposite   07. Mycelia Phase 1
04. Mycelia Biopolymer   08. Mycelia Phase 2
05. Mycoform + Acetobacter   09. Mycelia Phase 3

Design with Life

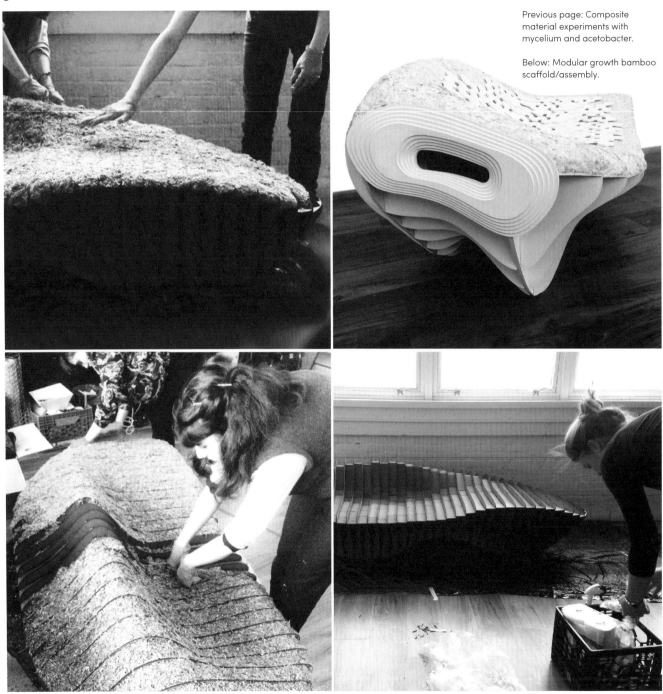

Previous page: Composite material experiments with mycelium and acetobacter.

Below: Modular growth bamboo scaffold/assembly.

Above: Mycelia growth close-up.
Below: Bamboo parametric ribs and mushroom mycelia surface grown from agricultural waste in seven days. The entire surface is fully compostable.

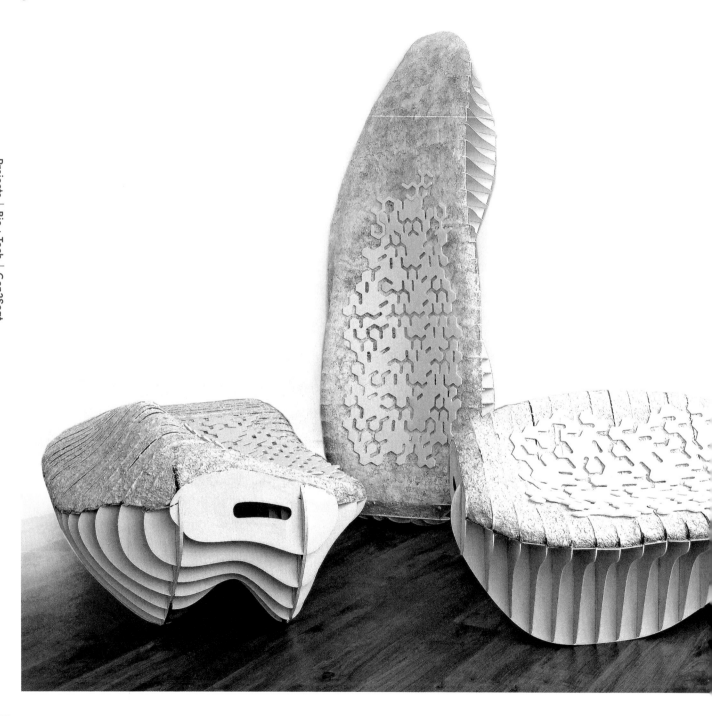

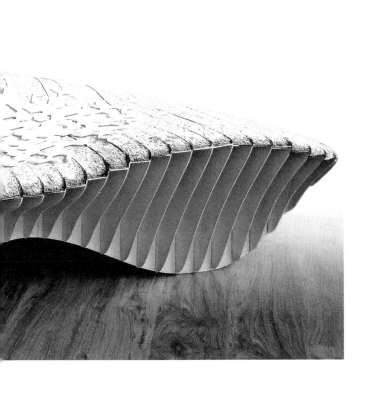

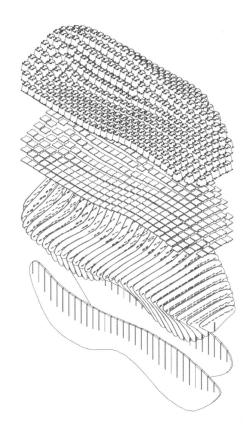

Left: Elevation curvatures.
Above: Multi-directional
interlocking mycoform module
assembly.

Design with Life

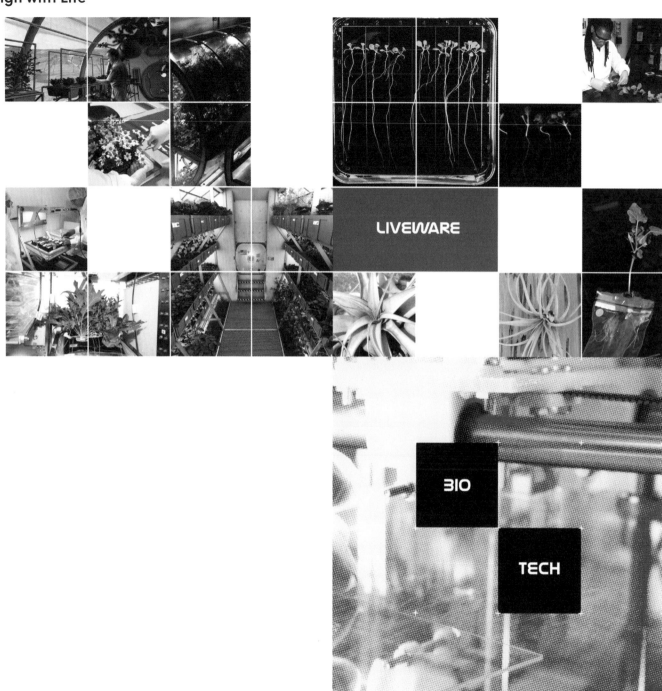

LIVEWARE

BIO

TECH

Liveware

Soft Root Aeroponic Chamber

As a continuation of the research into growing soft roots for use in living structural applications, we intend to design and fabricate a lightweight, modular alternative to the aeroponic system constructed with Treenovations in June 2016. Conceptualized as an individual 'spacesuit' for each plant, this apparatus generates and maintains a precisely conditioned adaptable environment in which growth can be promoted, monitored and controlled. Utilizing more sophisticated materials and technologies enable this system to become a transportable and deployable solution for growing programmable architectures on-site, as well as a smart monitoring device linked to an online database of life cycle analyses – aiming to iterate, discover and optimize the environmental conditions for maximally accelerated root growth over generations of plants. The eventual aim is to develop a living structural system, from which entire architectures can be 'grown-to-order'; pleaching the individual trees to form a composite structure.

Data Capture

The LIVEWARE functions as a data capture environment, recording the plant's biometrics as it develops, as well as the input parameters for growth. Over many iterations of this process, a comparative feedback process builds an understanding of the causal relationship between input parameters and the resulting health, form and growth rate of the plant. This phenotypical knowledge will enable us to push the limits of root growth rate, the primary prohibitive factor in developing practical structures made from living biomaterial. A visual output alongside a common graphical data display on a web page devoted to the documentation of this project would provide an open platform for publishing the results from the lab. This could be programmed, embedded tech automatically recording, analyzing and publishing the data to the web in real time, and plotting the progress of each plant in the system.

Data Output:
· CO2 Level (Canopy)
· Humidity (Root Chamber)
· Temperature (Root Chamber + Canopy)
· Solution pH / Chemical Constitution
· Net Weight

· Growth Time
· Photograph (Plan, Diameter)
· Photograph (Elevation, Height)
· Biological Samples
· Incident Light Conditions
Indicates parameter over which system provides complete control.

Controllable Input Parameters (Basic):
· Solution pH / Chemical Constitution
· Incident Light

Directionality, Photoperiod, Intensity, Spectrum
· Mister Phasing
· Auxin Application

Phenotype Development

Through precise control of the environmental parameters inside the 'space suit', a degree of formal variation will be achievable through their manipulation. This can be considered as a form of 'auto-espalier', programmable tree-shaping for which no human intervention or maintenance is required. The parameters are merely adapted in response to the growth feedback from previous iterations until a desired canopy form can be reliably achieved. For example, tightly controlled, localized exposure to light will enable the system to direct the directional tendency of each leaf's growth. This could be supplemented with the topical application of auxins to stimulate further cell division in the desired locations. These 'designed' phenotypes can then begin to assume the role of architectural elements in the bio-constructions, which result from their agglomeration, bearing the disposition of either a column, a series of mullions, a portal, a gable and so forth.

Expressive Exhibition

For our first prototype of this "veggie suit" an expressive, even sculptural piece will be imagined and constructed, one which seeks to playfully express the temporal shifts and events arising from the operation of the system as it maintains the environmental conditions for the plant. Trigger events such as mister operation, air pump operation, threshold breaches and time phase may all result in a visual, auditory or another sensory expression, such that the system

Design with Life

constitutes a responsive envelope. The goal is to engage and communicate to an observer the mode of operation of the system itself. This extends to visible metrics, programmed LEDs, inflatable sacs which translate the movement of air and water through the system into a performance.

Programmable Architectural Assemblage

The eventual conceptual goal of this research lies in a modular, adaptable bio-unit, designed to grow pre-configured bio-architectures using a common, infinitely replicable system. The geometry of the eventual architecture is defined by the arrangement of these units, which have a high degree of formal reconfigurability. Every composition, however, adheres to a principal set of geometric logics, defined foundationally by the scale of the human and the limits of the biological ability of the plants.

Temporal Phasing

The principle dictates the system in its prototypical composition is an architecture in itself, from the moment of its deployment through to its maturation into a living structure independent from artificial support.
The system also fulfills a number of functions with different periods of applicability relative to the life cycles of the plants.

1. Initial Environmental Control
This refers to the period during which the plant is fully reliant on the aeroponic system. It is growing roots at an accelerated rate yet attains its desired form and length.

2. Structural Support
This refers to the period after which the plant has achieved the desired root length and canopy form, but before the lignification process renders it supporting, or mutually supporting if pleached in a group. During this phase, the long, pliable taproot is exposed to the air, and the lower 10% is planted in soil (either at grade or at a predetermined level). As the 'planted' portion of the root is now surrounded by soil, the tactile stimuli encourage it to divide, bifurcating to yield many individual root tips. This begins the process of lignification, though it may take years before the exposed root attains sufficient mass to support itself, and hence a guiding 'scaffold' provides auxiliary support. At this time, the system's life-support components are completely or partially

removed, depending on the circumstance, leaving the plant to develop under natural conditions. In some cases, it may be desirable to continue to precisely control the growth of the canopy while the roots are left to develop naturally.

3. Supplementary Life Support
This refers to an interstitial period during which the root tip, having been planted, may have insufficient water uptake potential to support the canopy. In this case, supplementary aeroponic functionality may be maintained and phased out gradually.

4. Self-Supporting Living Bio-Architecture
This refers to the period after which the plants are self-sustaining and self-supporting, fulfilling their intended programmatic functions as a living bio-architecture.

Structural / Technical / Material

Seeing as the majority of the weight of the structure is contained in the water circulation system, this mass ought to be positioned closest to the point of suspension in an eponymous system – with the lightweight life-support elements hanging below this structure. The distribution of water weight can be seen as a means to adapt or transform the structure as needed, on the basis of:

1. Expandable Canopy Space – Soft vs. rigid elements, mode of expansion.
2. Extensible Root Chamber, material, mode?
3. Mister reservoir, better transmission efficiency, use of gravity.
4. Lighting fixture design.
5. Backing canvas/light reflector configuration.
6. LED integration.

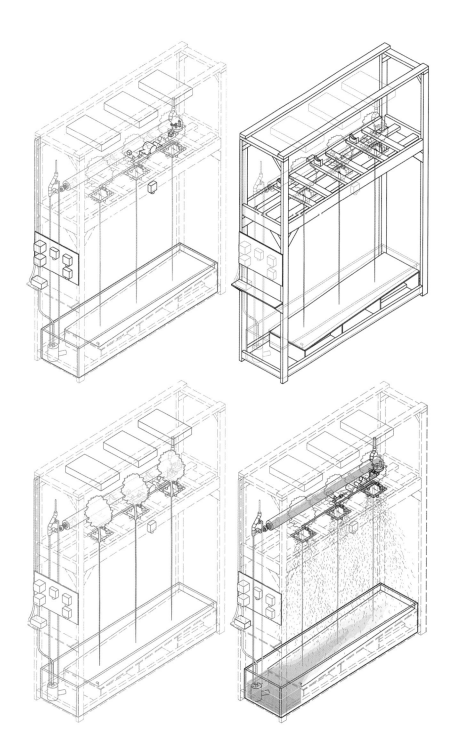

Soft root aeroponic chamber.

Design with Life

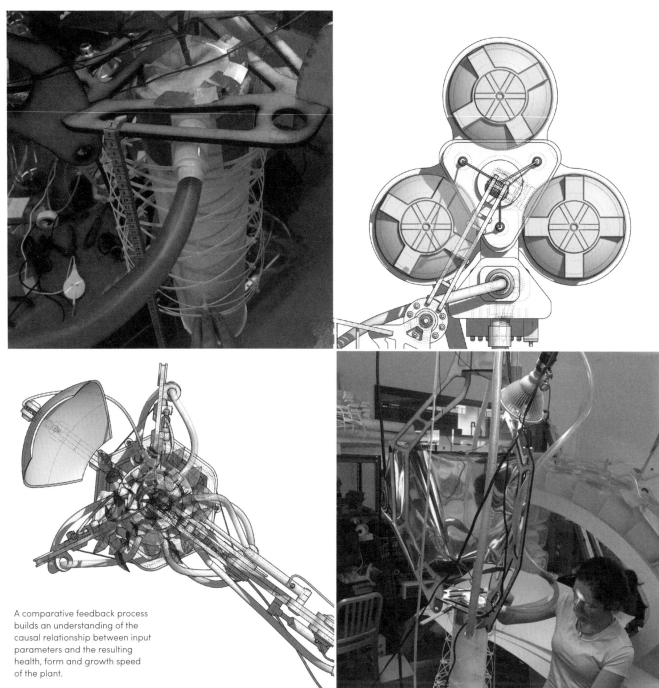

A comparative feedback process builds an understanding of the causal relationship between input parameters and the resulting health, form and growth speed of the plant.

146

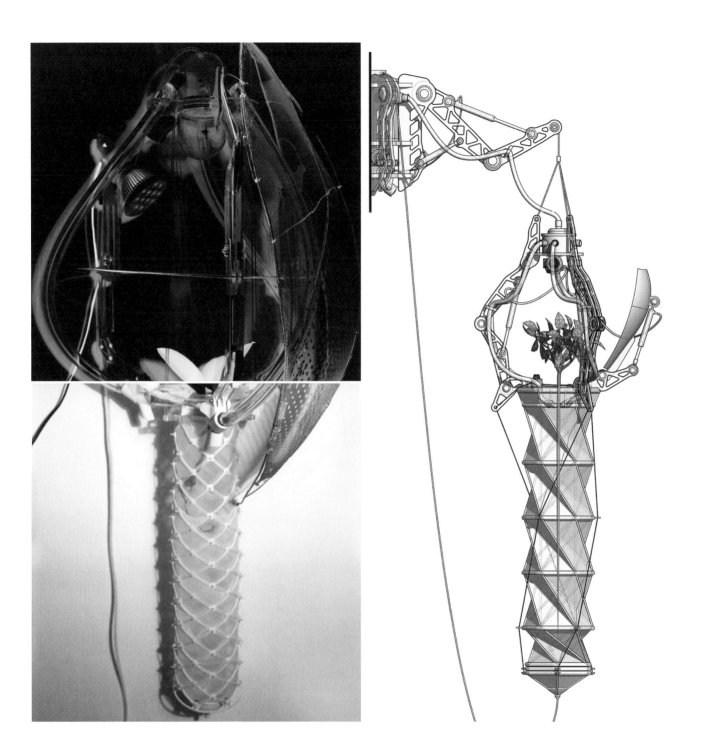

Design with Life

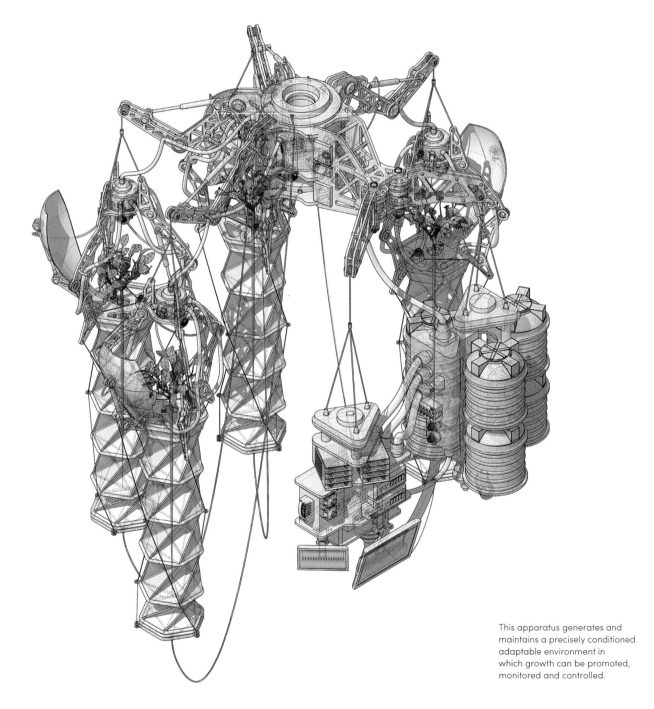

This apparatus generates and maintains a precisely conditioned adaptable environment in which growth can be promoted, monitored and controlled.

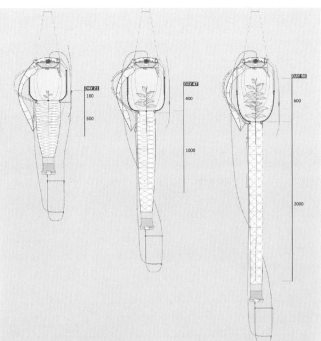

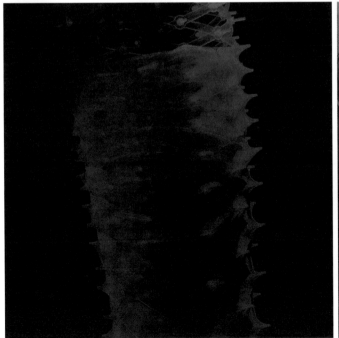

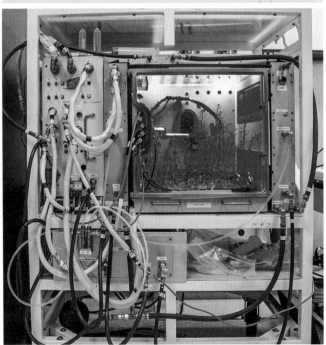

Design with Life

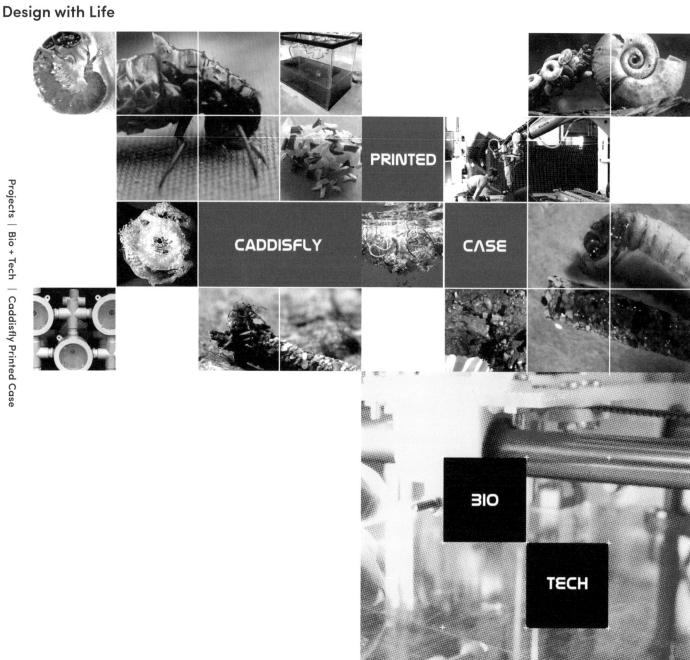

PRINTED

CADDISFLY

CASE

BIO

TECH

Caddisfly Printed Case

The rising anthropogenic emission of plastic waste is threatening water-based environments including most rivers and oceans. Microplastic, which is small particles degraded from domestic plastic consumer products, plays a critical role in exacerbating ecosystem stressors for aquatic animals. These microplastic waste particles are difficult to be observed by humans. They are exceedingly problematic to be recycled or cleaned due to their miniature size. However, through researching caddisfly larvae case architecture, we are able to find a potential solution to alleviate microplastic pollution.

Caddisflies spend most of their life living in fresh water. They secrete silk as a waterproof adhesive to bond miscellaneous natural geometric materials together for protection, camouflage, and prey capture. They create intricate shell-like structures that are incredibly sophisticated. Our intention is to explore the possibility of using caddisflies' ability to collect microplastic forms in polluted waterways. The caddisfly would use the discarded materials to build their protective shelter.

This phase of the caddisfly project is intended to produce solid methods of inducing larvae case manufacture by using our inputs in a controlled water tank. We are seeking optimized methods that encourage the insect to prototype and construct with commonly discarded ingredients. We built an aquarium that allowed us to adjust water flow speed, quantifiable waste content, nutrients, and oxygen level. Through regulating these factors, we observed different results of caddisflies' case architecture. Instead of humans trying to remove tiny elements of dispersed plastic, we are able to have the insect collect and assemble it for removal. The ultimate goal is to have them essentially behave like miniaturized 3d printers in order for us to easily harvest larger pieces of plastic waste.

Design with Life

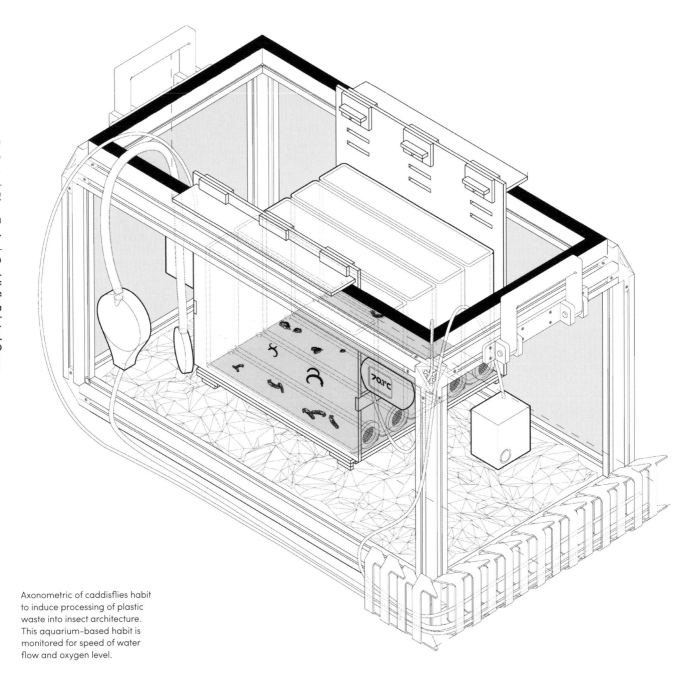

Axonometric of caddisflies habit to induce processing of plastic waste into insect architecture. This aquarium-based habit is monitored for speed of water flow and oxygen level.

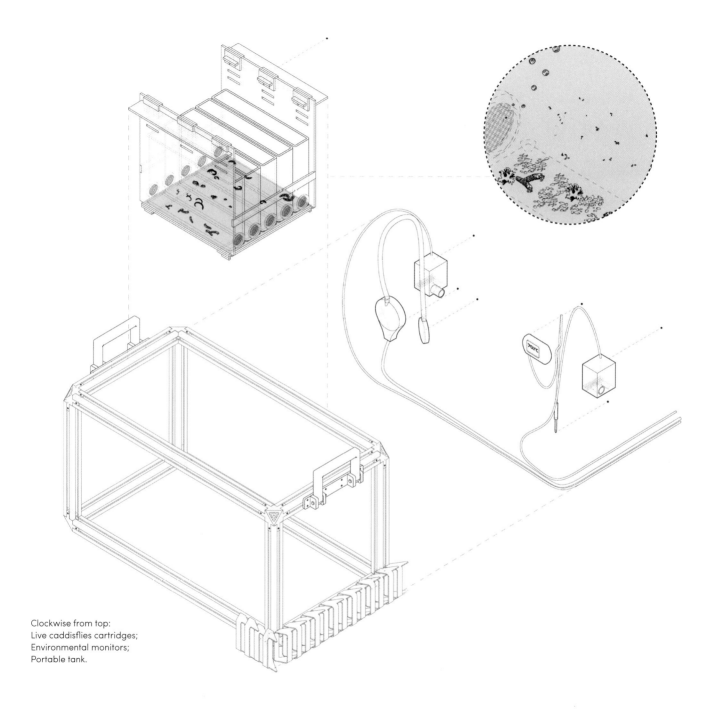

Clockwise from top:
Live caddisflies cartridges;
Environmental monitors;
Portable tank.

Design with Life

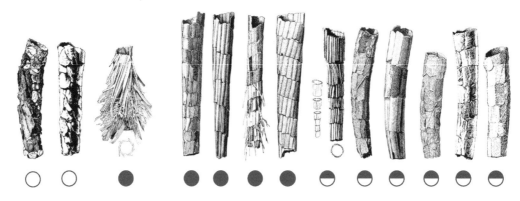

CASE TYPE

○ IRREGULAR

● SPIRAL WALL, RANDOM

◐ RINGS

Caddisflies' case types and formal logic built from puzzle-fitting irregular shaped pieces together.

Design with Life

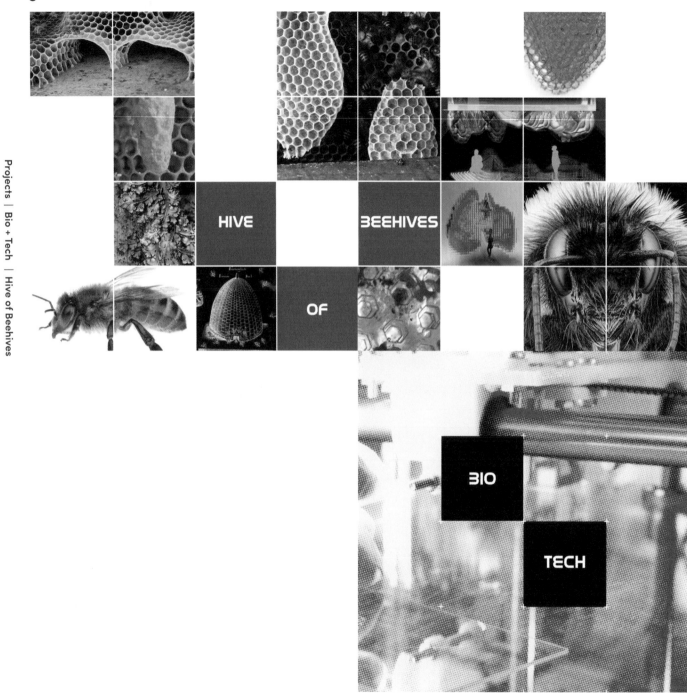

HIVE OF BEEHIVES

BIO TECH

Hive of Beehives

This ongoing research project was commissioned by the American Museum of Natural History. The aim was to create a unique central exhibition feature inside their insectarium wing for the new building. We desired to celebrate the North American Honey Bee and its life cycle, which includes the Waggle Dance and pollination. Also, the assignment was to educate the public about the issues surrounding the feared colony collapse disorder (CCD). After many thought-provoking concepts, we decided on the Hive of Beehives.

Essentially it was a chandelier type structure that supported one hundred fabricated hives in a permanent archival material. Some of the hives are exact replicas of ones found in nature while bees in a laboratory setting recreated others. As architects, we thought the bees themselves could be integral to the whole construction process.

We formed a highly divergent method of the lost wax process used in casting sculptural objects. In this version, bees would extrude wax material into the shape of a prefabricated form. Using 3D modeling software, we crafted a context model that serves as a precision scaffold for the bees. The bees would generate a wax hive colony inside that 3D printed geometric form. This bee-produced form is later scanned on a large turntable. The resulting geometry is made into a negative mold that is used to accept liquid pours from more permanent hardening materials. This interspecies (between human bee) process effectively turns the bee colony into a kind of analog computational element. All kinds of naturally produced inconsistencies and irregularities are captured within the design. Instead of a 3D model trying to mimic the shape of wax honeycomb structures, we use real bees to investigate and co-develop form making.

3D printed honeycomb scaled up twenty-four times from actual size.

Following pages
Left: Bee Printed Concrete: process of scanning natural honeycomb, 3D printing formwork and then casting in concrete.
Right: Honeycomb geometries cast in resin based off wax paper patterns.

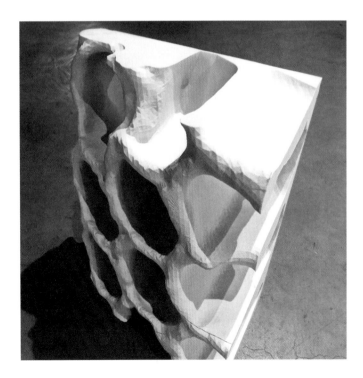

Design with Life

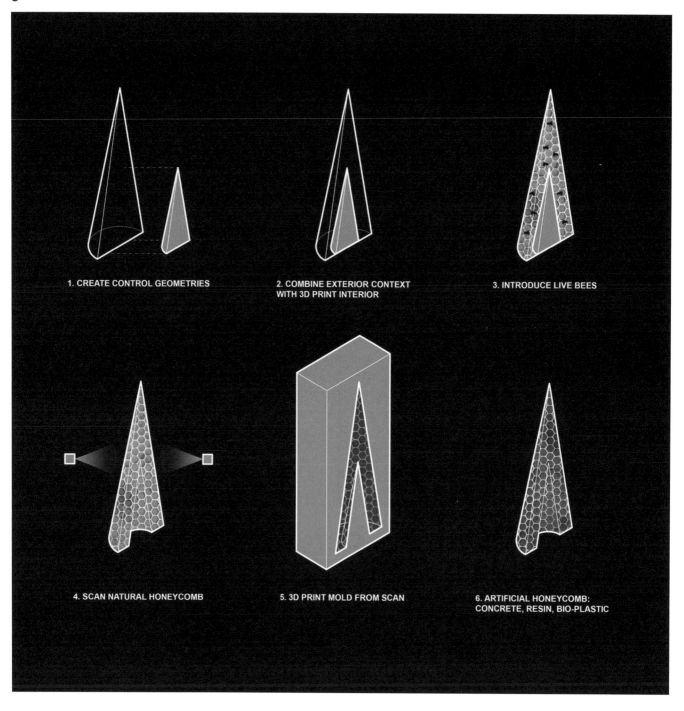

1. CREATE CONTROL GEOMETRIES

2. COMBINE EXTERIOR CONTEXT WITH 3D PRINT INTERIOR

3. INTRODUCE LIVE BEES

4. SCAN NATURAL HONEYCOMB

5. 3D PRINT MOLD FROM SCAN

6. ARTIFICIAL HONEYCOMB: CONCRETE, RESIN, BIO-PLASTIC

Design with Life

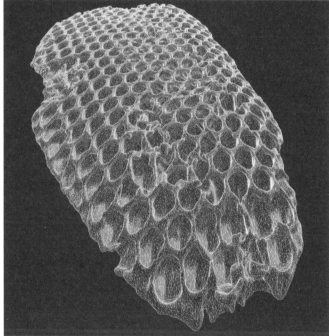

Above: Detail view of Hive of Beehives: Various hive types including those of Australian, Himalayan, and North American honey bee hives.
Left: 3D scan of one lobe of wild hive measuring 4.5" x 2.5" x 0.5".
Right: Honey driven clock that counts down the evolution of bees as it fills in the different hive types.

Following Pages:
Left: Patterning, lobe gaps, and lobe spread determined by local site conditions.
Right: Hive of Beehives installation featuring concentric arrangement of resin cast hives from around the world.

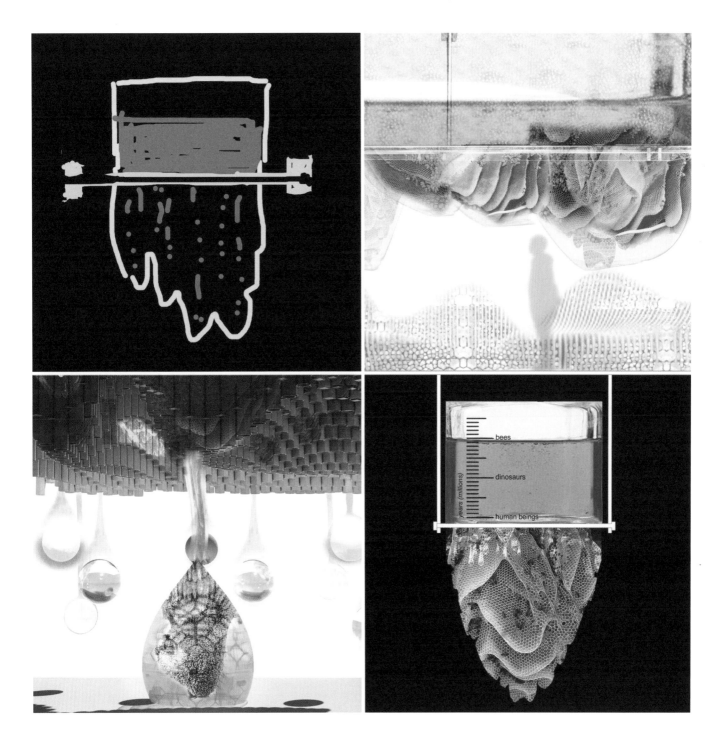

Design with Life

Design with Life

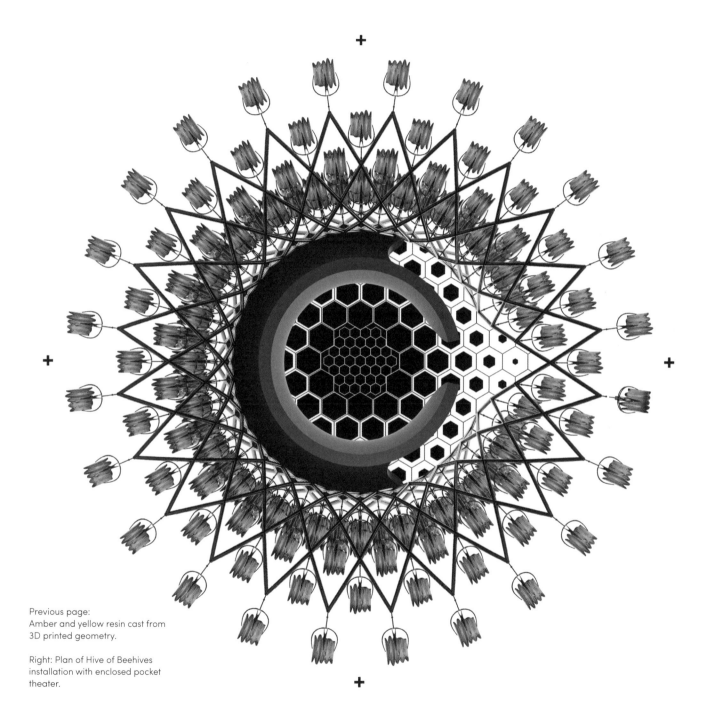

Previous page:
Amber and yellow resin cast from
3D printed geometry.

Right: Plan of Hive of Beehives
installation with enclosed pocket
theater.

Design with Life

URBANEERING
BROOKLYN

ECOLOGY

CIVIC

Urbaneering Brooklyn

Our primary assertion for Brooklyn 2110 is that all necessities are provided inside its accessible physical borders. We have designed an intensified version of Brooklyn that supplies all vital needs for its population. In this city, food, water, air, energy, waste, mobility, and shelter are radically restructured to support life in every form.

Whose job is it to create a city? Our intention is to jumpstart a new profession that can re-invent and negotiate the complex mix that encompasses a city. We have defined a radical new occupation to regenerate, pioneer, and sustain the future urban realm. These innovative multi-disciplinarian advocates are called Urbaneers. Their immense task is to manifest and facilitate the City 2.0 across the globe. Each Urbaneer is an individual with a different set of versatile abilities that merge previously disparate occupations. They range from combined ecological architects and engineers to action based urban planners and developers. Almost any recombined professional activities will work, so long as they meet the constantly changing needs of urbanization. Urbaneers perform in a role akin to Jane Jacobs, but at the magnitude and accomplishment of Robert Moses. An excellent historical example of an Urbaneer is Frederick Law Olmsted.

The strategy includes the replacement of dilapidated structures with vertical agriculture and housing merged with infrastructure. Former streets become snaking arteries of livable spaces embedded with; renewable energy sources, soft cushion based vehicles for mobility, and productive green rooms. The plan uses the former street grid as the foundation for new networks. By re-engineering the obsolete streets, we can install radically robust and ecologically active pathways. These operations are not just about a comprehensive model of tomorrow's city, but an initial platform for discourse. We think the future will necessitate marvelous dwellings coupled with a massive cyclical resource net. The future will happen, how we get there is dependent upon our planned preparation and egalitarian feedback.

Utilizing existing infrastructure as ecological generator.

Design with Life

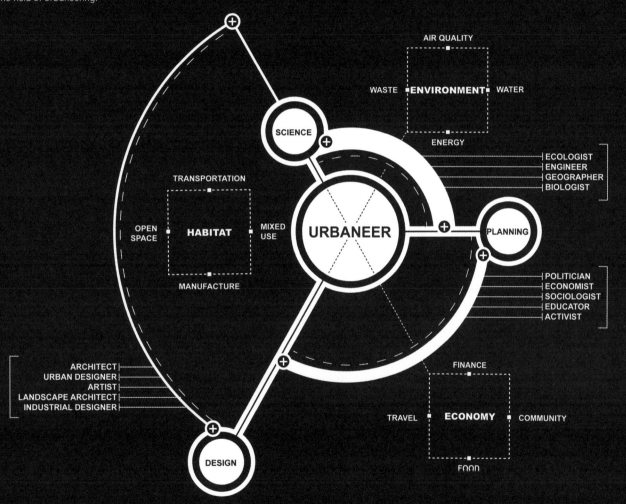

Previous page
Model perspective of city
center water + energy
works.

Below:
The field of Urbaneering.

AIR QUALITY

WASTE **ENVIRONMENT** WATER

ENERGY

SCIENCE

ECOLOGIST
ENGINEER
GEOGRAPHER
BIOLOGIST

TRANSPORTATION

OPEN
SPACE **HABITAT** MIXED
USE

MANUFACTURE

URBANEER

PLANNING

POLITICIAN
ECONOMIST
SOCIOLOGIST
EDUCATOR
ACTIVIST

ARCHITECT
URBAN DESIGNER
ARTIST
LANDSCAPE ARCHITECT
INDUSTRIAL DESIGNER

FINANCE

TRAVEL **ECONOMY** COMMUNITY

FOOD

DESIGN

Design with Life

Exploration of downtown Brooklyn with revised infrastructure, waterfront and energy facility.
01. Vinegar Hill
02. Manhattan bridge
03. Fort Greene
04. Docking armature water turbines
05. Water distribution facility
06. Biomass crop
07. Dumbo
08. Piezoelectric energy field
09. Brooklyn bridge
10. Brooklyn Queens expressway Estuarine canal system

Design with Life

Previous page
Above: Food, water, air, energy, waste, mobility, and shelter are radically reconstructed to support life in every form.
Below: Quadrant E + F urban plan: 1:1000.

Right: Infrastructure as spectacle.

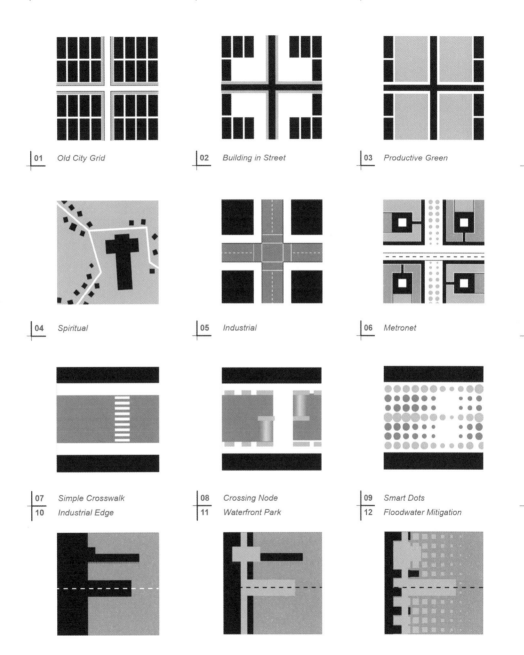

01 Old City Grid

02 Building in Street

03 Productive Green

04 Spiritual

05 Industrial

06 Metronet

07 Simple Crosswalk

08 Crossing Node

09 Smart Dots

10 Industrial Edge

11 Waterfront Park

12 Floodwater Mitigation

Design with Life

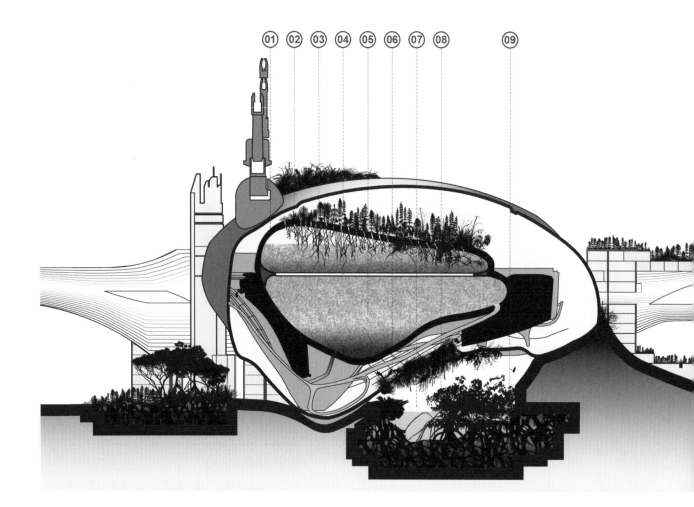

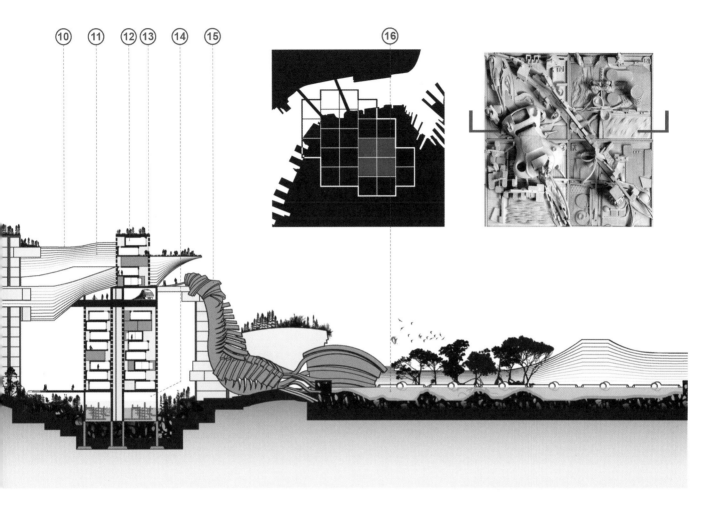

Section of city center water
+ energy works.
01. Water distribution facility
02. Aerobic ecological fluidized
    rooting bed
03. Open aerobic reactor bladder
04. Permeable membrane
05. Final clarifying settling
    bladder
06. Air purifying planted filter belly

07. Tidal surge and storm
    flood line
08. Estuarine canal outlet to the
    East River tidal strait
09. Permeable sponge enables
    hydrology of wetland and
    foothold for plant and
    organism growth
10. Brooklyn Queens Expressway

11. Connective transportation
    tubes
12. Housing merged with
    infrastructure and mobility
13. Areas of outside mobility
    and vegetated roofscapes
14. Hydroelectric turbines
15. Pedestrian transportation link
16. Aquaponic agriculture pool

Design with Life

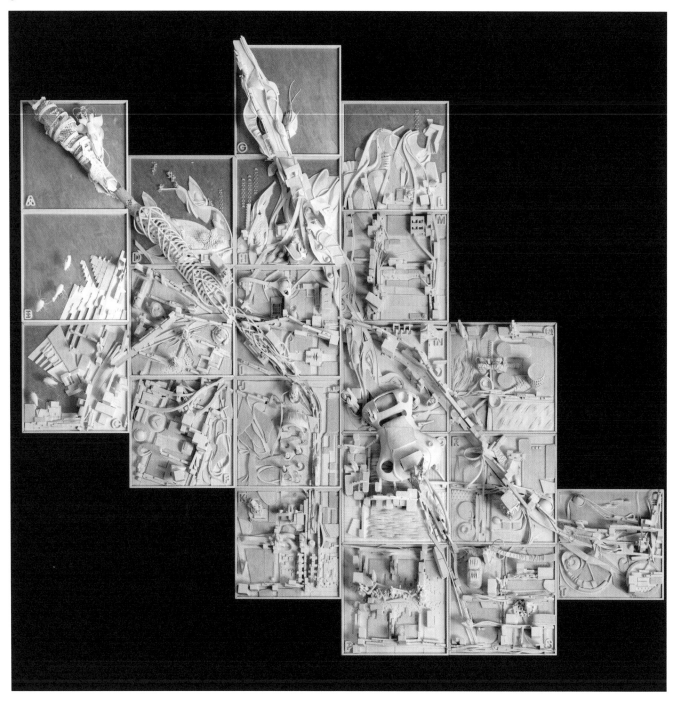

 **BROOKLYN**

POPULATION: 4,500

SITE

93%
PRODUCTIVE GREEN SPACE

11,500,000 sq. ft.
energy production farm

3,000,000 sq. ft.
water filtrating sponge & wetlands

0 sq. ft.
recreation park

OPEN SPACE

BROOKLYN WAS HISTORICALLY KNOWN AS "BROOKEN-LAND" BECAUSE NATURAL WETLANDS CARVED THROUGH THE CITY.

AREA: 15,000,000 sq. ft.
SCALE: 1"=600'

2010 **BROOKLYN**

POPULATION: 2,500,000

HEALTH

0%
PRODUCTIVE GREEN SPACE

0 sq. ft.
productive/ farm/ energy

0 sq. ft.
sponge/ wetlands/ water filtration

4,000,000 sq. ft.
recreation/ park

OPEN SPACE

PRESENT

AREA: 16,000,000 sq. ft.
SCALE: 1"=600'

Previous page:
Masterplan urban grid model of
Brooklyn, 2110.

Design with Life

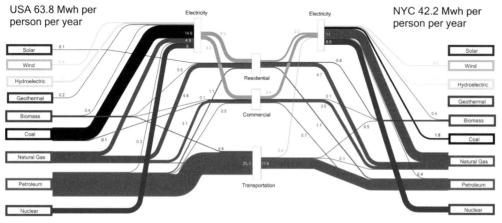

USA 63.8 Mwh per person per year

NYC 42.2 Mwh per person per year

Data for the US is obtained from the EIA. Data for NYC is estimated from EIA data for New York State and the inventory of greenhouse gas emissions done by PLANYC. Values below 0.05 are not displayed.

Above: Brooklyn bridge detail: Dumbo 2110.

Left: The field of urbaneering. Comparison of energy use for the United States and New York city 2020.

Following page: Future urban grain with fully integrated transport infrastructure.

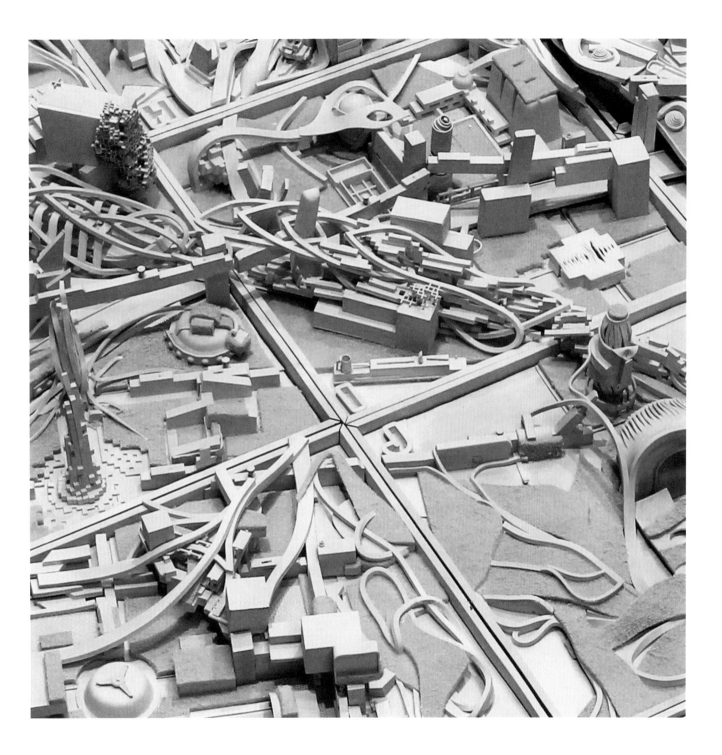

Design with Life

BROOKLYN
POPULATION: 5,000,000

FUTURE

75%
PRODUCTIVE GREEN SPACE

6,500,000 sq. ft.
energy production farm

5,000,000 sq. ft.
water filtrating sponge & wetlands

0 sq. ft.
recreation park

OPEN SPACE

AREA: 15,500,000 sq. ft.
SCALE: 1"=600'

2010 BROOKLYN
SITE
POPULATION: 2,500,000

0% RECYCLED WATER
fresh water is pumped in from up to 100 miles away

6% RENEWABLE ENERGY

400 MGA (million gallons annually) combine sewage overflow (CSO) a mix of strom and sewage water

EAST RIVER
CSO
untreated excess
runoff water

WATER SOURCE +

60 MGD (million gallons daily) filtration/collection/distribution primary system

60 MGD collection/distribution follows street grid runoff

23 MWH (mega watt hour/person/yr) non-renewable - petroleum/ nuclear/ nat. gas/ coal

ENERGY SOURCE

CSO's collect excess runoff including untreated sewage from the surrounding area which drains into harbor.

AREA: 16,000,000 sq. ft.
SCALE: 1"=1200'

PRESENT

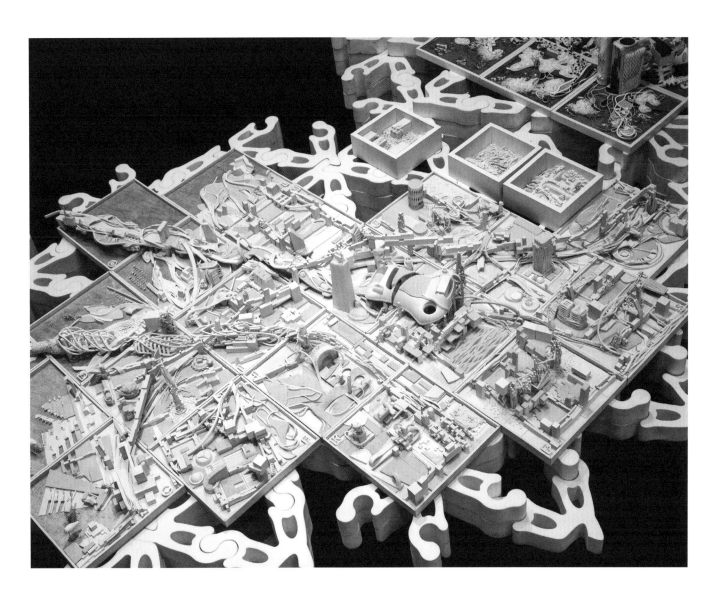

Brooklyn 2110.

Design with Life

2110 BROOKLYN
WATER
POPULATION: 5,000,000

100% RECYCLED WATER

120 MGD (million gallons daily)
filtration/collection/distribution
primary system

30 MGD
filtration/collection/distribution
secondary system

0 MGD
combine sewage overflow

WATER SOURCE

main tank collects from all
surrounding secondary
tanks

secondary water collection tank for
1,000,000 sq. ft. area

AREA: 15,500,000 sq. ft.
SCALE: 1"=600'

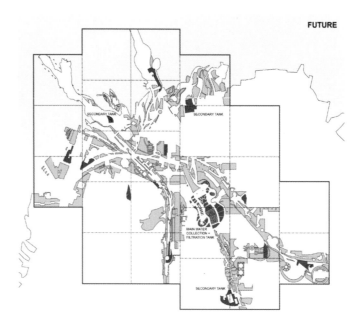

FUTURE

2110 BROOKLYN
ENERGY
POPULATION: 5,000,000

100% RENEWABLE ENERGY

23 MWH (mega watt hour/person/yr)
primary renewable system -
algae farms

20 MWH
secondary systems -
wind/ solar/ hydro

0 MWH
non-renewable -
petroleum/ nuclear/ nat. gas/ coal
ENERGY SOURCE

AREA: 15,500,000 sq. ft.
SCALE: 1"=600'

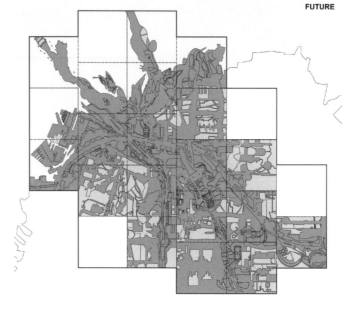

FUTURE

Right: Directives for new urban
ecology: The public park should
be the Green Brain of the city.
A. Biofuel head from local
   vegetative materials
B. Summer cooling mist outlets
C. Winter radiant heaters
D. Wi-Fi hotspot + seeders
E. Steward with organic
   fertilizers

Design with Life

NEW YORK

2106

ECOLOGY

CIVIC

New York 2106

Our project seeks to reinforce what is best about the city in both its forms and its life by speculating about the consequences of a radically new level of sustainability. We base our project on one clarifying hypothesis: in the future, New York will become self-sufficient in its vital necessities, including energy, food, water, air supply, employment, housing, manufacture, movement systems, waste processing, and cultural life. We propose transformation via a radical strategy: the reversal of figure and ground, of public and private property. We begin with citywide "green fill," the immediate transfer of half the aggregate of street space from the vehicular to the pedestrian and public realm. Terreform proposes covering New York City with vertical gardens and urban farms to achieve self-sufficiency.

Later, the streets become building sites and, as new, highly autonomous, buildings grow in intersections and wind their way down streets and avenues and through vacant lots, the old, deteriorated, fabric will fade away to be replaced both by an abundance of productive green space and by a new labyrinth of irregular blocks, a paradise for pedestrians. Fast movement will be accomplished underground in a superbly modernized subway and along the rivers and new cross-island channels. The city streets extended in their length but reduced in their area will support a marvelous technology we know to be just over the horizon, some fabulous and slow conveyance summoned with a whistle or collapsed into a pocket.

Downtown and Wall Street encapsulated with soft fertile infrastructure and biodiverse building skins.

Design with Life

Above: Aerial view of
Williamsburg Bridge.
Right: Site plan with reversal
of figure-ground

Following pages
Left: Diagrams of city blocks
becoming productive green
spaces.
Right: Comparison of historic
street hierarchy to proposed.

Design with Life

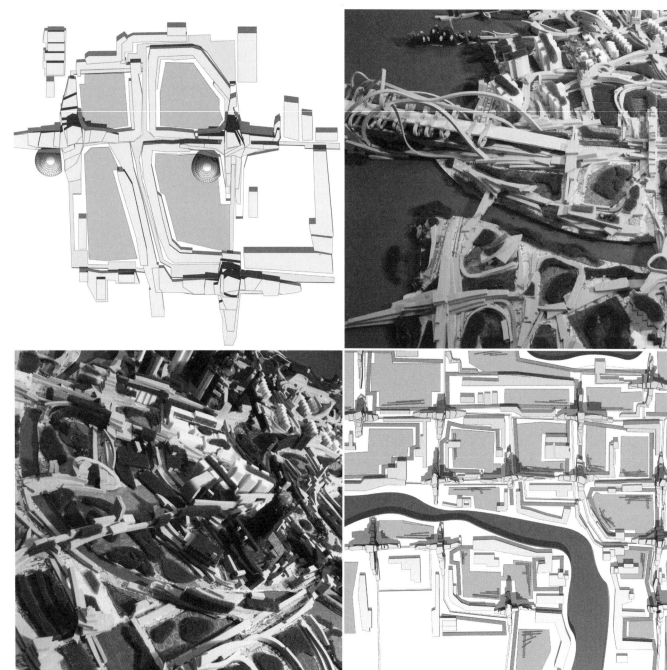

Design with Life

Lower East Side transformed.

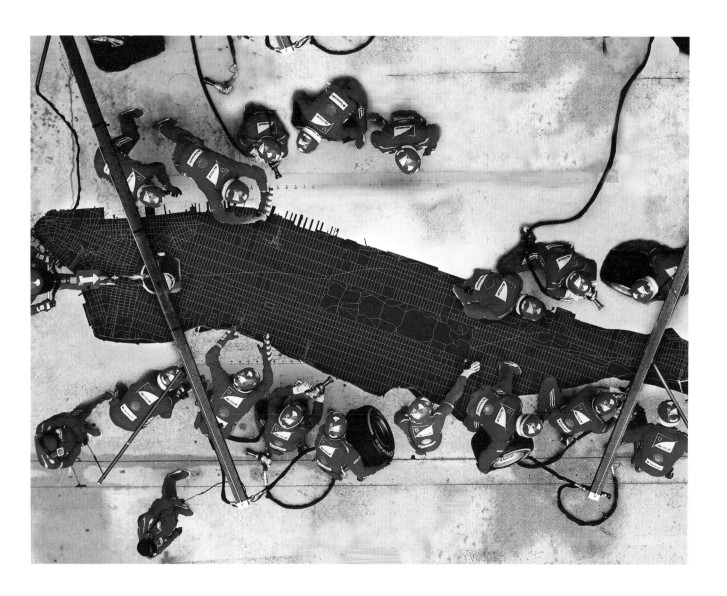

Urbaneering as collective act with
multitude of specialists.

URBAN TANGLE

PUBLIC

ACTION

Urban Tangle

Urban Tangle takes cues from the urban theories of the Situationists, seeking to translate psychogeographic experience into a reconfigurable sculpture.

Spatial excerpts from urban grids from global cities were analyzed, following an iterative geometric reduction process to fashion a family of interconnecting components.

These tracts were digitized, with the infrastructurally defined connection points allowing for a three-dimensional collage to be constructed - a 'cut-up technique' for the city. This creation process refers to the mechanism through which individual experience and memory shape the act of urban navigation and the parallel construction of the mind's narrative of the city. Each participant's contribution to the agglomerated assembly draws on their individual response to the act of building and to their knowledge of the urban tracts to which the elements refer. Multiple individual inputs coalesce to form an iteration of the whole specific to the actors involved in its construction. This collision of individual approaches creates a novel psychic object, as well a unique physical installation. This iterative 'cut-up' sculpture allows for the construction of limitless configurations of the urban grid, mirroring the infinite psychic constructions of the city mediated by the unique sensory experiences of each urban individual.

Community build in New York City.

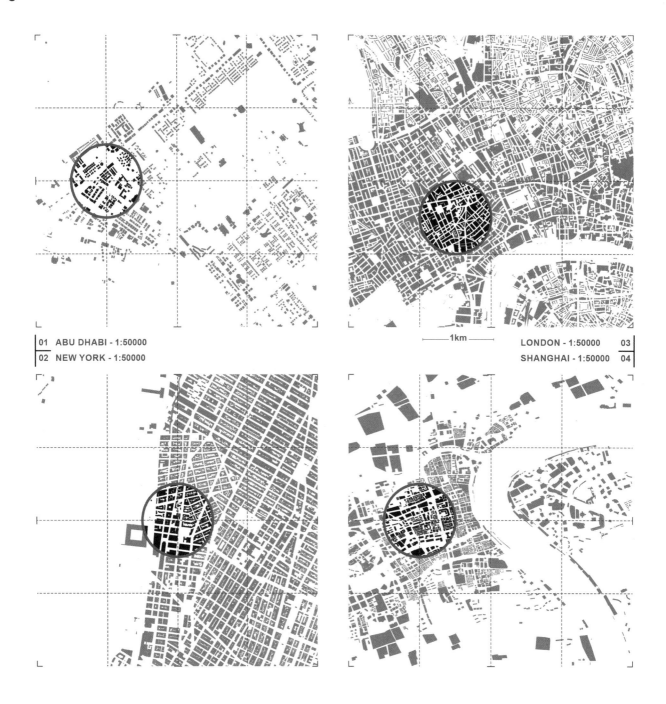

| 01 | ABU DHABI - 1:50000 |
| 02 | NEW YORK - 1:50000 |

1km

| LONDON - 1:50000 | 03 |
| SHANGHAI - 1:50000 | 04 |

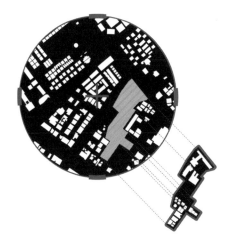

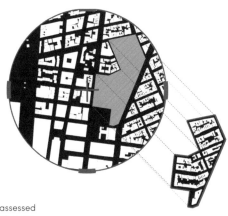

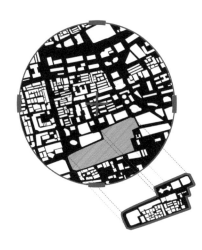

Each grid extract is assessed as form and void, before it is rationalized as a reproducible construction element.

Design with Life

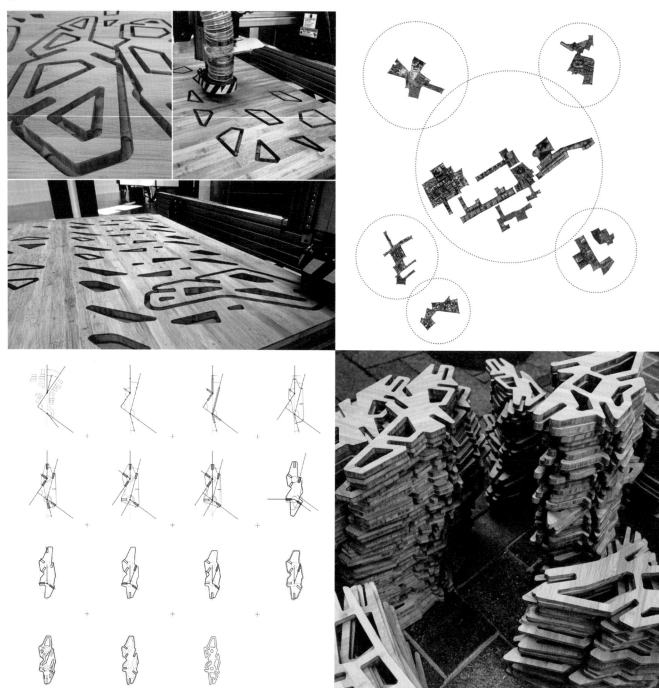

Previous page:
Above, left: Plyboo panels were
CNC milled, with map geometries
developed allowing for optimal
material efficiency.
Below, left: Tesselating component
geometry: Iterative derivation
process.
Above, right: Urban tracts
reassembled into a composite
grid plan.
Below, right: Components stack
by type.

Below:
Components stack by type.

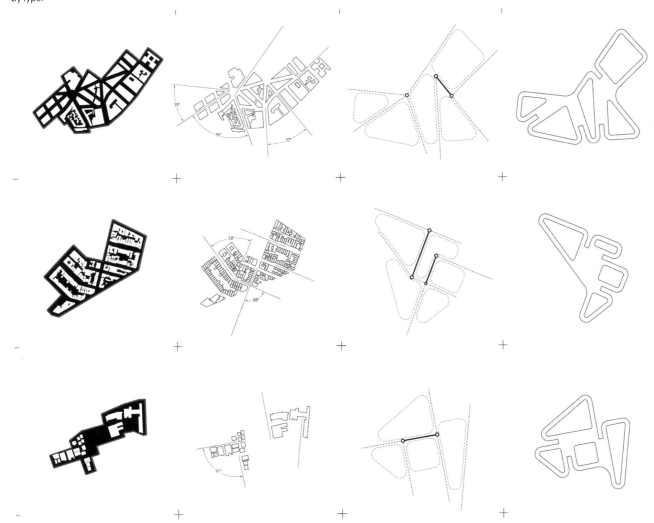

Design with Life

Studio built test.

Design with Life

Previous page: Urban Tangle live
community build: The degree of
organization is dependent upon
the experience and disposition of
the builders.

Above: Components assembled
on-site by the public.

Design with Life

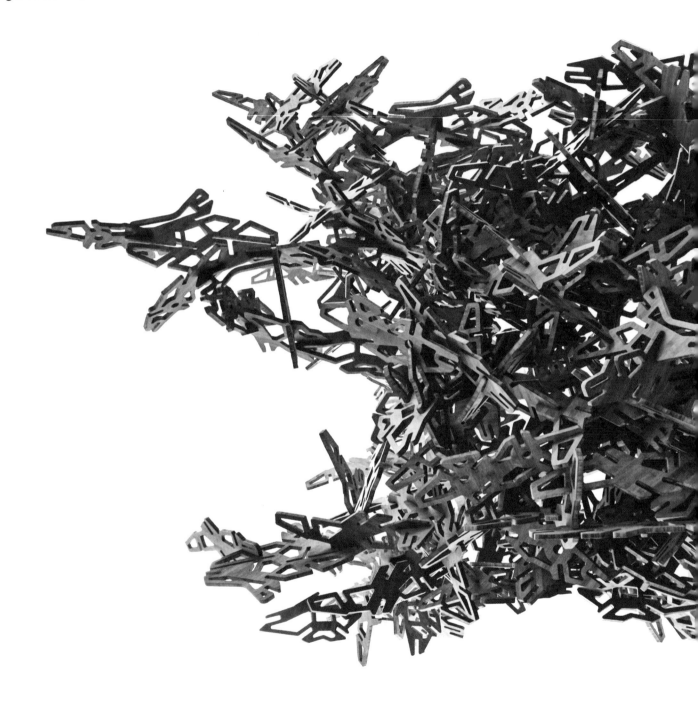

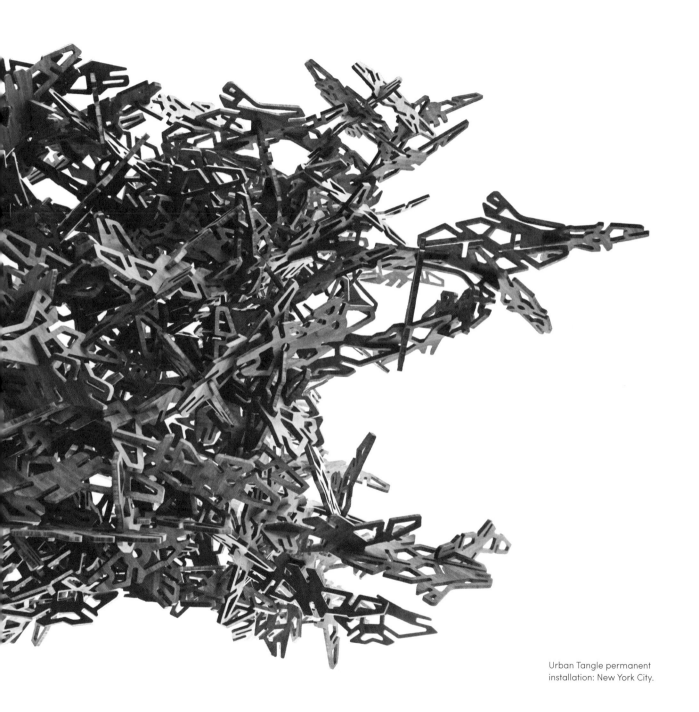

Urban Tangle permanent
installation: New York City.

Design with Life

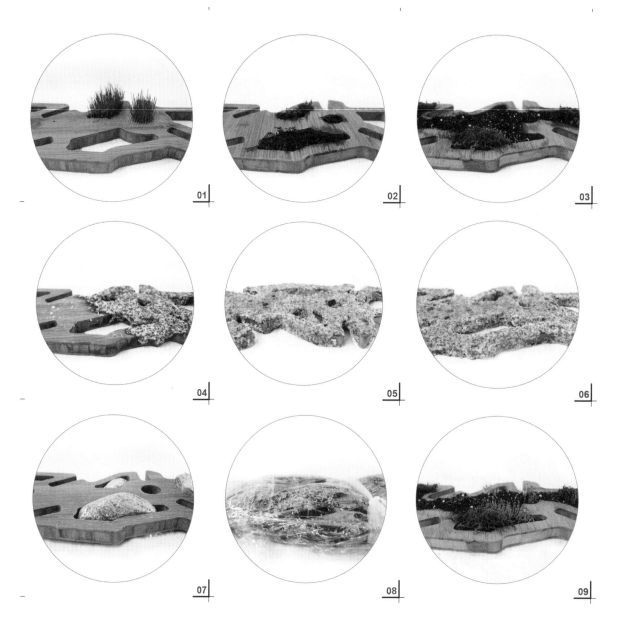

01
02
03
04
05
06
07
08
09

Experimental, biological integration.
01. Grass
02. Moss

03. Chia seeds with moss
04-06. Chia seeds with tissue paper.

Following page: Biodegradable public network map in the garden.

Design with Life

POWER OF
THE CITY

NO TAX
FOR
KILLING

IT'S TIME TO CHANGE
OUR NATIONAL PRIORITIES
BILLIONS FOR THE CITIES
AND ALL THEIR PEOPLE

OCCUPY WALL ST

PUBLIC

ACTION

Power of the City

As a part of the Occupy Wall Street Movement, this project demonstrates how 99% of the population is robbed of their due share of wealth by millionaires and billionaires, i.e. by the 1%. We stacked the residents of Manhattan on the top of the island. Each figure represent an income of $50,000 per year. The sharp peak clearly demonstrates the injustice of 1% of the Wall Street earners bringing home the whole island's wealth. An equal distribution will result into an alternative living income for every resident of the city. Power of the City embodies the frustration of many residents at the current economic climate. Corporations engaged in reckless and even unethical practices over the last decades, led to an unsustainable financial system that eventually fell apart. Favelas start to grow in Downtown NYC. Overtime, informal dwellings and vegetation take over growing into Green Wall Street and Archipelago of new islands.

Income mapped to Manhattan neighborhoods.

Design with Life

Projects | Public + Action | Power of the City

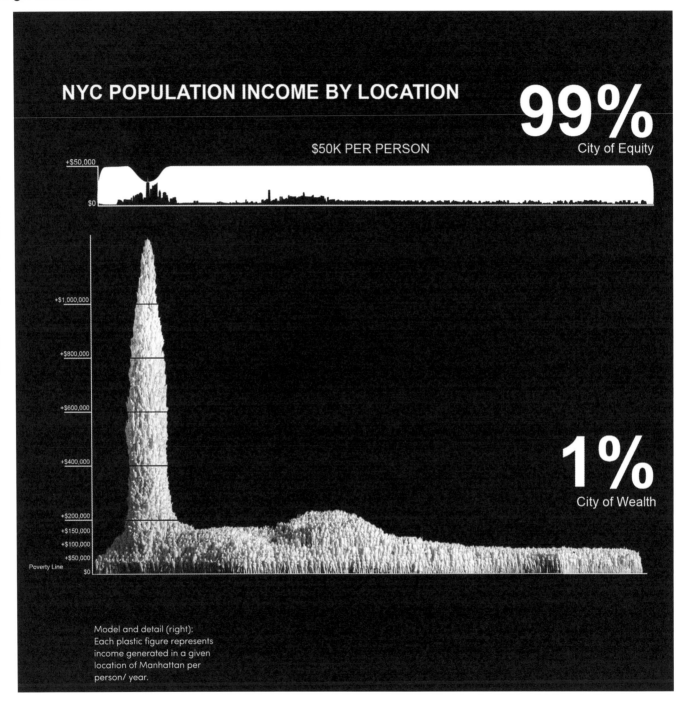

NYC POPULATION INCOME BY LOCATION

99%
City of Equity

$50K PER PERSON

+$50,000

$0

+$1,000,000

+$800,000

+$600,000

+$400,000

+$200,000

1%
City of Wealth

+$150,000
+$100,000
+$50,000
Poverty Line
$0

Model and detail (right):
Each plastic figure represents
income generated in a given
location of Manhattan per
person/ year.

Design with Life

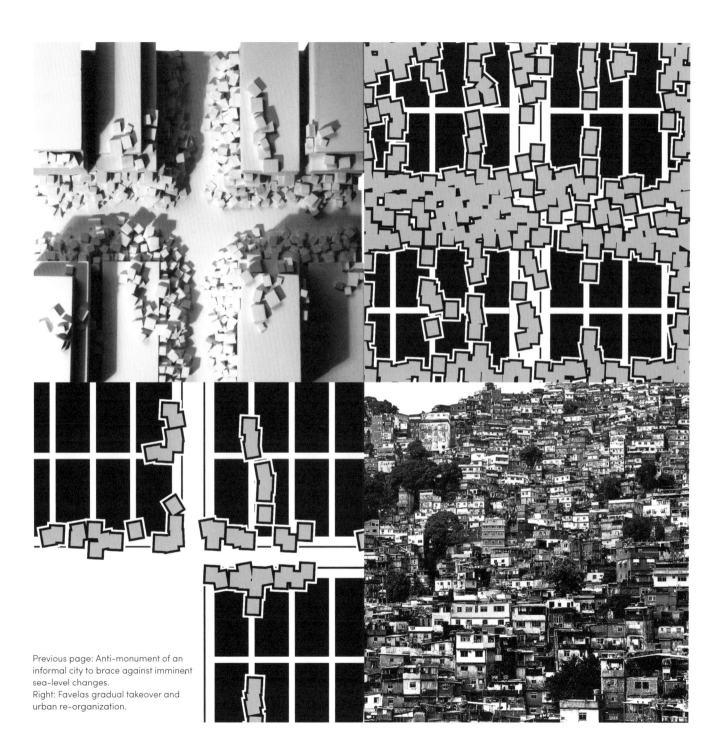

Previous page: Anti-monument of an informal city to brace against imminent sea-level changes.
Right: Favelas gradual takeover and urban re-organization.

Design with Life

GOVERNORS'

HOOK

WATER

RESOURCE

Governors' Hook

Governor's Hook focuses on the issue of stormwater retention in the Brooklyn Waterfront and feeds into a large research area of sea level affecting coastal areas and cities. We propose an investigation of adaptive reuse of former military vessels to create a riparian buffer zone that deals with issues of surges and flood management in New York Harbor. The goal is to combine the natural sedimentation techniques with the recycling of retired U.S. Naval ships from the National Defense Reserve Fleet [NDRF] and United States Navy reserve fleets to restore the natural water edge, to reinstate a diversified profile and to slow down the watercourse. This comprehensive model of the reimagined waterfront is based on one simple premise- instead of keeping the water out, the infrastructure is designed to let the water in. NY does not need to defend against water but instead share its presence with the existing estuary.

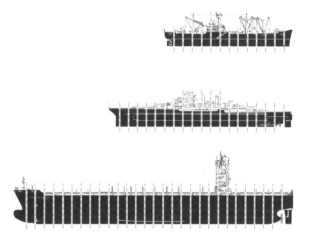

Below: View of integrated urban region: Governors' Island combined with Red Hook, Brooklyn.

Right: Ship breaking sections for reuse.

Design with Life

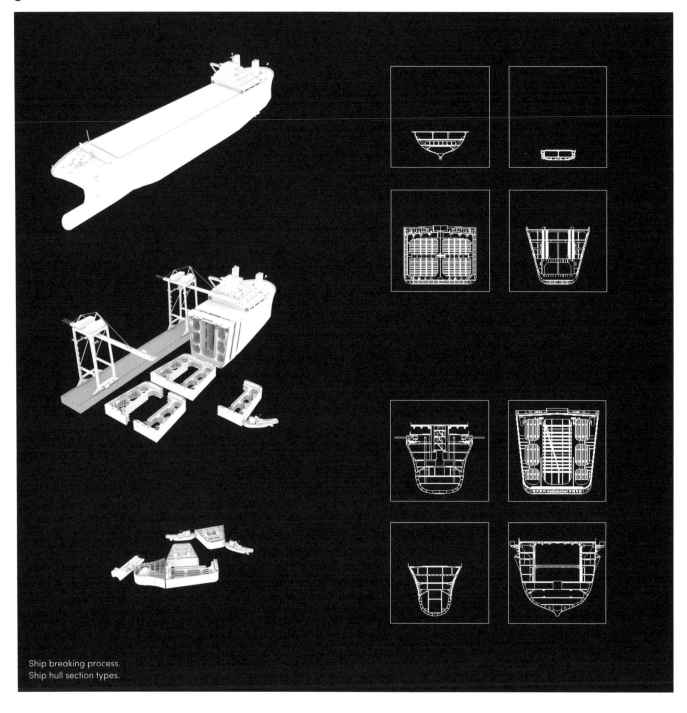

Ship breaking process.
Ship hull section types.

214

Sunken vessel acts
as artificial reef and
current control.

Design with Life

Master plan of Governors' Hook.

Following page:
Above: Office tower with active porous façade.
Below: Governors' Hook urban perspective.

Design with Life

Multi-scalar plan studies:
01. Borough: 434 hull sections
02. Neighborhood: 76 hull sections
03. Block: 34 hull sections

Following page:
Ship hull estuary: Water filtration and existing hard scape.

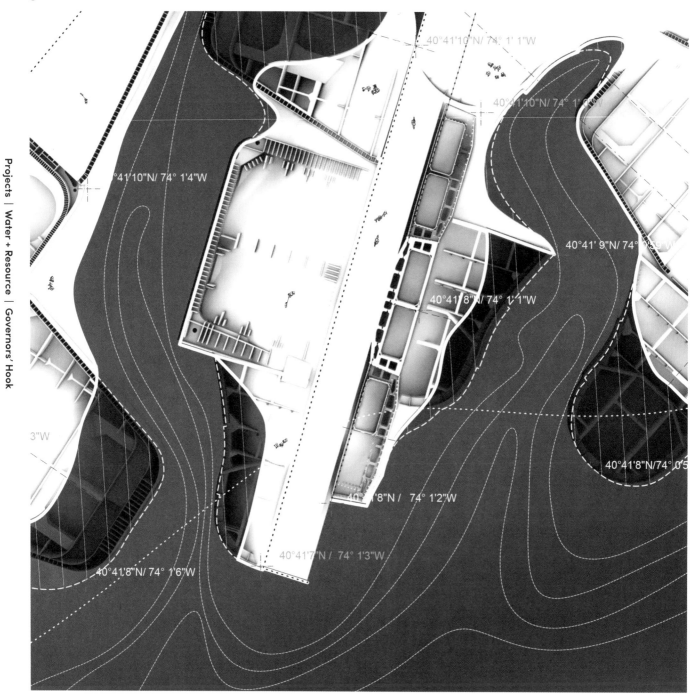

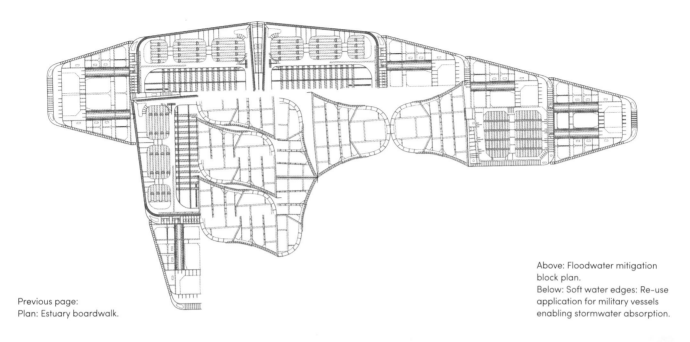

Previous page:
Plan: Estuary boardwalk.

Above: Floodwater mitigation
block plan.
Below: Soft water edges: Re-use
application for military vessels
enabling stormwater absorption.

GOVERNORS
ISLAND

RED HOOK

Previous page: Phytoremediation
piers, succession based plantings
and flood control barriers.

Right: Plan of sunken boat hull
sections along edges of Brooklyn.

Design with Life

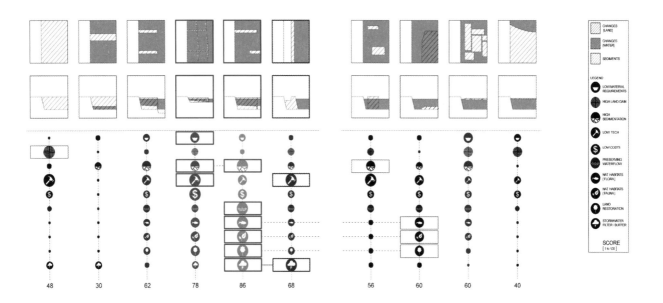

48   30   62   78   86   68   56   60   60   40

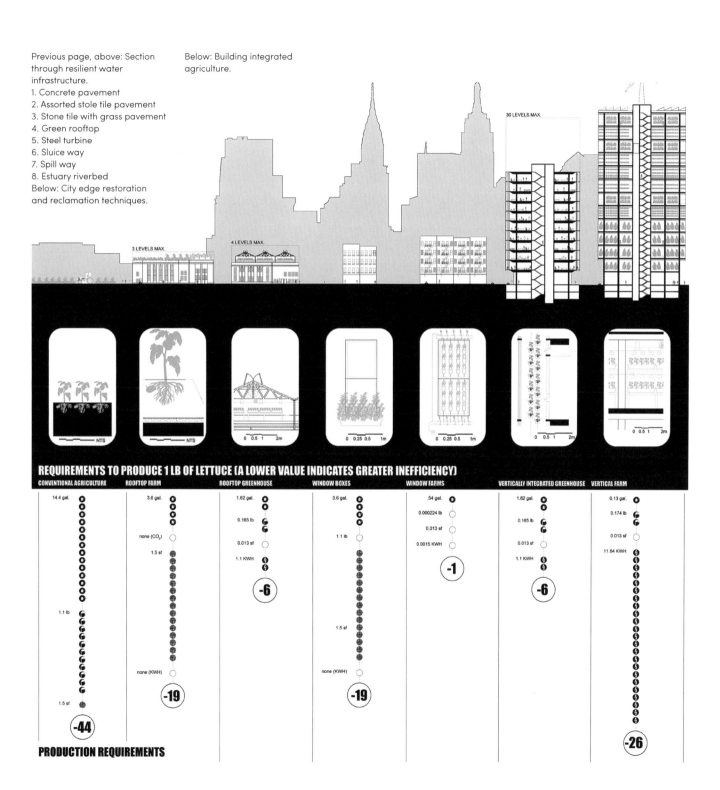

Previous page, above: Section through resilient water infrastructure.
1. Concrete pavement
2. Assorted stole tile pavement
3. Stone tile with grass pavement
4. Green rooftop
5. Steel turbine
6. Sluice way
7. Spill way
8. Estuary riverbed
Below: City edge restoration and reclamation techniques.

Below: Building integrated agriculture.

30 LEVELS MAX.

3 LEVELS MAX.

4 LEVELS MAX.

REQUIREMENTS TO PRODUCE 1 LB OF LETTUCE (A LOWER VALUE INDICATES GREATER INEFFICIENCY)

CONVENTIONAL AGRICULTURE

14.4 gal.
1.1 lb
1.5 sf

-44

ROOFTOP FARM

3.6 gal.
none (CO₂)
1.5 sf
none (KWH)

-19

ROOFTOP GREENHOUSE

1.62 gal.
0.165 lb
0.013 sf
1.1 KWH

-6

WINDOW BOXES

3.6 gal.
1.1 lb
1.5 sf
none (KWH)

-19

WINDOW FARMS

.54 gal.
0.000224 lb
0.013 sf
0.0015 KWH

-1

VERTICALLY INTEGRATED GREENHOUSE

1.62 gal.
0.165 lb
0.013 sf
1.1 KWH

-6

VERTICAL FARM

0.13 gal.
0.174 lb
0.013 sf
11.64 KWH

-26

PRODUCTION REQUIREMENTS

Design with Life

Revised estuary and slow
sediment build-up by 2052.

Design with Life

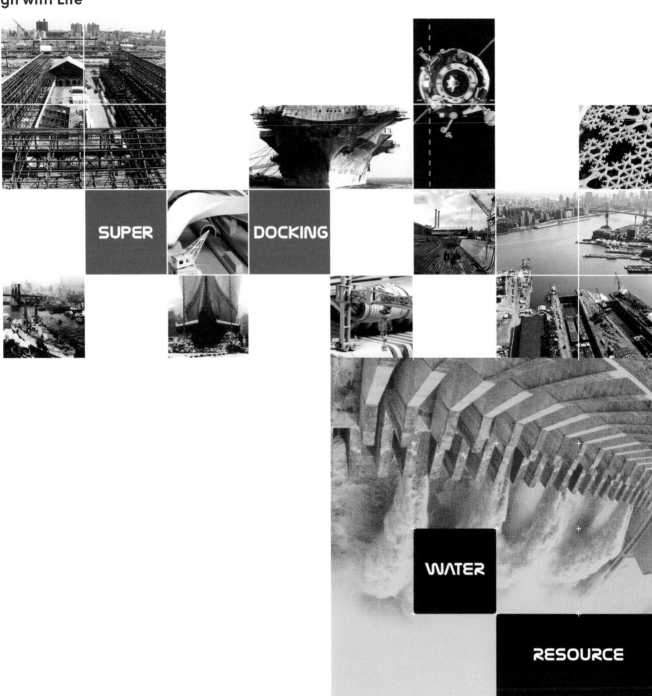

SUPER

DOCKING

WATER

RESOURCE

Super Docking Navy Yard

As a form of Urbaneering, this project continues to explore the possibilities of the architectural retrofit. On an urban industrial site in Brooklyn, New York, Super Docking imagines a self-sustained working waterfront as a center for clean industries that are incubators for new technologies. The designed landscape is adapted to local climate dynamics and is outfitted for a living infrastructure to seamlessly connect land and water. The project interfaces the historic dry-docks, which are retrofitted into five distinct research and production facilities; massive 3D digital prototyping/ scanning, replicable test beds for studies in limnology and restorative ecology, freight delivery of raw materials and finished goods, automated shipbuilding, and phytoremediation barges for CSO (Combined Sewer Overflow) issues.

The surface of the site mitigates architectural space and river flows. It supports programs to clean polluted water and sets the terrain for privileging pedestrian movement throughout the site. The project docks are highlighted by shapeable deployable structures and membranes. It is an industrial ecology landscape established to manage both manmade and natural systems, with reinforced land use needs.

The current urgency to aggregate areas for innovation with social and economic diversity is in demand. Our project encourages research, both as an industrial activity and as an ecological intervention. We wish to promote new products, jobs, green office spaces, and areas of knowledge exchange.

Repurposed dry dock detail:
High-volume 3D-print gantry
system.

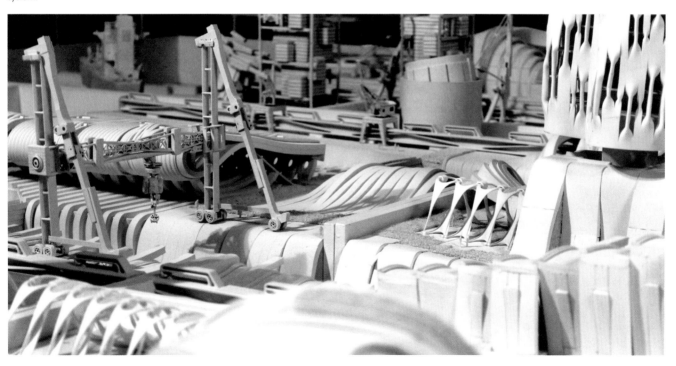

Design with Life

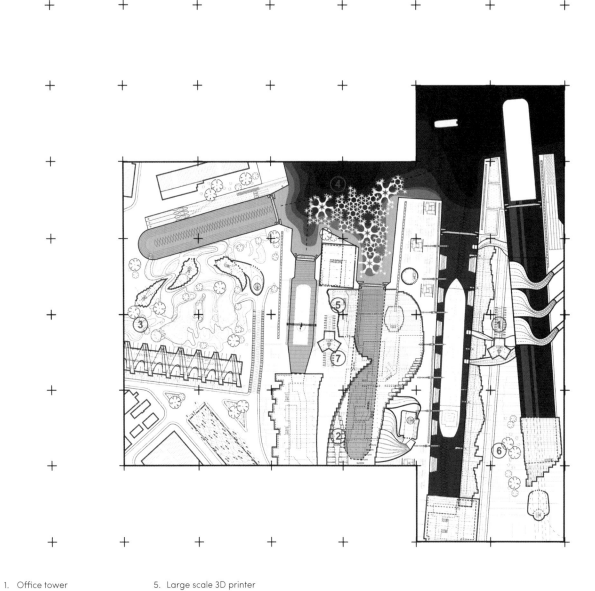

1. Office tower
2. Transformable surfaces for hydrological testing
3. Wetland test plots
4. Turbidity barriers
5. Large scale 3D printer
6. Hangar bay
7. Cleantech office tower
8. Refurbished dry dock
9. Existing buildings

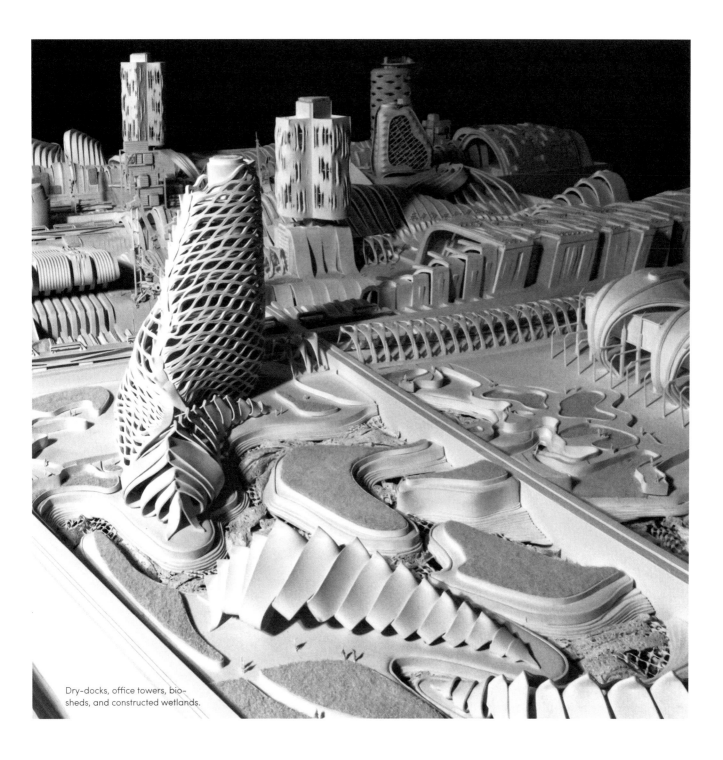

Dry-docks, office towers, bio-sheds, and constructed wetlands.

Design with Life

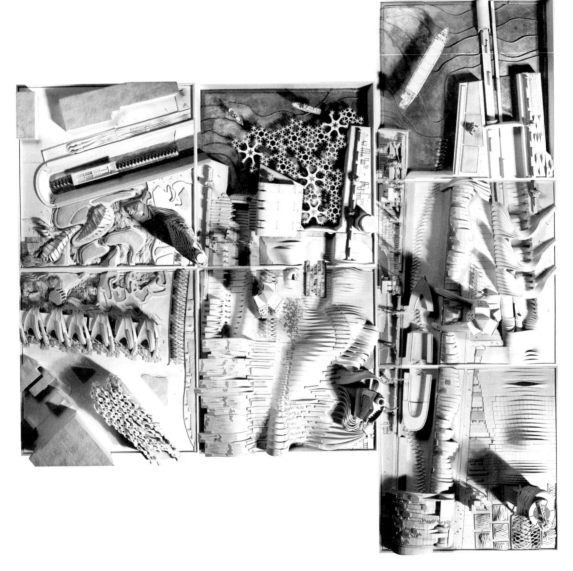

Masterplan and clean-tech micro-manufacturing program.

Following page: Self-sustaining functional dry docks for clean industry: incubators for new technology development.

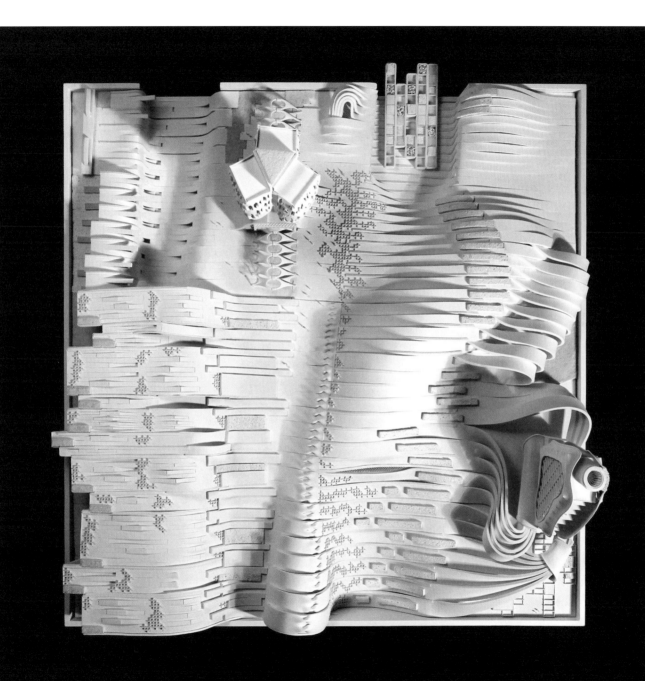

Design with Life

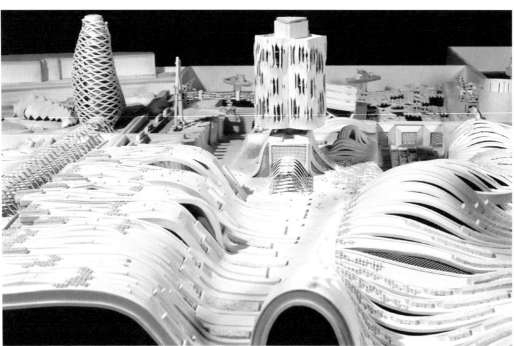

Left: Refurbished dry dock.
Below: Perspective of 3 landscape-integrated office towers.

Following page:
Aerial view of retrofitted docks for a maker village with spaces designed for large scale assembly and fabrication in future green industries.

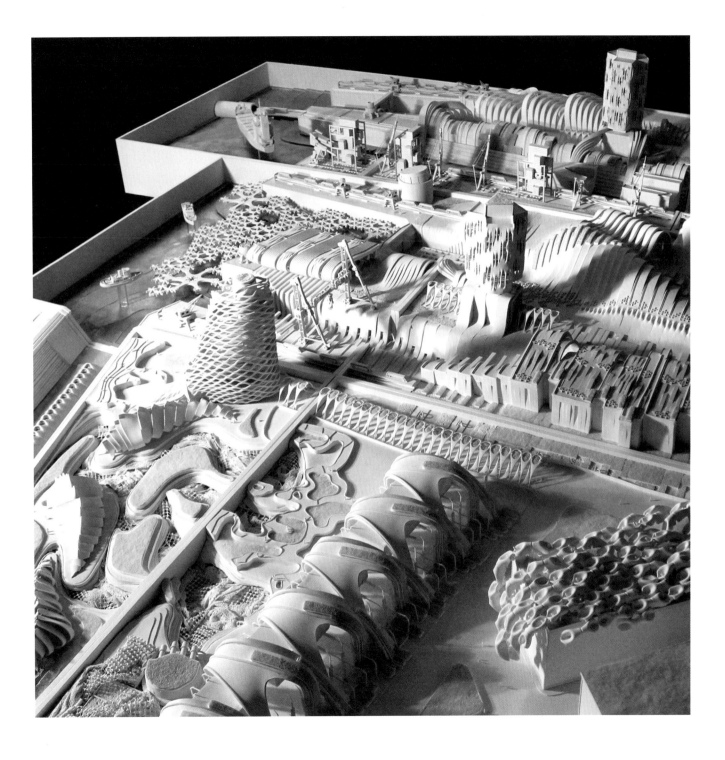

RAPID RE(F)USE

UPCYCLE

WASTE

Rapid Re(f)use

Imagine our colossal municipal landfills as sensible resource sheds to build our future urban and peri urban spaces. If so, what kind of effort is required to reuse their copious contents? Now that the bulk of humanity has chosen to settle in urbanized areas, waste management needs a radical revision. For hundreds of years we designed sites to generate waste. It is time we design waste to generate our cities.

America is the leading creator of waste on the earth, making approximately 30% of the world's trash and tossing out 0.8 tons per U.S. citizen per year. Ungracefully, our American value system is somewhat distressed. It seems value has devolved into feats of rampant affluenza and mega products scaled for super-sized franchise brands, big box retail, XXXL jumbo paraphernalia, etc., encapsulating a joint race for ubiquity and instantaneity in the U.S. mindset. Where does it all end up? Gertrude Stein cleverly pointed out; "away has gone away". The first step we must take is reduction; meaning a massive discontinuation of objects designed for obsolescence. Then we need a radical reuse plan. Our waste crisis is immense, what is our call to action?

New York City is disposing of 38,000 tons of waste per day. Most of this discarded material ended up in Fresh Kills landfill before it closed. The Rapid Re(f)use project supposes an extended New York reconstituted from its own landfill material. Our concept remakes the city by utilizing the trash at Fresh Kills. With our method, we can remake seven entirely new Manhattan islands at full scale. Automated robot 3D printers are modified to process trash and complete this task within decades. These robots are based on existing techniques commonly found in industrial waste compaction devices. Instead of machines that crush objects into cubes, these devices have jaws that make simple shape grammars for assembly. Different materials serve specified purposes; plastic for fenestration, organic compounds for temporary scaffolds, metals for primary structures, etc. Eventually, the future city makes no distinction between waste and supply.

New York has, over the last few centuries, become one of the world's most densely packed cities. But what if you could redraw the city's map – and build it from scratch? If we were designing New York today, how different would it look? The New York City would balance the relationship between the information networks that the metropolis depends on and Earth's finite resources. All vital components of life would be monitored and attuned to the needs of every organism, not just humans. Supplies of food and water, our energy and waste and even our air would be sensibly scrutinized. Thanks to masses of miniaturized low-cost electronic components deployed across the city, communication becomes far easier. New York will grow and adapt to millions of new minds entering it every day. The city would make sure every need is provided for within its borders. How we provide nutrients, transports, and shelter would be updated. Dilapidated buildings would be replaced with vertical agriculture and new kinds of housing would join cleaner, greener ways to get around the city. What were once streets become snaking arteries of livable spaces, embedded with renewable energy sources, low-tech, green vehicles for mobility and productive nutrient zones.

Design with Life

Above: One Hour Tower: 24 hours,
36,200 tons of compacted waste.
Right: Landfill fire.

Design with Life

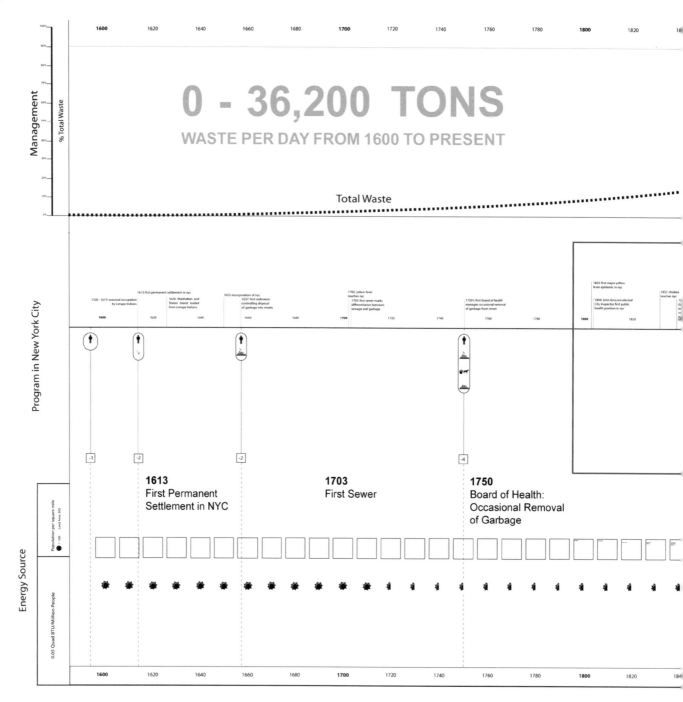

0 - 36,200 TONS

WASTE PER DAY FROM 1600 TO PRESENT

Total Waste

1613
First Permanent
Settlement in NYC

1703
First Sewer

1750
Board of Health:
Occasional Removal
of Garbage

Projects | Waste + Upcycle | Rapid Re(f)use

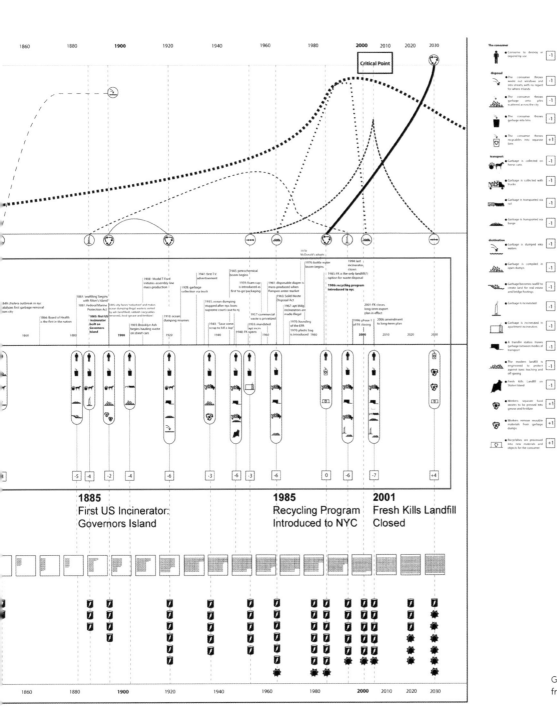

1885
First US Incinerator:
Governors Island

1985
Recycling Program
Introduced to NYC

2001
Fresh Kills Landfill
Closed

Garbage in New York City
from 1600 to 2030.

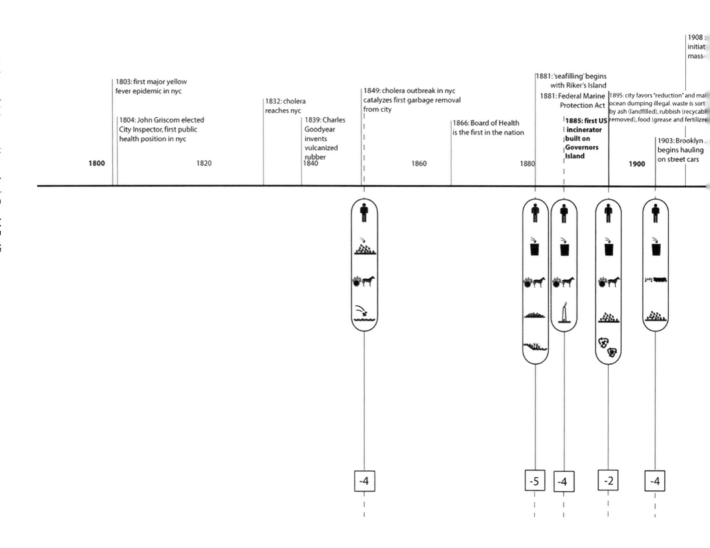

1803: first major yellow fever epidemic in nyc

1804: John Griscom elected City Inspector, first public health position in nyc

1832: cholera reaches nyc

1839: Charles Goodyear invents vulcanized rubber

1849: cholera outbreak in nyc catalyzes first garbage removal from city

1866: Board of Health is the first in the nation

1881: 'seafilling' begins with Riker's Island

1881: Federal Marine Protection Act

1885: first US incinerator built on Governors Island

1895: city favors "reduction" and mak ocean dumping illegal. waste is sort by ash (landfilled), rubbish (recyclabl removed), food (grease and fertilize

1903: Brooklyn begins hauling on street cars

1908 initiat mass

1800   1820   1840   1860   1880   **1900**

-4   -5   -4   -2   -4

NYC waste timeline.

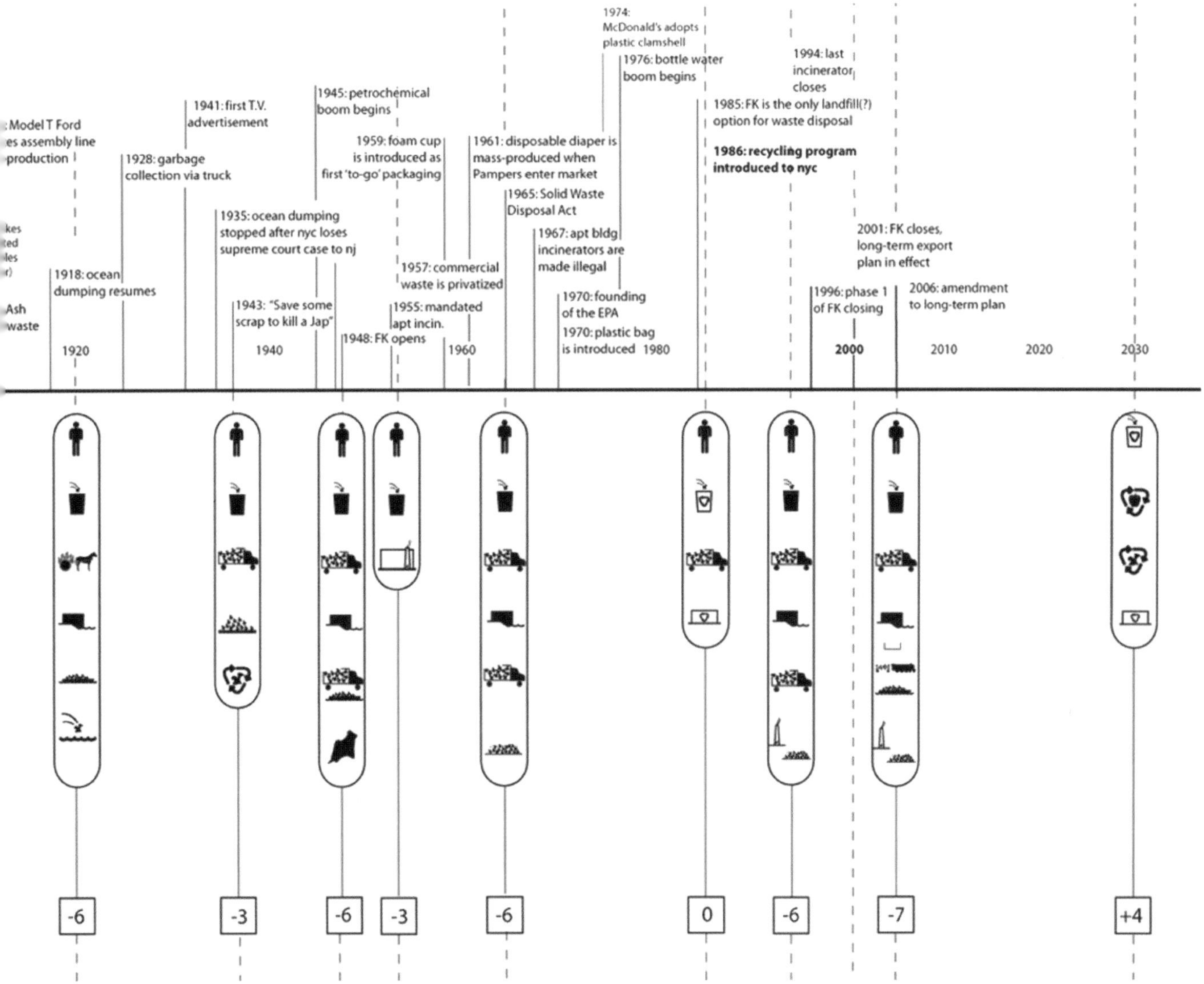

Timeline annotations (left to right):

: Model T Ford
es assembly line
production

kes
ted
les
r)

Ash
waste

1918: ocean
dumping resumes

1920

1928: garbage
collection via truck

1935: ocean dumping
stopped after nyc loses
supreme court case to nj

1943: "Save some
scrap to kill a Jap"

1940

1941: first T.V.
advertisement

1945: petrochemical
boom begins

1959: foam cup
is introduced as
first 'to-go' packaging

1955: mandated
apt incin.

1948: FK opens

1957: commercial
waste is privatized

1960

1961: disposable diaper is
mass-produced when
Pampers enter market

1965: Solid Waste
Disposal Act

1967: apt bldg
incinerators are
made illegal

1970: founding
of the EPA

1970: plastic bag
is introduced   1980

1974:
McDonald's adopts
plastic clamshell

1976: bottle water
boom begins

1985: FK is the only landfill(?)
option for waste disposal

1986: recycling program
introduced to nyc

1994: last
incinerator
closes

1996: phase 1
of FK closing

2000

2001: FK closes,
long-term export
plan in effect

2006: amendment
to long-term plan

2010   2020   2030

Scores (left to right): -6   -3   -6   -3   -6   0   -6   -7   +4

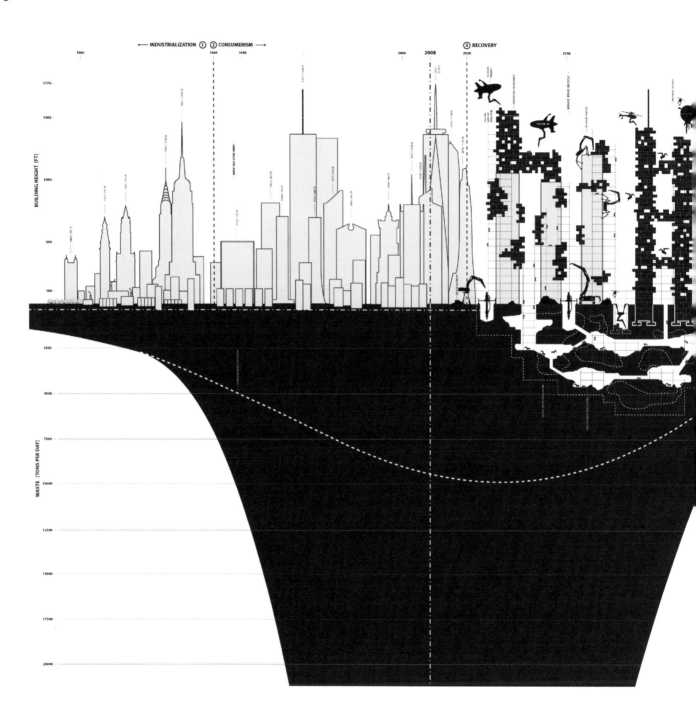

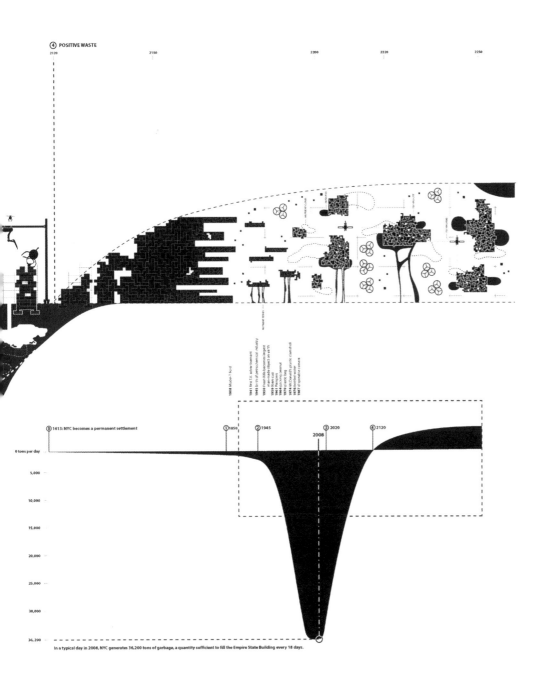

④ POSITIVE WASTE

| 2120 | 2150 | 2200 | 2220 | 2250 |

1908 Model T Ford

1941 first T.V. active transient
1945 birth of petrochemical industry
1950 Fresh Kills becomes largest man-made object on earth
1959 foam cup
1961 Pampers
1966 polymeric aerosol
1974 Mr. Owen's plastic clamshell
1976 bottled water
1987 disposable contacts

⑩ 1613: NYC becomes a permanent settlement

① 1850 ② 1945 ③ 2020 ④ 2120

2008

0 tons per day

5,000

10,000

15,000

20,000

25,000

30,000

36,200

In a typical day in 2008, NYC generates 36,200 tons of garbage, a quantity sufficient to fill the Empire State Building every 18 days.

Design with Life

Above:
01. Composite compacted waste brick bound using mycelial growth.
02. Individual hyphae–mycelium root structure.
03. Aluminum waste.

Right: Deployable smart brick transport.

Hunter–seeker landfill
mining bot.

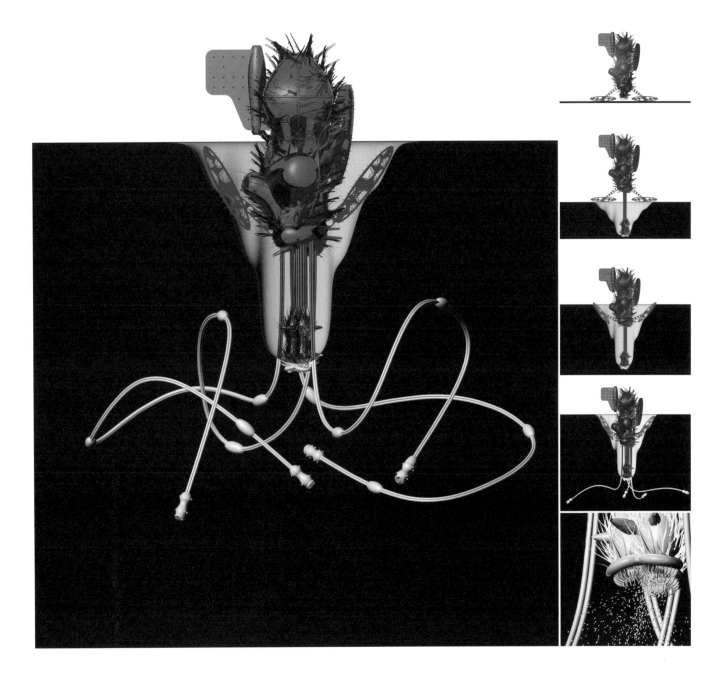

Design with Life

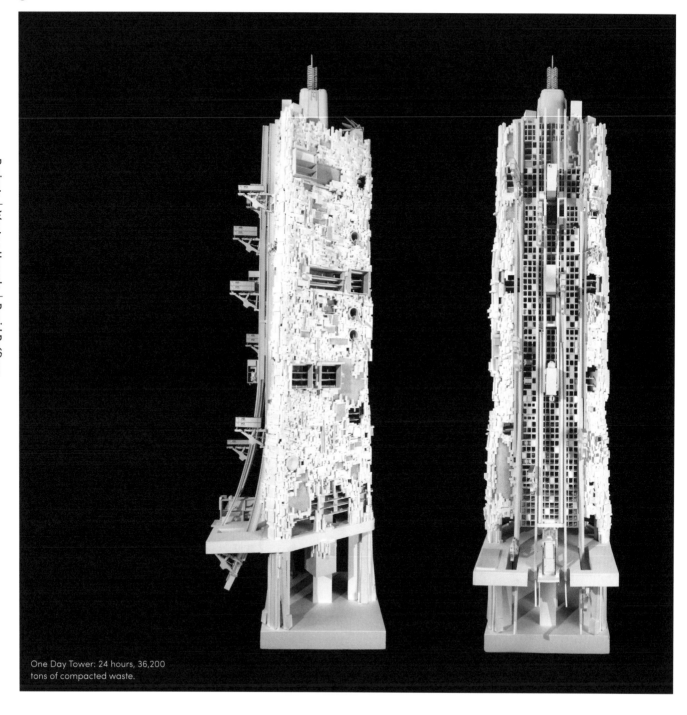

One Day Tower: 24 hours, 36,200
tons of compacted waste.

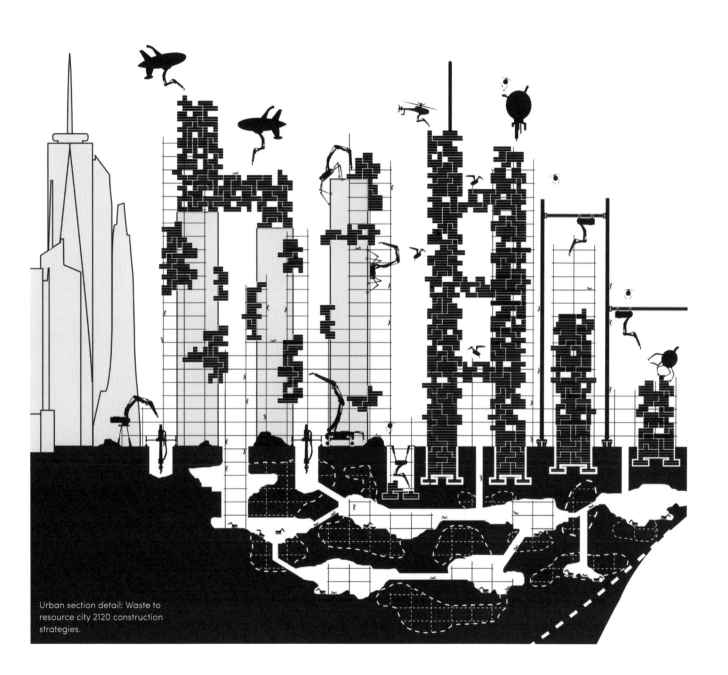

Urban section detail: Waste to resource city 2120 construction strategies.

Design with Life

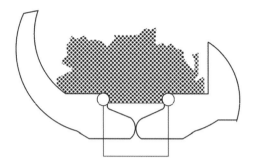

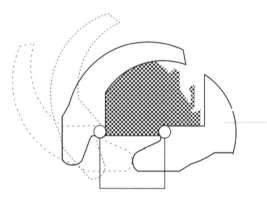

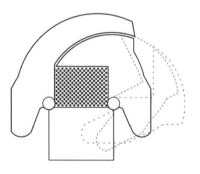

Diagrams of jaws shaping waste.
Puzzle-fit compacted refuse
facade.
Right: Continuous environments:
Trash as nutrient.

Following page: One Day Tower:
24 hours, 36,200 tons of compacted waste.

+ 3D WASTE PRINTERS

SPID

HANG

BLIM

PELI

HELO

LOON

+ DIGGERS

DIGS

DRIL

+ SUPPORTS

PUZZ

WIND

FLY HAB CITY

Design with Life

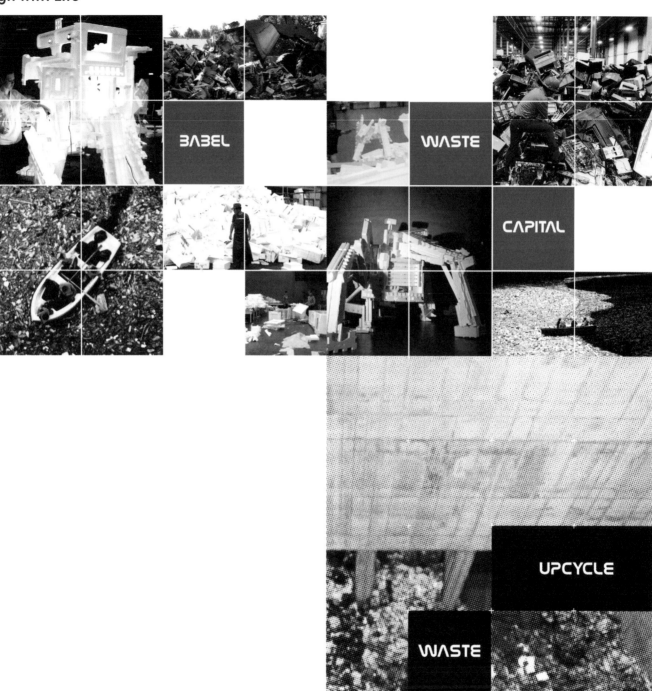

Babel Waste Capital

A testament to global sameness and affluenza induced conduct, the Babel Waste Capital up-cycles what the city throws away. Styrofoam packaging is collected from the neighborhood and erected as a tower in a few short hours. This sculpture represents an extension of a city reconstituted from its own refuse materials. The star form represents a single 30 second flash of Styrofoam e-waste produced in New York City from packaging materials for new refrigerators, microwave ovens, speakers, vacuum cleaners, and other electrical appliances. Our city disposes of heavy volumes of consumer e-waste daily. This project rethinks andupcycles what the people throw away. Styrofoam packaging was collected from local neighborhoods and transformed into a didactic installation. The aim is to confront the public with the trash our city produces in just moments. In the future, we shall make no distinction between waste and supply. Here waste is up-cycled into usable systems for building or sculptural folly. Exhibited at the Metropolitan Museum of Art with DJ Spooky and Terreform ONE as: "Of Water and Ice - A Concert of Compositions Based on Water and Arctic Rhythms" in Grace Rainey Rogers Auditorium. Also shown at New Museum, Ideas City street fair: An installation made from discarded Styrofoam rises in front of Raumlabor's Spacebuster, a mobile inflatable pavilion commissioned by the Storefront for Art and Architecture.

Follies made from discarded styrofoam trash to build public awareness.

Design with Life

The form represents a single 30 second flash of styrofoam e-waste produced in New York City from packaging materials.
Following page: Assembly and subsequent disassembly.

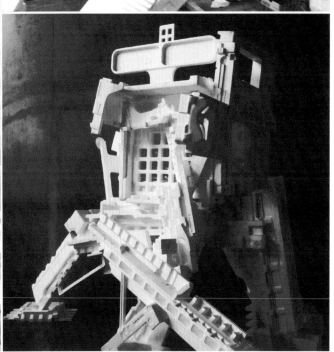

Design with Life

Previous page: Models in context and under construction.

Below: Babel: Recycled styrofoam sculpture.

Design with Life

Exhibited at the Metropolitan Museum of Art with DJ Spooky and Terreform ONE as: "Of Water and Ice

A concert of compositions based on water and arctic rhythms" in Grace Rainey Rogers auditorium.

New Museum, Ideas City
street fair.

Design with Life

HOMEWAY

RESILIENCE

HOUSING

Homeway

How can our cities extend into the suburbs sustainability?
We propose to put our future American dwellings on wheels.
These retrofitted houses will flock towards downtown city
cores and back. We intended to reinforce our existing
highways between cities with an intelligent renewable
infrastructure. Therefore, our homes will be enabled to flow
continuously from urban core to core. Our proposal envisions
an immense and vital solution to a fundamental problem:
American suburbs fail to work efficiently. In the next 25 years
we will build 56 million new homes that will consume 18.8
million acres of virgin land and emit 7.3 billion tons of CO_2
per year. These frameworks of development need to be
rethought to meet our ecological carrying capacities. Why
should we put further energy into past inferior patterns?
America needs to deliver dwellings closer to our existing
main infrastructural arteries. We cannot continue to
overextend our thinly disturbed resource lines.

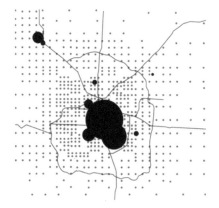

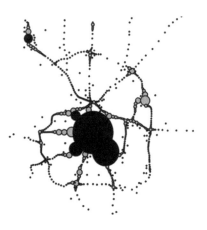

Above: Nodal urban expansion
concept.
Left: Multigen freedom: Multi-
generational housing for America.

Design with Life

01. Dwelling units
02. Family room + driver's cabin
03. Drivetrain mechanisms

Following page: Smart infrastructure corridors.

Design with Life

Infrastructure ecology.

Following page: Homeway
sectional model: Inhabited urban
superhighway.

Design with Life

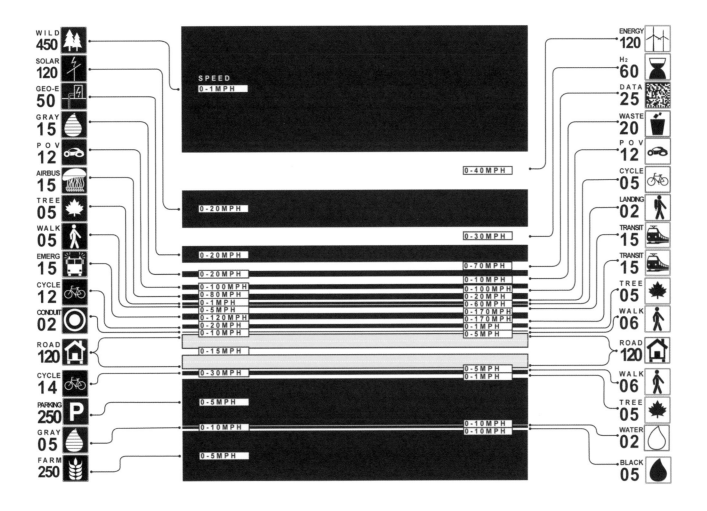

WILD 450	SPEED 0-1MPH	ENERGY 120
SOLAR 120		H₂ 60
GEO-E 50		DATA 25
GRAY 15		WASTE 20
POV 12	0-40MPH	POV 12
AIRBUS 15		CYCLE 05
TREE 05	0-20MPH	LANDING 02
WALK 05	0-30MPH	TRANSIT 15
EMERG 15	0-20MPH 0-70MPH	TRANSIT 15
CYCLE 12	0-20MPH 0-10MPH	TREE 05
CONDUIT 02	0-100MPH 0-100MPH 0-80MPH 0-20MPH 0-1MPH 0-60MPH 0-5MPH 0-170MPH 0-120MPH 0-170MPH 0-20MPH 0-1MPH 0-10MPH 0-5MPH	WALK 06
ROAD 120	0-15MPH	ROAD 120
CYCLE 14	0-30MPH 0-5MPH 0-1MPH	WALK 06
PARKING 250	0-5MPH	TREE 05
GRAY 05	0-10MPH 0-10MPH 0-10MPH	WATER 02
FARM 250	0-5MPH	BLACK 05

Previous page:
Left: Homes mobilized and traversing corridor.
Right: Mobile home highway swarm.

Above: Speed and energy source relationship diagram.

Mobile concept dwelling.

Design with Life

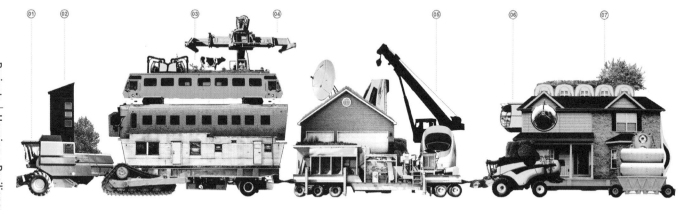

Previous page:
Above:
1. Drivetrain assembly
2. Modular hab block
3. Mobile micro-farm
4. Loading winch
5. Assembly unit
6. Driver's cabin
7. Rooftop agriculture

Below: Mechanized dwelling
transport typologies.

Top view along interstate
showing the regional condition
between cities.

Design with Life

FAB

TREE HAB

RESILIENCE

HOUSING

Fab Tree Hab

Our dwelling is composed with 100% living nutrients. Here traditional anthropocentric doctrines are overturned, and human life is subsumed within the terrestrial environs. Home, in this sense, becomes indistinct and fits itself symbiotically into the surrounding ecosystem. This home concept is intended to replace the outdated design solutions at Habitat for Humanity. We propose a method to grow homes from native trees. A living structure is grafted into shape with prefabricated Computer Numerical Controlled (CNC) reusable scaffolds. Therefore, we enable dwellings to be fully integrated into an ecological community.

A methodology new to buildings yet ancient to gardening is introduced in this design - pleaching. Pleaching is a method of weaving together tree branches to form living archways, lattices, or screens. The trunks of inosculate, or self-grafting, trees, such as Elm, Live Oak, and Dogwood, are the load-bearing structure, and the branches form a continuous lattice frame for the walls and roof. Weaved along the exterior is a dense protective layer of vines, interspersed with soil pockets and growing plants. Prefab scaffolds cut from 3D computer files control the plant growth in the early stages. On the interior, a clay and straw composite insulates and blocks moisture, and a final layer of smooth clay is applied like a plaster to dually provide comfort and aesthetics. Existing homes built with cob (clay & straw composite) demonstrate the feasibility, longevity, and livability of the material as a construction material. In essence, the tree trunks of this design provide the structure for an extruded ecosystem, whose growth is embraced over time.

The seasonal cycles help the tree structure provide for itself through composting of fallen leaves in autumn. Seedlings started in such a nutrient rich bed may provide the affordable building blocks for a new home typology, firmly rooted to place. Likewise, realization of living structures would introduce forest renewal to an urban setting. Building of these homes occurs throughout a longer time period, yet the benefits are enjoyed as long as the tree live, after which another wave of renewal begins.

In congruence with ecology as the guiding principle, this living home is designed to be nearly entirely edible so as to provide food to some organism at each stage of its life cycle. While inhabited, the homes gardens and exterior walls continually produce nutrients for people and animals. As a direct contributor to the ecosystem, it supports an economy comprised of truly breathing products not reconstituted or processed materials. Imagine a society based on slow farming trees for housing structure instead of the industrial manufacture of felled timber.

50% Living Home Design: An alternate proposal that uses mixed traditional prefab construction with living surfaces. A mosaic of materials, components, and spaces evolved for this dwelling, asserting that nature and people are mutually beneficial. The built-form sanctions life at all levels. Soil pockets serve gardens, native species, and the water cycle. Minute channels within the grid framework collect and direct rainfall. The mass-flows from life within the home feed ponds and nutrient producing compost. Participating in the logic of the home, the people determine their consumption patterns to ensure that outputs become inputs for other processes.

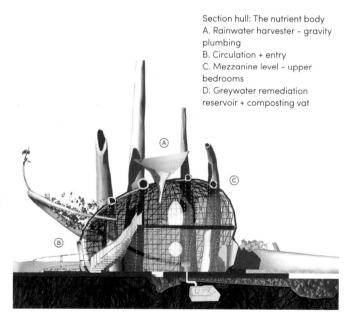

Section hull: The nutrient body
A. Rainwater harvester - gravity plumbing
B. Circulation + entry
C. Mezzanine level - upper bedrooms
D. Greywater remediation reservoir + composting vat

Model of completed habitat.

Above: Traditional methods of
arboreal manipulation.
Below: Local biota and flora
grafted living structure.

Design with Life

Left: Solar orientation plan. Arboreal growth sequence.

Following page:
Above: Fab tree hab town.
Below, left: Fab tree hab in suburban context.

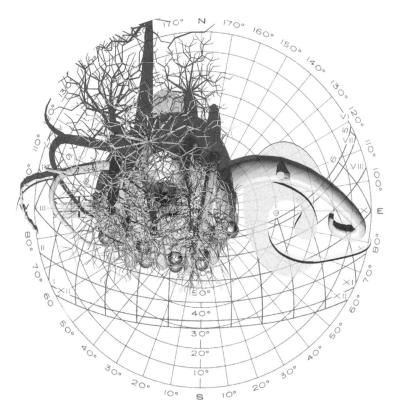

A. Rainwater harvester
B. Soy-based plastic operable
   windows
C. Buoyancy-driven ventilation
D. Cool air intake at floor level
E. Expandable vine surface
   lattice
F. Rammed earth pavers
   + tile flooring

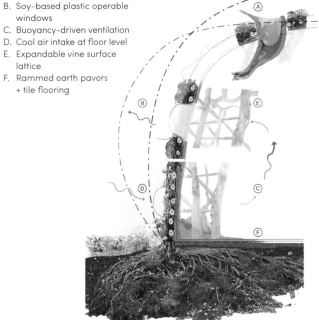

Design with Life

Below: MATscape grid encoded as an interpretation of the climatic inputs.

Following page: MATscape various tiled gradients in section and plan towards a functional green tech-fabric.

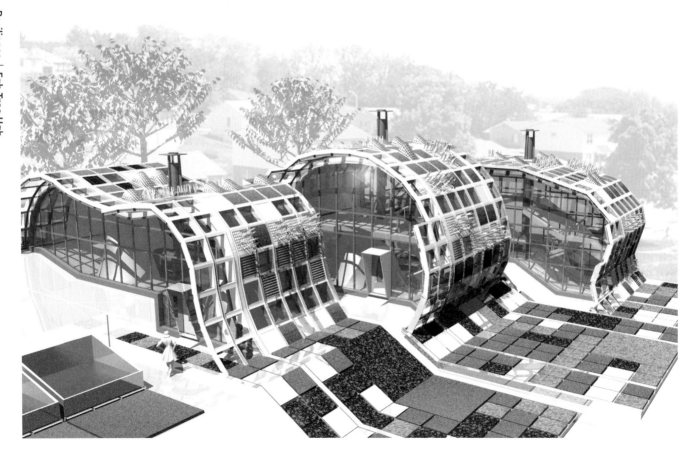

278

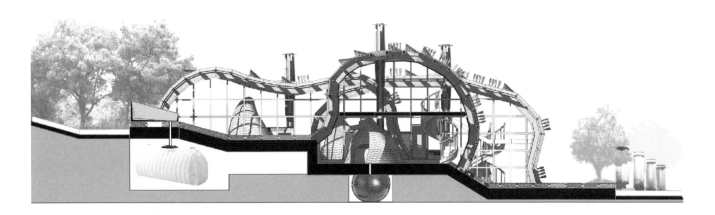

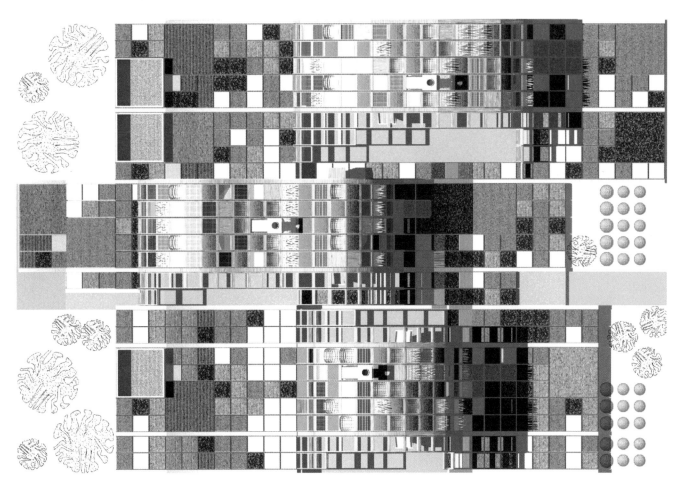

Design with Life

POST

CARBON

CITY-STATE

ENERGY

REGENERATIVE

Post Carbon City-State

Carbon output from cities is embedded in everyday life, directly affecting climate change and rising sea levels everywhere in the world. New York City's sea level rise is projected to reach a high estimate of 11 inches by the 2020s and 31 inches by the 2050s. Instead of only investing in mitigation efforts and building for resiliency, what if we let the East and Hudson River submerge parts of Manhattan and rebuild the new city in its surrounding rivers? We accept the inevitable and prepare for the aftermath by imagining the Post Carbon City-State, a future Manhattan cleansed through the physical and spatial inversion of the East and Hudson River. New bulk/use zoning envelopes maximize solar exposure, regulate population size, and optimize resources. Zoning occupies more area that extends into both the Hudson River and East River. It is a bold combination of plans for the East River redirection and drainage by T. Kennard Thomson (Really Greater New York) and the Hudson River infill strategy by William Zeckendorf (New York City's Dream Airport). Grafting Manhattan to physically join with New Jersey, Brooklyn, Queens and Governors Island is the definitive advancement structure for the whole city.

Ecological reclamation of the street and multiplane urban agriculture with mass transit below ground.

Design with Life

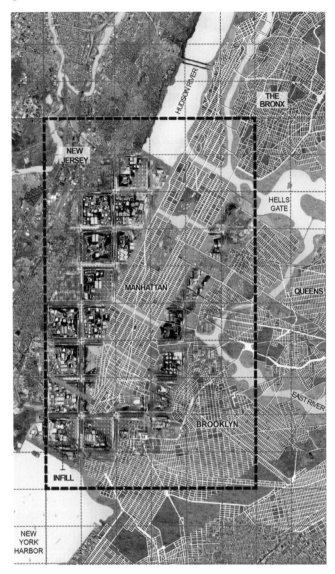

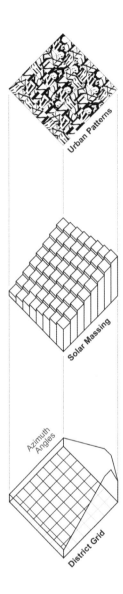

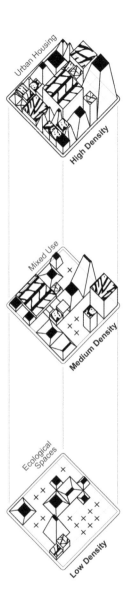

Above: Water re-routing grid.
Right: Block density typologies and solar massing strategy.

Following page:
Above: Solar massing and energy infrastructure.
Below, left: Corridors replanted as a fabric of productive green spaces.

Below, right: Vacuum-forming and rubber fabrication.

Previous page:
Left: Energy stations bordering Central Park.
Right: Grafting Manhattan to physically join with New Jersey.

Right: Hudson and East River allowed to infiltrate Manhattan.
Below: Up-cycled car tire pattern grid detail.

Design with Life

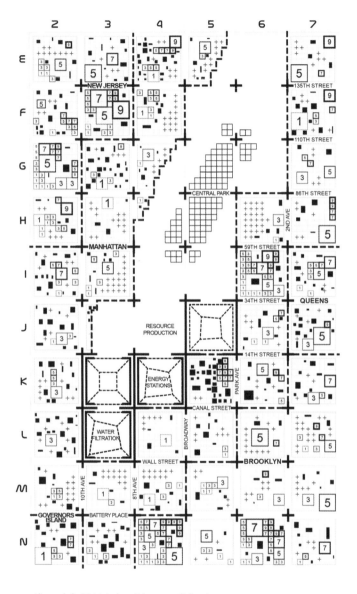

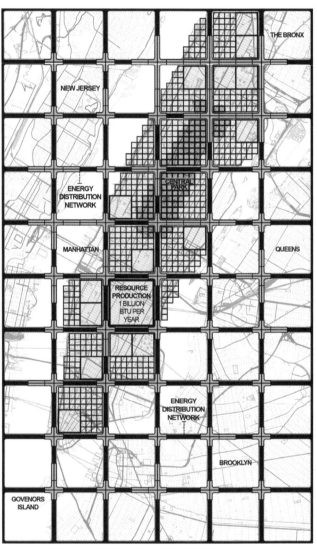

Above, left: District plan: Urban zoning density matrix.
Right: Resource production grid.

Following page:
Above: Post Carbon City-State model.
Below: Aerial view of Manhattan, Central Park.

Design with Life

New 42nd Street with trackless trains, living machines, riparian corridor, vertical wind turbines, facade biodiversity, urban agriculture, and new civic spaces.

PERISTALCITY

ENERGY

REGENERATIVE

Peristalcity

"Peristalcity" is a tall building made of a cluster of shifting pod spaces. The pod skins alter the volume locations within. This soft, pliable, sealed, and non-mechanical innovation encapsulates volumetric structures. Textile reinforced hoses execute a peristaltic action. Thus, the modules are enabled to create an articulated motion that is symbiotically connected to an urban armature. By employing a dynamic spatial application against the traditional organization of core and space, we dissolved the dichotomy between circulation and habitable environments. We have eliminated typological stacking where experiences are vapidly suggested to be diversified by simply designating floors to social practices. Instead, we propose a spatial layout that establishes heterogeneous movements, and not just assorted practices, as the criteria for a dynamic assemblage.

Below: Dwelling pod units + peristaltic pathway.

Right: Plan of muscle elevator skin.

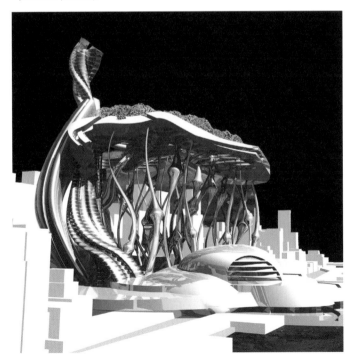

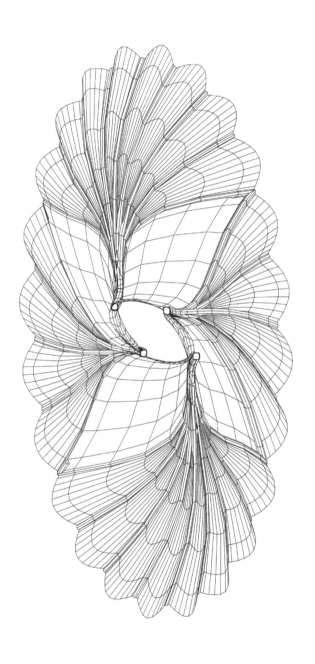

Design with Life

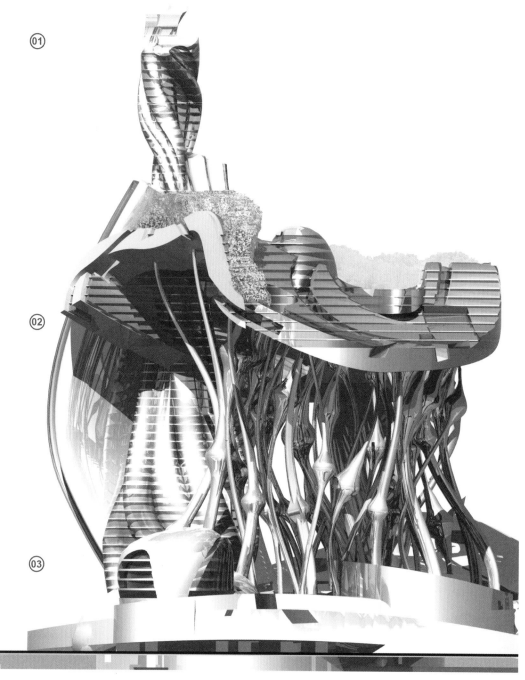

01

04

05

02

06

03

07

Armature building with
urban pod cluster.
01. Upper level tower
02. Dwelling pod units
    + peristaltic pathway
03. Public auditorium
04. Biosphere centre
05. Observation park
06. Sky bridge
07. Lower plinth

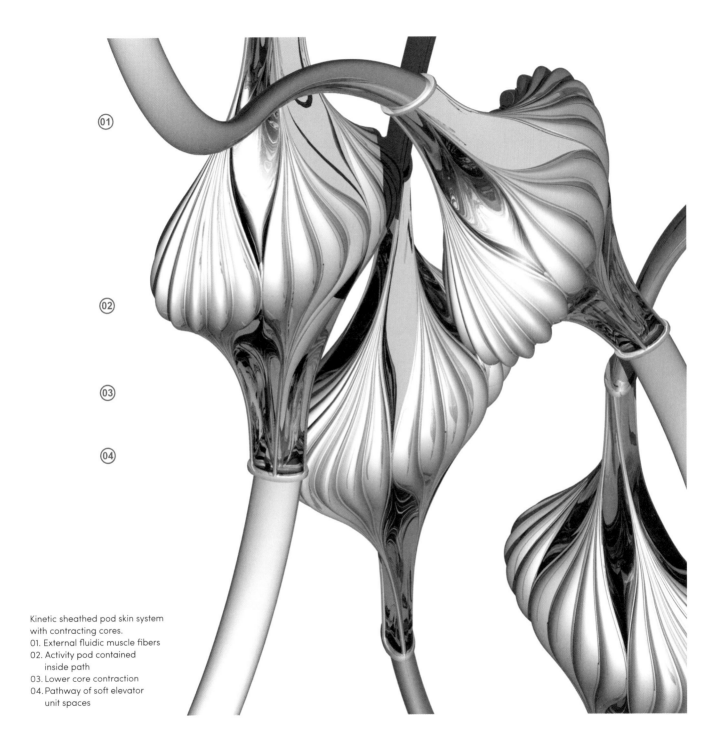

01

02

03

04

Kinetic sheathed pod skin system
with contracting cores.
01. External fluidic muscle fibers
02. Activity pod contained
      inside path
03. Lower core contraction
04. Pathway of soft elevator
      unit spaces

Design with Life

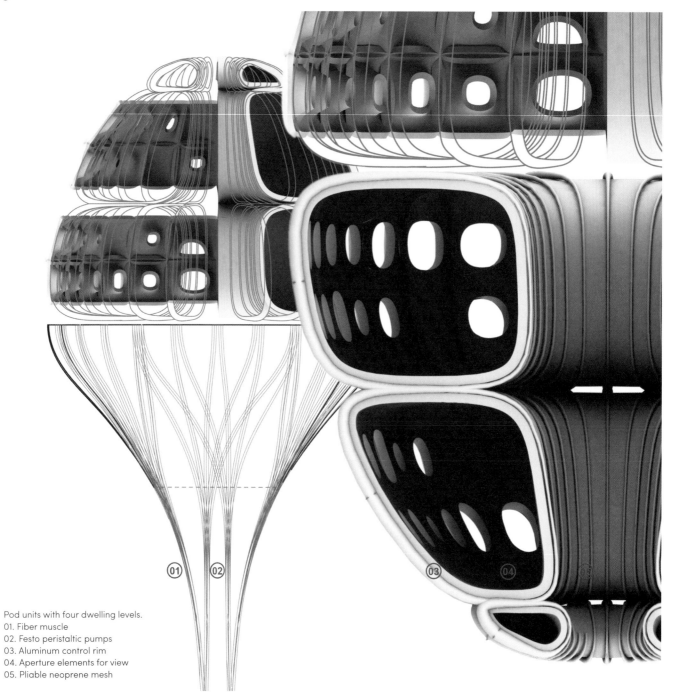

Pod units with four dwelling levels.
01. Fiber muscle
02. Festo peristaltic pumps
03. Aluminum control rim
04. Aperture elements for view
05. Pliable neoprene mesh

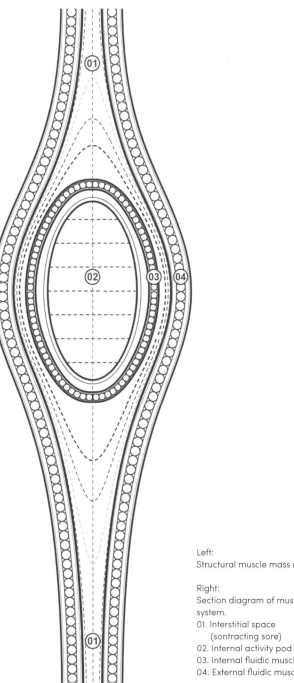

Left:
Structural muscle mass model.

Right:
Section diagram of muscle
system.
01. Interstitial space
    (sontracting sore)
02. Internal activity pod
03. Internal fluidic muscle fibers
04. External fluidic muscle fibers

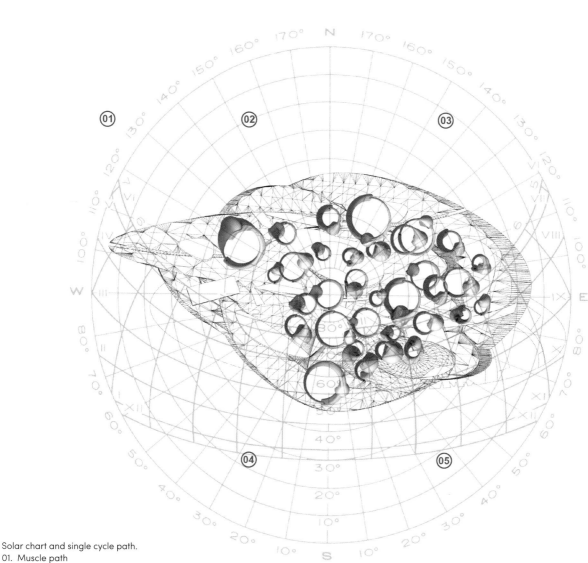

Solar chart and single cycle path.
01. Muscle path
02. Plinth
03. Auditorium space
04. Port at Hudson
05. Westside park gateway

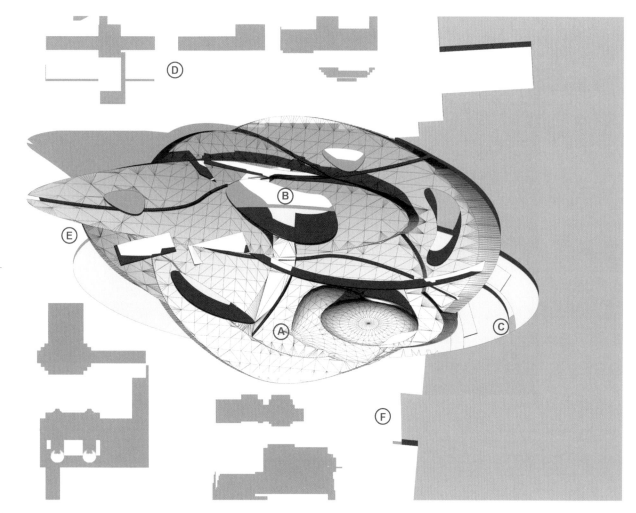

Plinth at west side railyards.

A. Main auditorium
B. Open to mezzanine below
C. Public dock – viewing plaza
D. Existing buildings
E. Park for esidents
F. Henry Hudson underpass

Design with Life

SCHOOL OF
THE EARTH

ENERGY

REGENERATIVE

School of the Earth

In 2061, Gallatin will celebrate the 300th birthday of Albert Gallatin, the founder of our school. At the same time, sea levels will have risen, but not yet to the point of making Gallatin a beachfront property, weather patterns will be increasingly erratic and damaging, and the Western world will be at a point where it can no longer ignore the impacts of climate change. This is why our School of the Earth has been placed in the year 2061: it is a year of significance for both NYU and climate change predictions. Our hope is that Gallatin as School of the Earth will stand a beacon of hope and innovation for climate adaptation in the future of Gallatin, New York University, New York City and hopefully the world.

The entire world is an ecosystem, nothing is in isolation, and therefore our education does not exist in a vacuum. In the new design, the historical context of the development of the university and climate change will be visible. This can take many different forms: a permanent installation on Indigenous claims to the land or climate change, teaching about native environmental methods and habitats, photo essays on climate change around the building, constantly screening documentaries on climate change, and guest speakers on the history of climate change. We will have a renewed understanding of how humans have gotten to the point where they are affecting the climate and causing the issues that we are redesigning our school to combat.

There must be environmental understanding and information woven into all education. Comprehension of climate change and the environment around us will not be relegated to environmental studies and science students; instead it will be incorporated into all education. Gallatin is full of creative students that are deeply involved in arts and humanities and will therefore have to find ways to incorporate environmental awareness into all aspects of education, not just the obvious choices. Possible ideas include green murals, climate-awareness performance art pieces, and other humanities-based understandings of climate change. Gallatin is an interdisciplinary school and we should make climate and environmental awareness an active part of that interdisciplinary education.

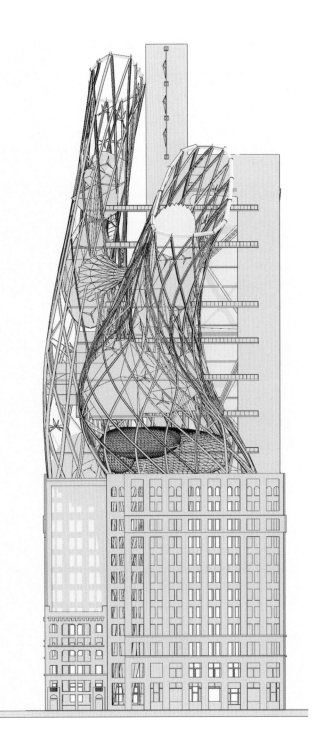

Washington Place elevation drawing.

Design with Life

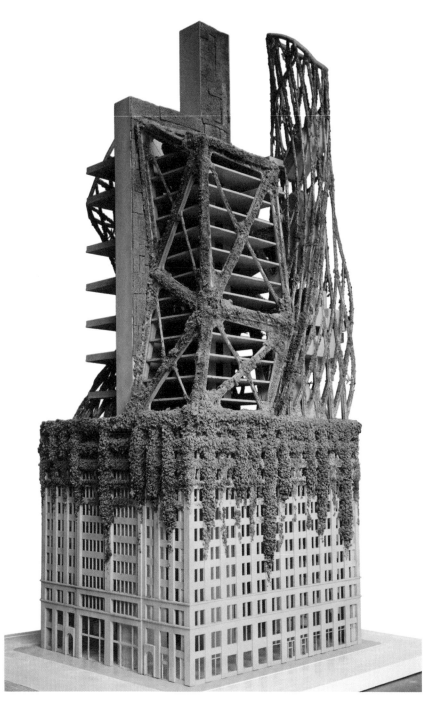

Left: Physical model perspective from corner of Broadway and Waverly Place.
Next page, right: Exterior perspective and corresponding physical model photograph of assembly spaces within the school.

Following pages:
Left: Broadway and Mercer Street elevation photographs of physical model. Right: Aerial rendering of The School of the Earth within its context.

Design with Life

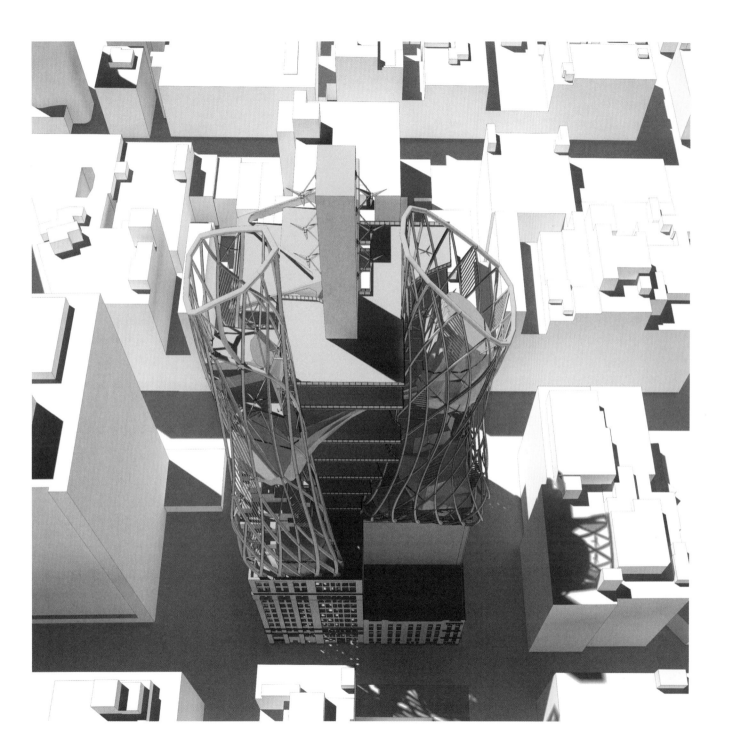

Design with Life

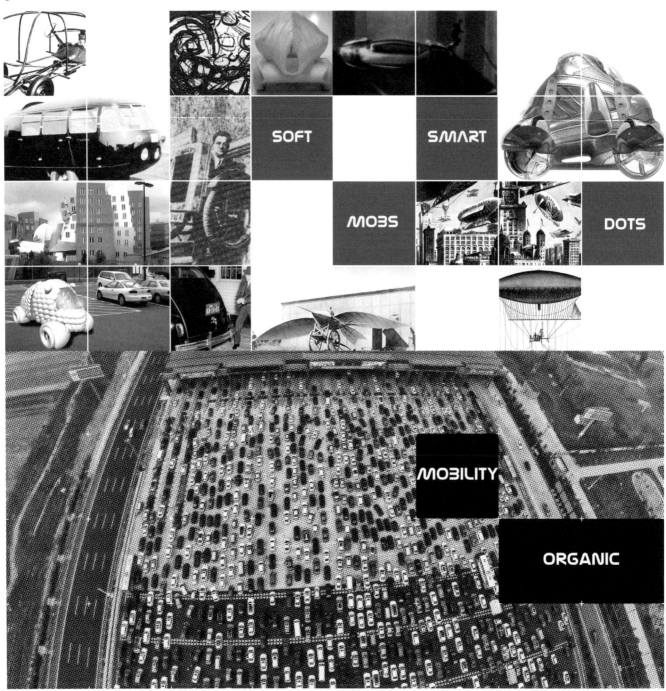

SOFT

SMART

MOBS

DOTS

MOBILITY

ORGANIC

Soft Mobs & Smart Dots

Smart Dots is a radical strategy for rethinking the crossroad by "injecting" a system of intelligent environmental elements -"smart dots"- that can spread out from the core to the periphery, reorganizing the streetscape. The design scheme is a critique of the hard boundaries that the automobile inflicts to the function of the streetscape, where people are forced to move around cumbersome barriers and often dangerous metal cars. Our future street is a soft, gradient field: a "pixelated" urban landscape of distributed functions, with no hard borders between different street occupancies.

Soft Mobs invokes a new technological and material arrangement for adapting cars to cities in pliable organized movements -"soft mobs,"- while it also suggests the use of softer vehicles where users can be in direct contact with the street. While architects and urban designers mostly take cars as a given and are content to design streets and public spaces around car movement, here we challenge and reverse this well-worn assumption.

The design is organized in three phases 2008, 2020 and 2028 respectively. In Phase 2008, we suggest taking minor design interventions as immediate safety measurements against continual conflicts of pedestrians with automobiles. Phase 2020, signals a transition period, where car lanes are narrowed, pedestrian zones are widened, bicycle bollards are introduced with new car technology and gentle congestion. Already in Phase 2020, we are suggesting the placement of environmental "smart dots," or green modules that filter rainfall, greywater, and at the same time, slow down traffic separating smoothly walking zones, bicycles and transportation zones. Phase 2028 is the future embodied in "pixelated" surfaces, gradient green zones, and living self-sufficient machines that provide their own energy, generating electricity through air movement. In the future, giant benevolent air-cleansing blimps dangle tentacles to collide spongy seats in a playful catch-and-release plan for people moving about town. All life is enveloped in a sentient ecology of street, mobile systems, and people.

The flexible body jetpack moves in flocks that bump and glide. Tugged along in groups for longer distances these devices run on hydrogen peroxide. The intention is to have multiple units air-towed to conserve power until a specific destination is reached. Individual jetpacks may decouple from the flock and head to a more localized point.

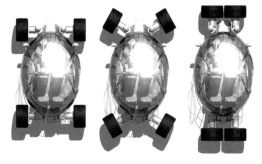

Above: An integrated facade with SOFT car rails for vertical travel of freight and passengers.
Below: Each wheel operates autonomously and intelligently and the motion of the wheels is controlled and coordinated by sophisticated software.

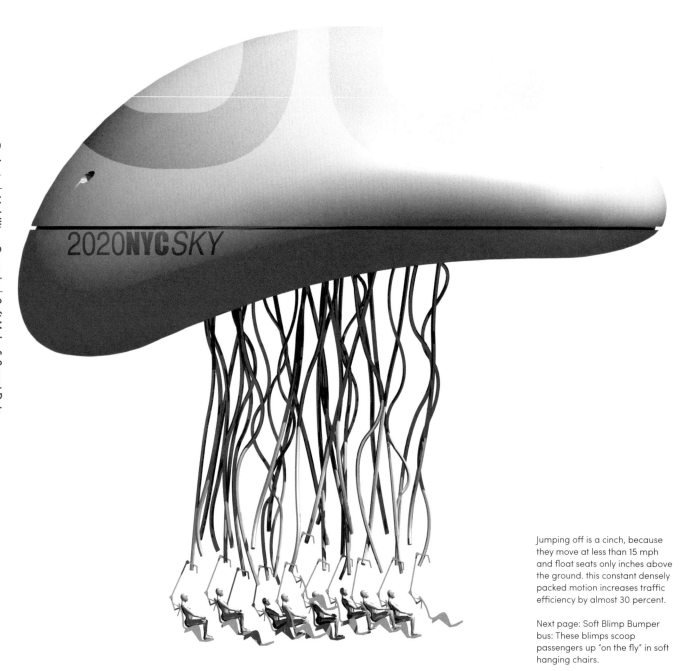

2020**NYC**SKY

Jumping off is a cinch, because they move at less than 15 mph and float seats only inches above the ground. this constant densely packed motion increases traffic efficiency by almost 30 percent.

Next page: Soft Blimp Bumper bus: These blimps scoop passengers up "on the fly" in soft hanging chairs.

Design with Life

Future metropolitan transit infrastructure: 2028.

Design with Life

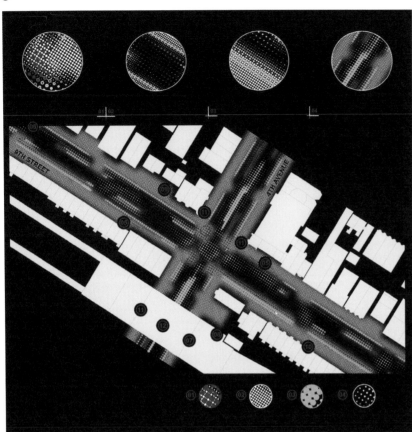

Left:
1. Pedestrian pathways
2. Green spaces
3. Bicycle zones
4. Car zones
5. Bus stops
6. Car parking
7. Bike storage
8. Water closet
9. Info kiosks
10. Café
11. Subway exits
12. Bridge

Below: Taxonomy of smart dots in the street.

Below: Smart Dots and Soft Mobs may function as a prototypical strategy for inserting soft plazas in various street intersections. we can rethink the city as whole by making nodal changes that may grow to infiltrate the rigid grid that we currently live in.

Design with Life

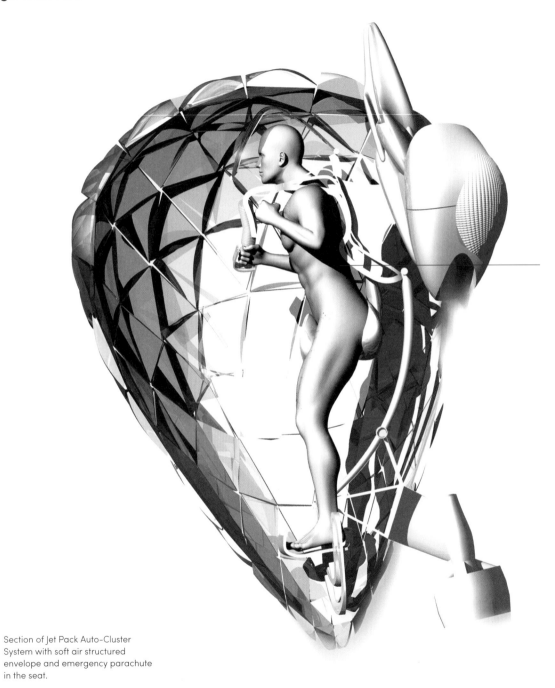

Section of Jet Pack Auto-Cluster System with soft air structured envelope and emergency parachute in the seat.

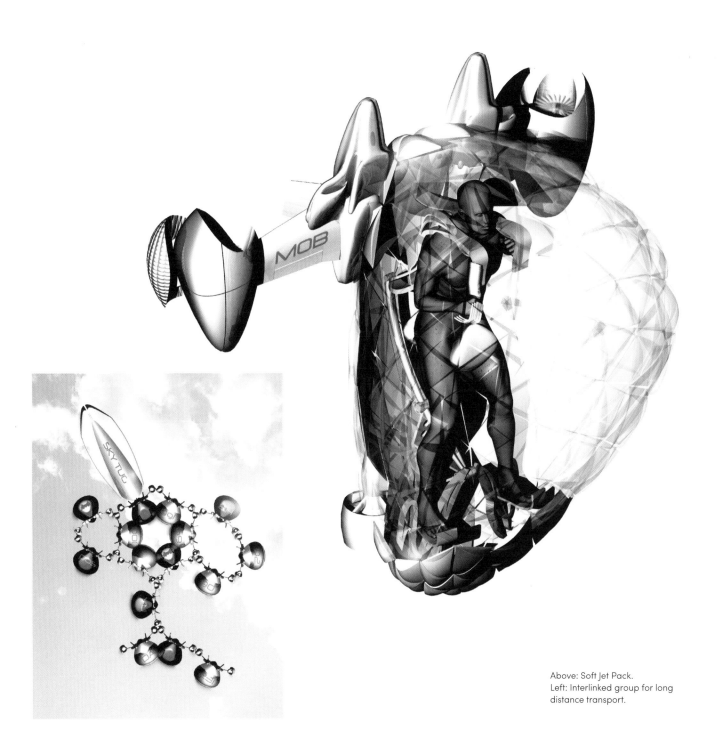

Above: Soft Jet Pack.
Left: Interlinked group for long distance transport.

Design with Life

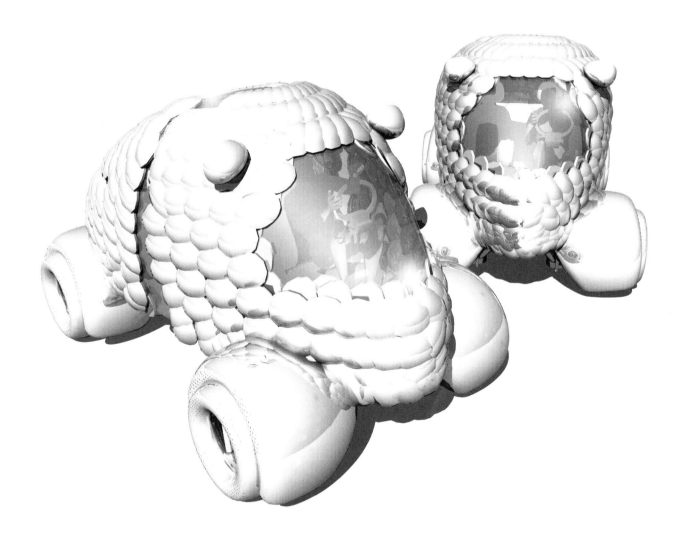

Above: S.O.F.T. – Sustainable Omni
Flow Transport, flocking vehicle.
Prototype: XO Lamb concept car.

Following page:
Above, left: City flows and altered
patterns.
Right: Mini stacking electric cars.

Below: Cars move as slow organic
swarms in the streets called
"gentle congestion".

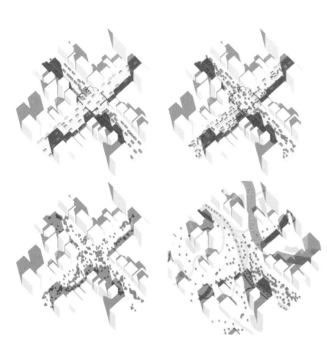

Design with Life

Soft dynamic cabin + "S" frame truss.

Articulated H–Type chassis in
a signature vehicle series.

Design with Life

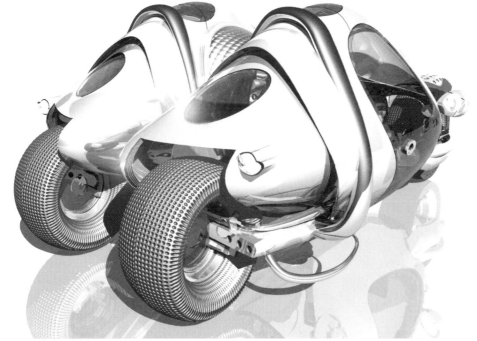

Above: Smart solar charging and urban stacking storage station.
Left: Athlete car (G)Race: Two drivers in collaboration.

Following page: Soft floating micro-island gyms on waterway paths.

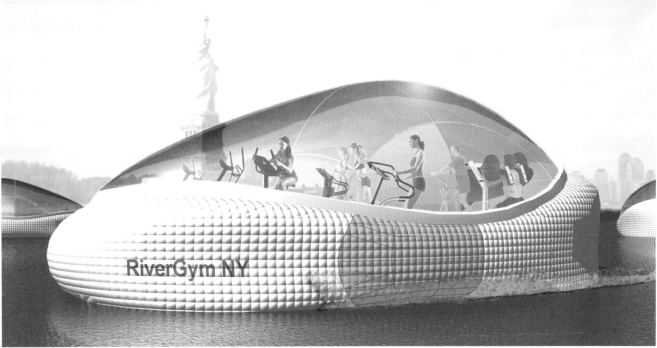

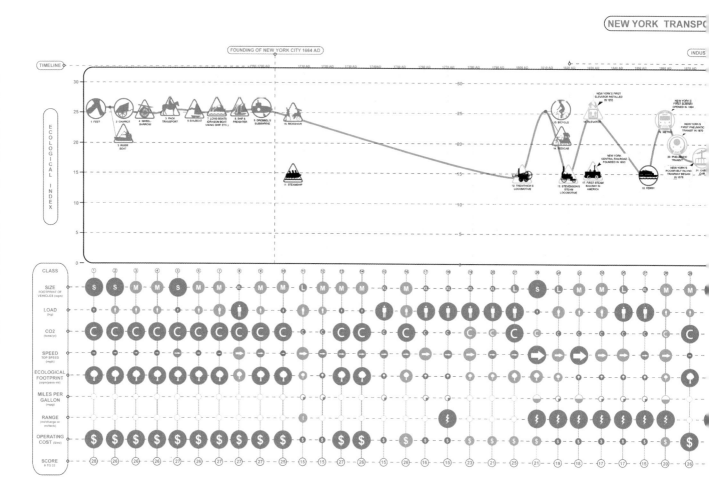

NEW YORK TRANSPO

FOUNDING OF NEW YORK CITY 1664 AD

INDUS

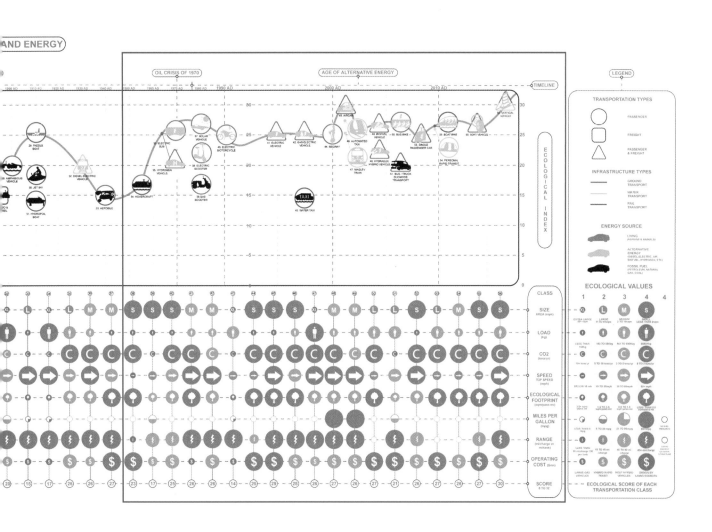

Detail of New York transportation
and energy chart.

Design with Life

CRICKET SHELTER

WELLNESS

FOOD

Cricket Shelter

The UN has mandated that insect sourced protein will become a major component in solving global food distribution problems. This impacts people globally, since continuing to raise livestock is not possible at our current rate of consumption and resource extraction.

It is a well-established fact that industrialized animal agriculture accounts for a fifth of all human greenhouse gas emissions. With global demand for meat projected to double by 2050, the industry's land requirements constitute one of the most significant drivers of deforestation in the world. This project proposes an alternative: with 1% of the greenhouse gas emissions and requiring 0.001% the land to produce the same amount of protein annually as cattle farming, we feel that environmental destruction need no longer be the consequence of ensuring our food supply. Cricket Shelter is a prototype for an urban farming strategy that minimizes the ecological footprint of protein-rich food production.

The continuous impact of climate dynamics, armed conflicts, non-stop urbanization, and economic upheavals present a distinct need for a hybrid architectural typology to deliver parallel solutions for food and shelter in distressed regions. Our proposal is a dual-purpose shelter and modular insect farm in one structure.

Raising cattle, pigs, and chickens for meat all require immense amounts of fresh water, land and energy. Breeding insects for food typically takes three hundred times less water for the same yield of protein. Our project aims to maximize access to nutrient resources and to support local communities in anticipation of post-disaster scenarios. This also targets societal upgrading strategies in both developed and developing countries as the temporary shelter easily converts to a permanent farming system/eatery after the crisis has dissipated.

Cricket Shelter is a self-sufficient, interconnected array of structural pods that fosters an optimal environment for supporting the life cycle of crickets. The embedded ecosystem was developed to permeate the structural system, each independent module linked by tubes connecting the elements to render the crickets "free-range". Whereas in many parts of the world entomophagy is more common but contamination is more likely, Cricket Shelter's innovative process offers a sanitary and hygienic solution.

Cricket Shelter was conceived as a hybrid architectural typology delivering parallel solutions for food and shelter in distressed regions throughout the world. As a modular structural system, it lends itself to simple construction and deconstruction in various site-specific orientations, making it easy to educate consumers on use and maintenance. As an architectural object, the shelter can contribute to the public realm inhabiting vacant lots, pocket parks, and rooftops, bringing agriculture and entomophagy into focus for the local populations. In this way we can fulfil our aim of educating the public about their role in sustainable consumption.

Below: Industrial livestock.

Following pages:
Left: Global entomophagy.
Right: Mesh tubing simulating preferred environment and serving as a means of transportation.

Design with Life

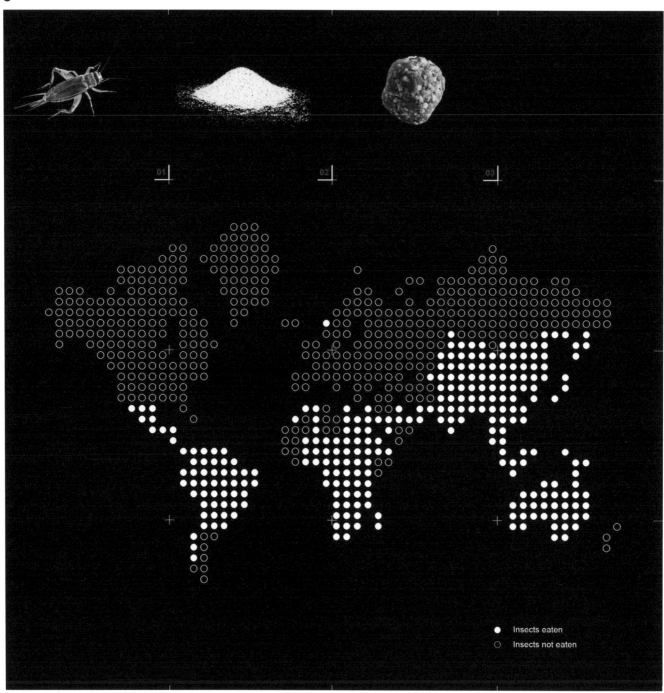

01

02

03

- ● Insects eaten
- ○ Insects not eaten

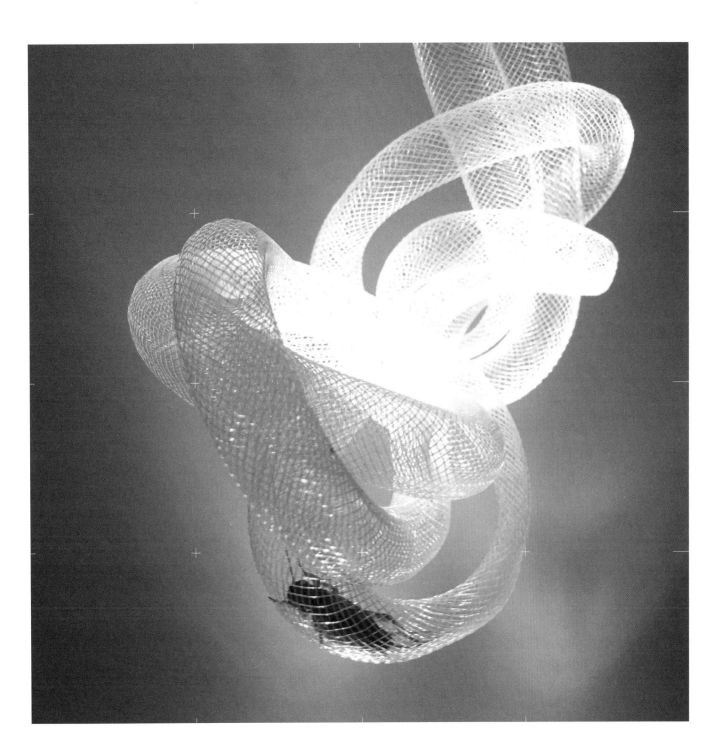

Design with Life

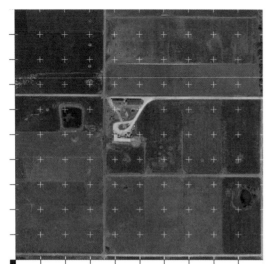

100 ACRE RURAL CATTLE OPERATION, INTENSIVE LAND USE.

100 ACRES OF URBAN GRID, CONTAINING 1.24 ACRES OF DISTRIBUTED MODULAR CRICKET FARMS.

98 ACRES   **1 YEAR**   **2000kg PROTEIN**   **3 ACRES**   **1 YEAR**   **2000kg PROTEIN**

98%

LAND AREA PER 100 ACRES REQUIRED WITH TYPICAL RURAL INDUSTRIAL CATTLE FARMING.

3%

LAND AREA PER 100 ACRES REQUIRED WITH FREE-RANGE URBAN CRICKET FARMING.

300×

WATER REQUIREMENT FOR CATTLE.

1×

WATER REQUIREMENT FOR CRICKETS.

100×

GREENHOUSE GAS EMISSIONS BY CATTLE.

1×

GREENHOUSE GAS EMISSIONS BY CRICKETS.

60%

INEDIBLE LIVE WEIGHT WASTED IN BEEF PRODUCTION.

15%

INEDIBLE LIVE WEIGHT WASTED IN CRICKET FLOUR PRODUCTION.

Above: Land intensivity comparison.
Following page: Connected modular bio-units.

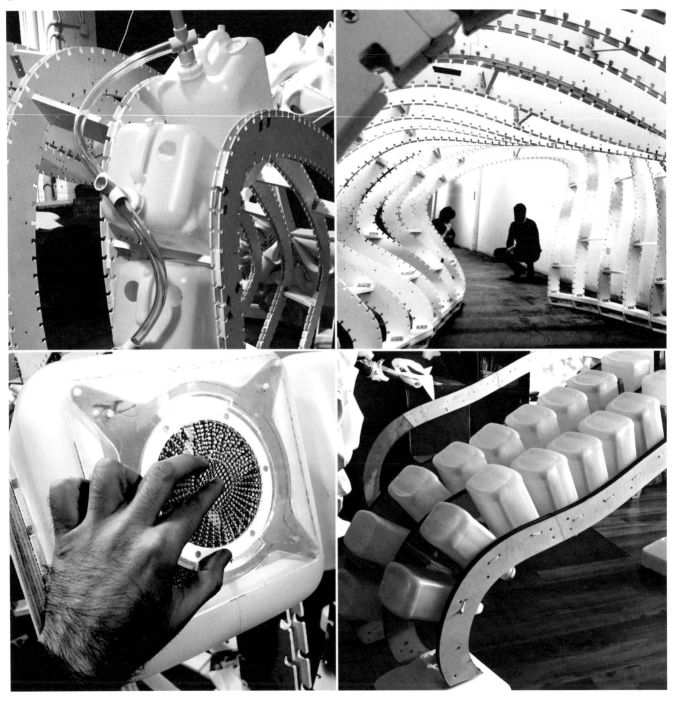

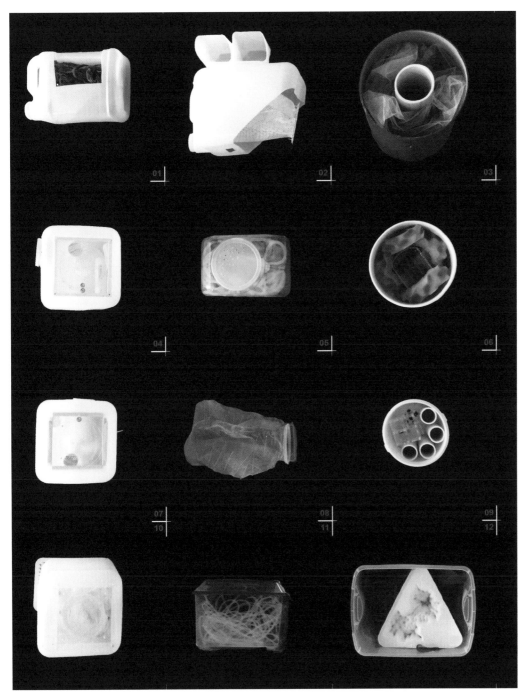

Left: Iterative development of bio-unit forms.

Previous page: From top left, clockwise: Assemblage of bio units into structural ribs; Structural ribs spline construction; Bio-unit infill prototyping; Dial lock attached to bio-unit.

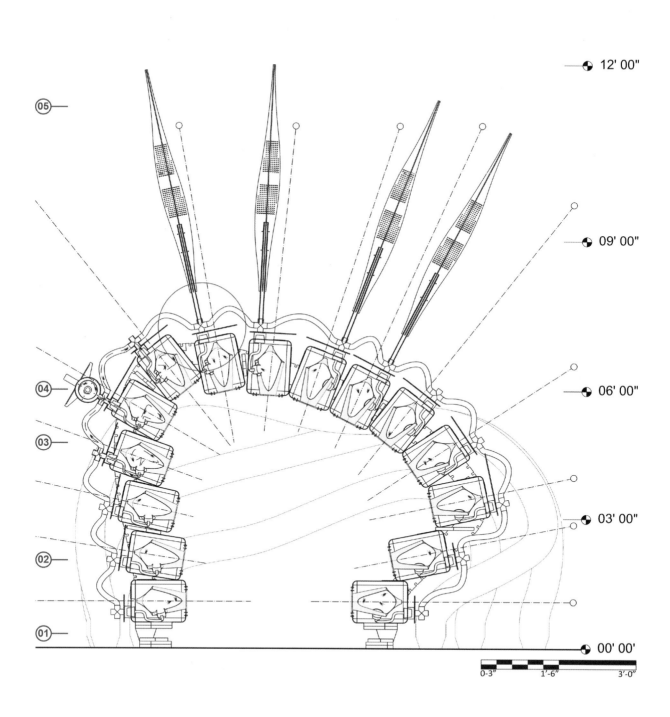

12' 00"

09' 00"

06' 00"

03' 00"

00' 00"

0-3"　　1'-6"　　3'-0"

05

04

03

02

01

Previous page:
Section of linked bio-unit for
cricket life.
01. Foundation
02. Cricket habitat
03. Mobility tube
04. Sex/birthing pod
05. Ventilation wind quill

Right: Exploded module assembly
with structural ribs.
01. Dial lock
02. Mounting plate
03. 5-gallon module
04. Semi-rigid sack
05. Structural rib
06. Shading louver
07. Wind quill

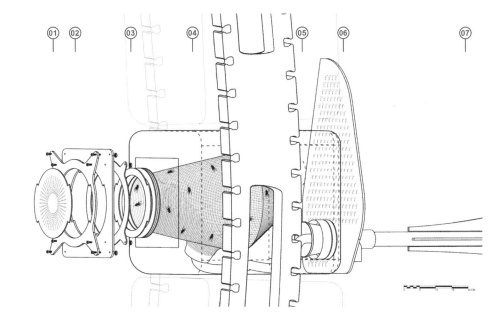

Cricket lifecycle analysis through
growth phases.

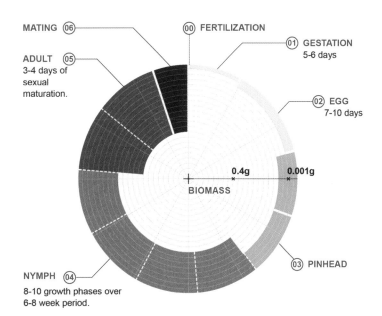

MATING 06

00 FERTILIZATION

01 GESTATION
5-6 days

ADULT 05
3-4 days of
sexual
maturation.

02 EGG
7-10 days

0.4g   0.001g

BIOMASS

03 PINHEAD

NYMPH 04

8-10 growth phases over
6-8 week period.

Design with Life

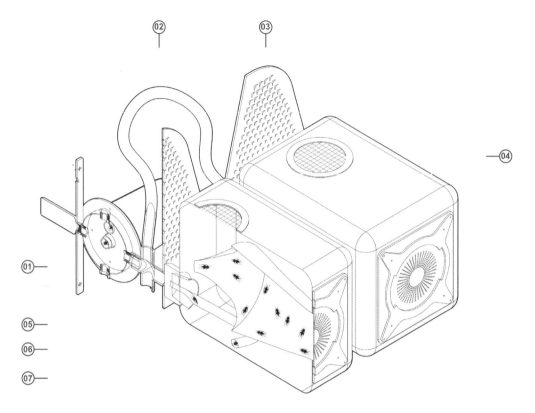

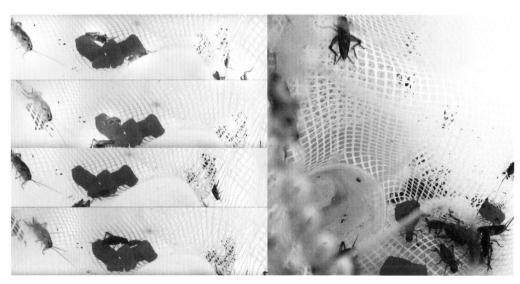

Above: Sectional perspective: Linked birthing pods, habitats, and louvers.
01. Sex pod
02. Mobility tube
03. Shading louver
04. Ventilation mesh
05. Nylon mesh tube
06. Semi-rigid weave sack
07. 5-gallon module

Left: Crickets consuming food gels to enhance flavor.

Following page: Interior view of 224 bio-units for 22,000 crickets.

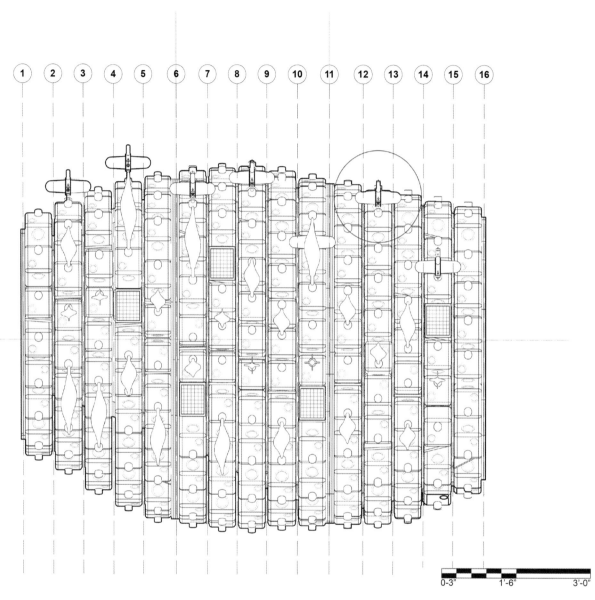

1 2 3 4 5 6 7 8 9 10 11 12 13 14 15 16

0-3"   1'-6"   3'-0"

Above: Plan view of cricket shelter.

Following page:
Above, left: Component stack by type, pre-construction on site. Right and below: Each grid extract is assessed as form and void, before it is rationalized as a reproducible construction element.

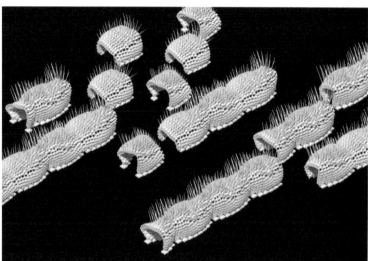

Design with Life

Climate-adaptive free-range insect super-colony.

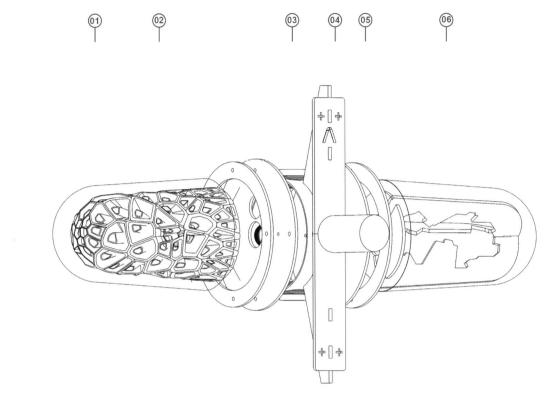

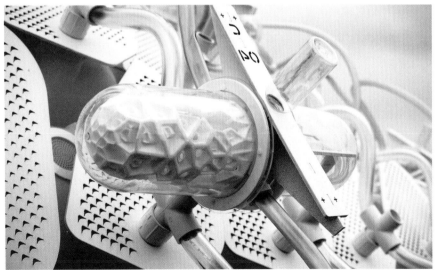

Above: Sex/birthing pod detail with multi-use chamber and feeders.
01. Ventilation grille
02. Circulation apparatus
03. Semi-rigid sack
04. Dial lock assembly
05. Semi-rigid sack
06. Dial lock assembly
Left: Sex/birthing pod detail.

Following page:
Disassembled sex pod elements.
A. Ventilation grille
B. Circulation apparatus
C. Semi-rigid sack
D. Dial lock assembly

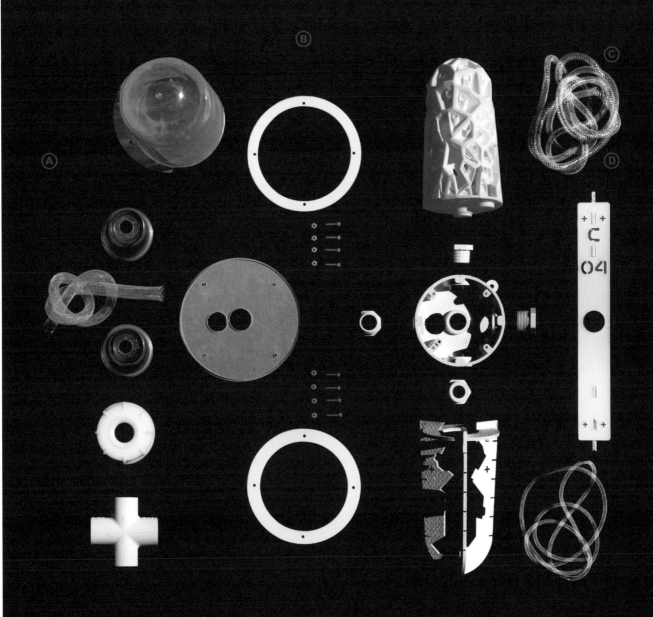

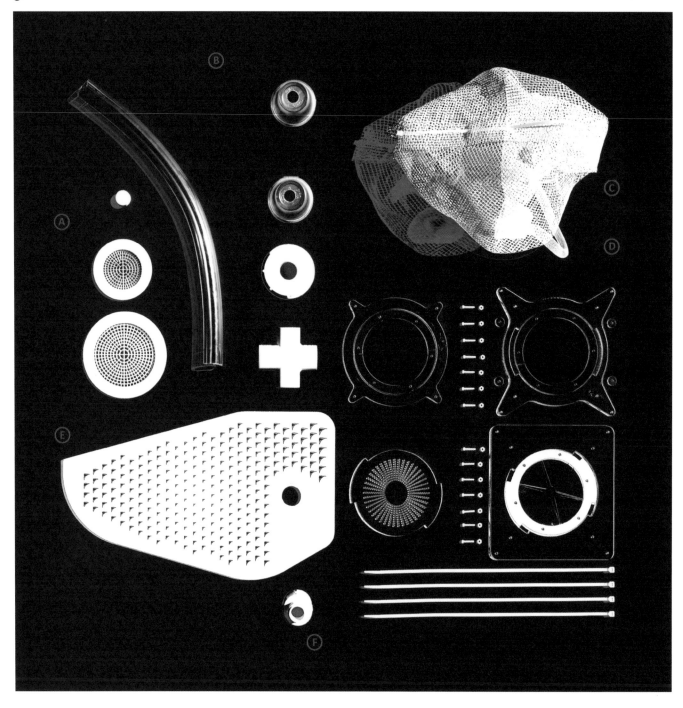

Previous page:
Bio-unit components
disassembled:
A. Ventilation grille
B. Circulation apparatus
C. Semi-rigid sack
D. Dial lock assembly
E. Perforated louvre

Right: Advanced insect farming
prototype.

Design with Life

Brooklyn Navy Yard, climate-adaptive free-range insect super-colony.

Design with Life

PLUG-IN

ECOLOGY

WELLNESS

FOOD

Plug-In Ecology

The Plug-In Ecology; Urban Farm Pod is a "living" cabin for individuals and urban nuclear families to grow and provide for their daily vegetable needs. It is an interface with the city, potentially touching upon urban farming, air quality levels, DIY agronomy techniques in test tubes, algal energy production, and bioluminescent light sources, to name a few possibilities. It can be outfitted with several optional systems to adapt to different locations, lighting conditions, and habitation requirements. While agricultural food sources are usually invisible in cities such as New York, the pod archetype turns the food system itself into a visible artifact, a bioinformatic message system, and a functional space.

The Plug-In Ecology cabin sphere prototype uses a robotic milled rotegrity ball for the under-grid structure made of reclaimed flat packed materials. A fully operable sub irrigation system and shaped foam panels serve as sleeves for the potting elements and agronomy tissue culture for micropropagation. A digital monitoring platform relays information about specific plant health to the web. Our vision for future iterations of the pod is to naturally grow structures over time, within a new form of mediated arboreal culture, to integrate the biological and mechanical elements more closely, to transform the object into one that grows and changes symbiotically. The Plug-In Ecology project sets out a direction for healthy biological exchanges with urban inhabitants, and to contribution to the life of urban ecosystems that mediate between autonomy and community.

Terreform ONE is committed to promoting the principles of ecotourism and responsible travel. It is important to determine if your trip conserves and improves the places you visit. These mini-lodges are composed of prefabricated pleached structures. Each unit has access to composting toilets, gray water systems, and solar powered lighting.

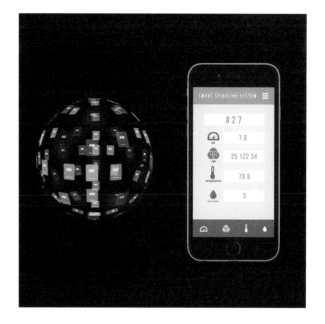

Right: Spirulina growth
monitoring app.

Design with Life

Projects | Food + Wellness | Plug-In Ecology

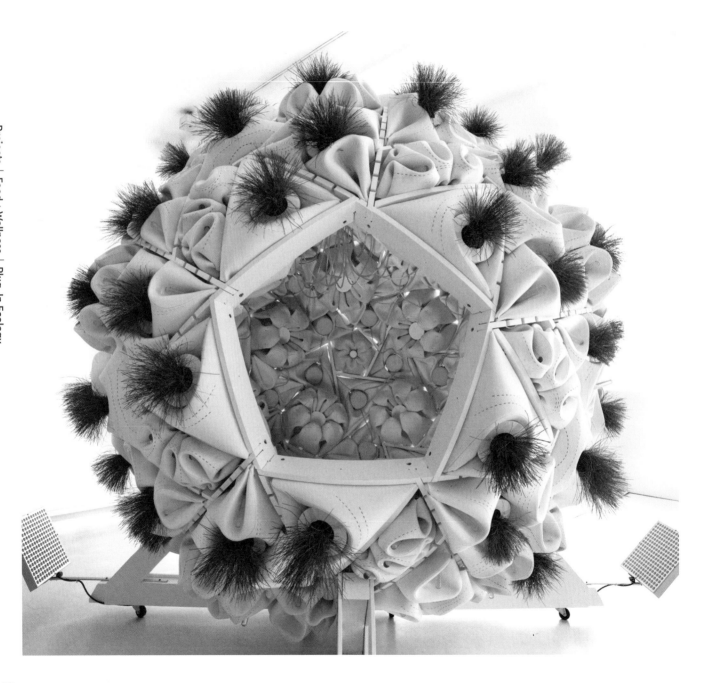

Previous page: Robotically-milled
rotegrity sphere section.

Above: Interior view with gravity-fed
irrigation system and Led artificial
grow lights.

Design with Life

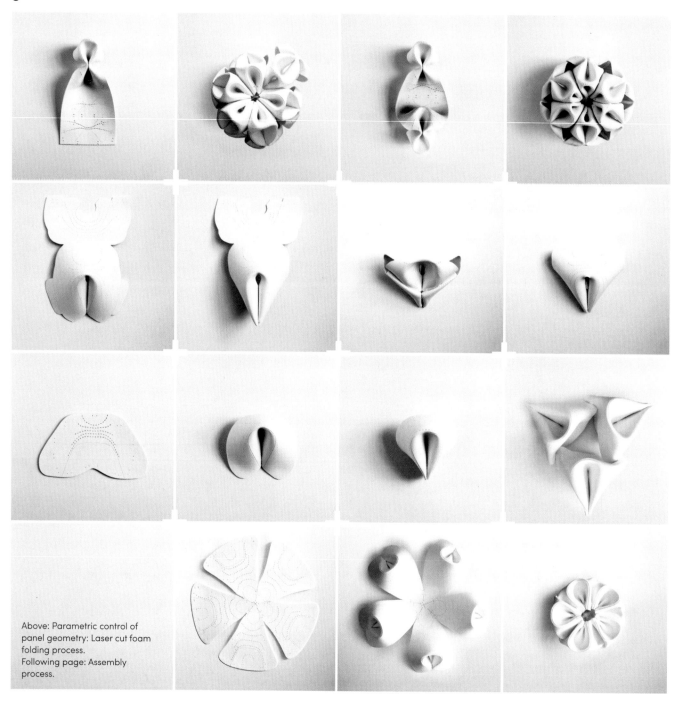

Above: Parametric control of panel geometry: Laser cut foam folding process.
Following page: Assembly process.

Design with Life

Previous page:
A. Gradual water reservoir
B. Sub-irrigation lines
C. Test Tube plant cell cultures
D. Zero petrochemical panel
E. Gravity controlled casing

Above: Willow balls, potential application supporting ecotourism.

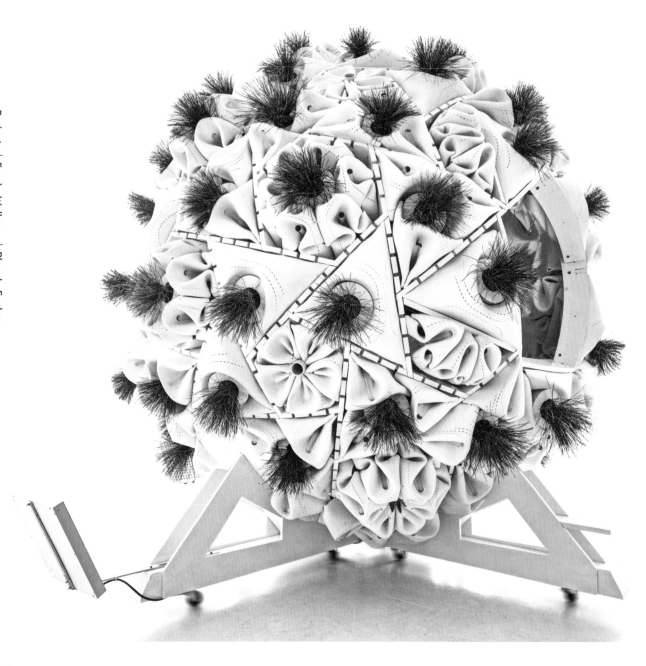

Previous page: A living
deployable structure for urban
food production, air quality, and
DIY test tube gardening.

Above: Rotegrity sphere, section.
Below: Assembly diagram
depicting CNC routed structure.

ONE PRIZE
ONE LAB

ONE Prize

ONE Prize is a platform on which creative pioneers can combine social infrastructure and design-based methods to save cities before an extreme climate shift. We promote all the winning projects and explore the possibilities of implementation in New York City and in areas like it around the world.

In 2014, ONE Prize proposed to design a collaborative teaching facility and public outreach center for socio-ecological design within the Brooklyn Navy Yard, for ONE Lab, a new school for design and science. The "Smart Dock" would include spaces for lectures, events, and design studios for approximately thirty graduate level students. It would function both as a visual reference and spatial matrix for ONE Lab, and as a unique interdisciplinary research laboratory for industrial design, synthetic biology, landscape ecology, art, architecture, and master planning.

The 2013 competition was a call for action to stormproof cities, ecosystems and social structures; to combine engineering and quality-of-life design to sustain the existence of future generations. Low-income housing communities in cities around the word are frequently in areas prone to natural disaster. As the effects of climate shift worsen these areas need to be storm-proofed by establishing a link between existing social structure and innovative design. ONE Prize 2013 aimed to deploy sophisticated design to alleviate storm impact through various urban interventions such as protective green spaces, barrier shorelines, alternative housing, waterproofing technology, and public space solutions.

The ONE Prize 2012 competition was powered by the idea that social, ecological, and economic struggles can simultaneously be addressed through collaborative action and innovative design. Situated in the context of a struggling U.S. economy and the tension of stagnant unemployment, ONE Prize 2012 was a call to put design in the service of the community, to reinvigorate deindustrialized and depressed urban areas, and to repurpose spaces for economic growth and job creation. It aimed to explore the socially, economically, and ecologically regenerative possibilities of urban transformation and design.

The 2011, Water as the 6th Borough, competition turned its focus to New York and its waterways, concentrating on recreational space, public transportation, local industry, and the native environment in the city. Contestants responded to the design brief with a great diversity of strategies, with waterfront farmers markets, parkways, playgrounds, and expo sites, five-borough local and express ferry loops, floating marine habitats, on-river shops, parks, wind farms, and even an airport, floating exhibition halls, recreational and commuter barges, oyster, fish, and shrimp farms, and interlinked bike share, car share, and ferry transit hubs.

The inaugural competition in 2010, From Mowing to Growing: Reinventing the American Lawn, was launched the context of larger issues concerning the environment, global food production and the imperative to generate a sense of community in our urban and suburban neighborhoods. From Mowing to Growing was not meant to transform each lawn into a garden, but to open us up to the possibilities of self-sustenance, organic growth, and perpetual change. We sought specific technical, urbanistic, and architectural strategies not simply for the food production required to feed the cities and suburbs, but the possibilities of diet, agriculture, and retrofitted facilities that could achieve that level within the constraints of the local climate.

In the five years of running, the ONE Prize Competition was an overwhelming success. The competition announcements were published in 2,406 magazines, websites and blogs and it was translated into 18 different languages. The ONE Prize Jury contained the Speaker of the City Council, two NYC commissioners, NYSERDA director, the presidents of nonprofit & environmental organizations, leading designers, and academics. 586 teams and 4,256 team members, representing 22 different countries submitted their work. The ONE Prize Competition captured the imagination of the design community from around the world. The ability to provide cash awards to the winners played an important part in achieving the desired impact. Over the five years, Terreform ONE raised and distributed $65,000 of prize money. Congratulations to all the ONE Prize winners!

ONE Prize / ONE Lab

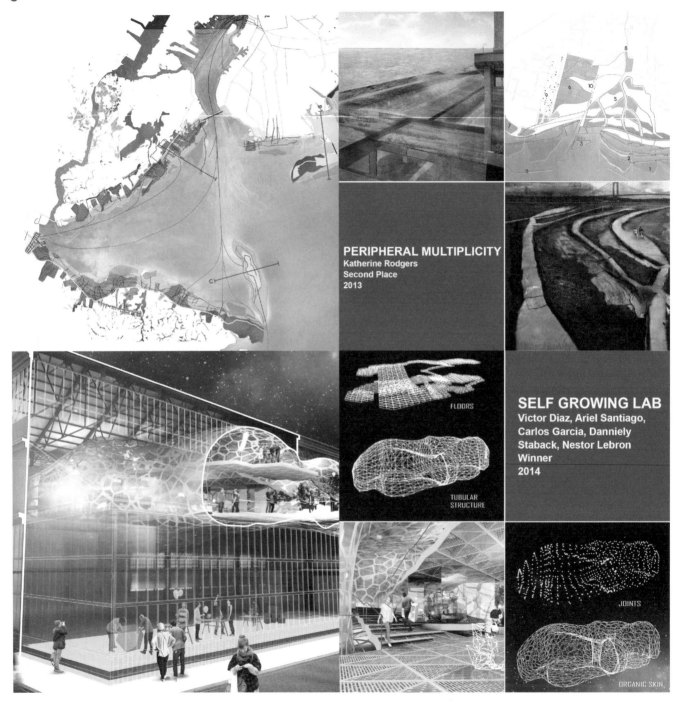

PERIPHERAL MULTIPLICITY
Katherine Rodgers
Second Place
2013

FLOORS

TUBULAR
STRUCTURE

SELF GROWING LAB
Victor Diaz, Ariel Santiago,
Carlos Garcia, Danniely
Staback, Nestor Lebron
Winner
2014

JOINTS

ORGANIC SKIN

KOGAMI
Ben Devereau
Finalist
2013

SKOOL HAUS
Nikole Bouchard + Vanessa Moon
Honorable Mention
2014

Design with Life

DYNAMIC CAPACITIES
Kenya Endo
Winner
2013

PURIFY

INTERCEPT

STORE

PARALLEL NETWORKS
Ali Fard + Ghazal Jafari
Winner
2011

CO₂

ONE Prize / ONE Lab

SUPER LEVEE
URBAN FARM
AGENCY architecture LLC
Winner
2010

PLASTIC RELIEF
Joseph Varholick
Finalist
2013

Design with Life

ONE Lab

The ONE Lab (1L) is an urban non-profit school involved in research and education. 1L professes a new awakening in the power and role of designing with technology in urban areas. We have uncovered a necessity for an independent, interdisciplinary think tank, or pedagogical "silo breaker zone," in which to inquire, rouse, debate, conduct experiments, and rethink the potential of humanity at all scales. We do not see design and technology belonging to any individual mindset; instead we envision design to be totalizing, comprehensive, and global in reach.

We search for harmonized global and local solutions that can open the sociopolitical borders that all too often separate design from people. The overarching aim is to develop a language of technological design that can create proximity between individual responsibility and the current global environmental crisis. We perceive environmental problems as an issue of human alienation from the natural world, and our initiative will explore ways in which design can reformat this separation. Innovation, for us, is the answer to sustainable cities and ecosystems.

COMMUNITY OUTREACH

ONE Lab advocates urban thinking by cultivating community organizers and activists. Today, city government and grassroots movements require more demands than traditional silo encapsulated professionals can procure. We must break away from insular territories of knowledge and redefine the limits of future neighborhoods. Urbaneers have the technical knowhow combined with conceptual exuberance. To redefine our urban community, we need to redefine the supportive disciplines that instigate it. In its simplest form, an Urbaneer is someone with an existing career track that adds a consecutive qualified activity to focus on cities. This focal point can be in concepts of waste, food, water, air quality, mobility, energy, and culture. Our educational venture, ONE Lab, is poised to cultivate this change. Our school boosts people into an advanced intellectual filter towards the recalibration of the city. As members of an urban community, Urbaneers can serve to better inform leaders or become leaders themselves.

LONG-TERM VISION

Our Urbaneering program at ONE Lab aspires to create a vision of the next city. The mission is to form heterodox approaches urgently needed in the age of natural resource scarcity. We seek synchronized global and local solutions that can open the sociopolitical borders that all too often disconnect design from people. We perceive environmental problems as an issue of human alienation from the natural world, and our initiative will explore ways in which design and science can reformat this separation. Innovation, for us, is the answer to equitable cities and eco-systems.

The City 2.0 needs a new breed of communicator. A person skilled in the art of cites beyond the typical planners, civil engineers, and architects of today. These fields need a multifaceted filter of reason to incorporate a profound comprehension of place. An Urbaneer posits the solutions to urban problems that normally take multiple disciplines to solve. Why can't an architect design a transportation system, or an ecologist design a building complex, or an automotive engineer design an urban landscape? We are looking to merge the edification and skills needed to reform the city of today.

MAIN LESSONS

We desire to learn more about mechanisms of change that reach the public. How can city thinkers communicate and receive continuous feedback to the denizens of a place? Its vitally important to investigate theories and projects such as the Masdar City, Smart Cities, and Landscape Urbanism and redistribute their cathartic elements elsewhere. Every city is different, yet successful principles and patterns of dwelling are known. These are the methods to transfer into other environs. Through innovative education, this is possible.

ONE Lab develops its pedagogy based on the needs of interdisciplinary workshops and improvised studio areas. This rarefied mixture of different knowledge sets near formulated a unique alliance. At this juncture, freely organized teams produce solutions that can span multiple fields of expertise around the world. Eventually, we seek to create ONE Lab Urbaneer charters around the world.

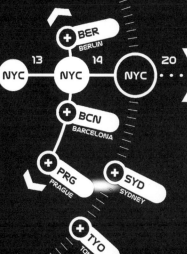

ONE LAB

EVOLUTION

2009
–
2020

BARCELONA
BERLIN
CAPETOWN
MOSCOW
MUMBAI
NEW YORK
PRAGUE
SEOUL
SHANGHAI
SYDNEY
TOKYO

09 10 11 12 13 14 20

ICN SEOUL
PVG SHANGHAI
SVO MOSCOW
BER BERLIN
NY NYC NYC NYC NYC NYC
BCN BARCELONA
PRG PRAGUE
SYD SYDNEY
TYO TOKYO
CAP CAPETOWN
BON MUMBAI

Design with Life

Design with Life

CONTRIBUTING AUTHORS

Extinct Eden and Ultrabionic

ANNA BOKOV

The Extinct Eden project is an acutely deliberate model based on one of the Early Modern renditions of biblical Eden and its collapse, known as *The Garden of Earthly Delights*.

The massive changes in climate dynamics since the first measurement of the Keeling Curve in 1958 make us question the division between the man-made and the natural environment, between man and nature. While it was believed to be a sign of progress at the onset of the industrial revolution, this divide has proven not only unproductive in the long run but also downright dangerous. The entire argument has shifted towards the socio-ecological realm, affecting humankind as well as fauna and flora.
Our planet is during its sixth wave of extinction. We are seeing the greatest loss of plants and animal species since the disappearance of the dinosaurs 65 million years ago. Can rethinking the built realm lead to a sustainable strategy for preserving non-human species? What if we were to design for life forms beyond our own?

The dialogue on the opposition or union of man and nature is by no means new. It goes back to the idyllic narrative of the Garden of Eden, which can be considered the primal environment designed by divine will for humans as well as for animals and plants. Eden, a metaphor for a sanctuary where humankind is in harmony with nature, remains an unattainable phenomenological state. Yet it offers some of the clearest precepts for dwelling in congruence with all creatures of the Earth.

A related second project entitled Ultrabionic has a more prescribed topological approach. Yet its fundamental combined principals of formwork, experimental materiality, geomorphology, and biological life are strangely similar in scope to the previous work.

From the onset of the information age in the design fields, about two decades ago, there has been a distinct vector attempting to re-create digital aliases for organic, natural forms, even as the digital technologies available at the time did not easily allow for that. For example, Reiser + Umemoto, Foreign Office Architects, Karl Chu, and many others have been mining the natural world for architecturally usable language—re-proposing organic geometries, patterns, and structures.

During the first decade of the 21st century, the finesse and sophistication of the digital mimicry progressed rapidly, blooming into something known as performative design—where computer generated matter was not just formed a certain way to evoke natural systems, but was ostensibly ready to perform in an analogous way. Digitally generated models were no longer static and limited to a certain aesthetic, rather they became dynamic and functional, especially with the emergence of robotics—bringing us closer to not simply replicating the natural world but to eventually becoming a part of it.

In the past, digitally generated proposals tended to favor an obsessive logic attempting to mimic natural

geometries, leaving behind the human dimension, such as the subjective, the subconscious, the corporeal, the creative. More importantly, the digital process of making and, ultimately, of creating utilizes different means and methods than those historically associated with human creativity. Traditionally, the phenomenon and culture of creativity has been intrinsically tied to discovery and experiment through making, through engaging our bodies in the process, through working with physical matter. No doubt digital technologies will eventually remedy that—in the post-sustainable world. Already there is an emergence of sensor-based technologies that allow for informal, intuitive interaction between the human (body) and the machine (think the recent installation at MoMA by Random International, the Rain Room). In the post-sustainable world, further fusion and ultimately the erasure of the boundary between the digital and the physical seems inevitable—yet so far the advance seems to be largely one-way.

The Utrabionic Project anticipates that shift. It utilizes simple algorithms and basic physical laws to produce relatively complex geometries—geometries that tend to resemble natural forms, both in their distinctiveness and (handmade) imperfection. Yet it is not only the formal quality of the work that is important; rather, it is its focus on making, i.e. creating, as an organic process that links the work with nature in a fundamental way that is both proto- and post-sustainable.

Diversity of organic forms, structures, and textures (the result of countless natural processes—physical, chemical, geological, biological) provided a continuous source of inspiration and served as a reference for the project, defining the selection of typologies and templates. Made from easily available materials, such as plaster[1], Bioforms (as they are called) are the result of series of experiments that fuse the programmed, the accidental, and the intentional. The form generating process took advantage of the methodical creative intervention as it entered in

dialogue with "naturally" occurring processes and directed them. The creative method was based on the exploration of the possibilities of material self-organization, in this case the self-organization of liquid matter, using mechanical forces and through the interaction with foreign shapes and textures to produce unique organic forms. The resulting forms invite associations with structures and formations created by natural processes such as growth, decomposition, erosion, turbulence; others recall the activity of biological species such as anthills, beehives, or corals. Overall the production can be described as an articulated synthesis of physical laws, such as gravity or tension, with algorithmic processes and base geometries.

1 Other materials are used along with plaster, such as wax, rubber, clay, bronze, and even certain unexpected ones, such as chocolate, meringue, jelly... It is important to note that the objects can be experienced individually or as spatial modules, as fragments that compose a bigger whole.

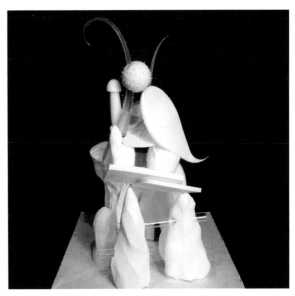

Partial model of The Garden of Earthly Delights by Hieronymus Bosch.

Special thanks to Margaux Wheelock-Shew.

Looking Backwards and Around

CHARLES C. MANN

"You go to war with the army you have, not the army you might want or wish to have at a later time.
Donald Rumsfeld, 8 Dec 2004

The future belongs to cities, but that future belongs to the past. The cities themselves—they belong to the countryside.

In 2008 humankind crossed a line it had never passed before. For the first time as many people lived in cities as lived in rural areas. The speed of the change was breathtaking. Two centuries ago, only 3 percent of the world's population lived in cities. By 2050 the figure may be as high as 70 percent. The world's urban population has been growing at an average rate of 2.16 percent per year for the last two decades.

Sociologists looked at this change with foreboding. Rising urbanization meant atomization, anomie, and anonymity. Farmers dispossessed by mechanization poured into cities and created slums. Metropolitan governments, already corrupt and inefficient, were overwhelmed by the new arrivals. Crime rates soared, water and sewage systems collapsed. Mumbai, Lagos, Jakarta, Nairobi, Mexico City, São Paulo—all were cautionary tales about the perils of gigantism.

Environmentalists looked at the rise of megacities and saw hope. Rising urbanization meant smaller ecological footprints, they said. Compared to their country cousins, city-dwellers consume less water, use fewer pesticides and herbicides, and burn smaller amounts of fossil fuels. Bring on the cities! environmentalists cried. More than that, cities were good for the wild areas around them. The logic was easy: The denser the city, the emptier the countryside! The emptier the countryside, the more room for Nature!

As the physicist Geoffrey West has demonstrated, per-capita infrastructure costs decrease with increasing city size—one reason that big cities are said to be greener than their smaller cousins. On top of that, similar scaling laws appear in economic quantities: average wages, patents per capita, restaurants per capita, the gross urban domestic product. In each one of these, big cities always do better than smaller ones. "The bigger the city," West writes, "the more each person earns, creates, innovates, and interacts." Ecological excellence and economic efflorescence, all in one urban package! What's not to like?

Excited environmentalists got on the urban train and held meetings with designers. From these meetings emerged brochures and PowerPoints showing cities as hyper-modern playgrounds surrounded by deep forests and lush savannas. Inside the urban boundary was a zone of self-actualization and personal liberty in which the sociologists' worries had been overwhelmed by exuberant technological gymnastics and virtuous urban planning. Just outside the urban boundary was the zone of charismatic megafauna, a gorgeous rewilder jumble of feathers, fur, and fish, a space for ecosystem services and ecological penitence.

Notably absent from these visions was the steel grip of history, even in its modern jargonized form of "path-dependence." An example: Cities often begin their existences as ports. That past may come back to haunt them, because coastal cities are vulnerable to the sea-level rise associated with climate change. The world has 136 big, low-lying coastal cities with a total population of about 550 million. Climate change threatens all of them. A study in Nature in 2013 estimated that if no preventive actions are taken annual flood costs in these cities could by 2050 reach as much as a trillion dollars. Other research teams have arrived at similarly extreme estimates. Coastal flooding could wipe out up to 9.3 percent of the world's annual output by 2100 (a Swedish-French-British team in 2015). It could create losses of up to $2.9 trillion in that year (a German-British-Dutch-Belgian team in 2014). It could put as many as a billion people at risk by 2050 (a Dutch team in 2012). Test cases occurred in 2017, when storms inundated Houston, San Juan, and Jacksonville within a few weeks of one another. If the damages grow fast enough, the resources devoted to mitigation and reconstruction will more than outweigh the savings due to urbanization.

On a parallel track, cities that grow large have historically tended to become financial centers. Almost inevitably their governments and cultures become captives of wealth, which in turn leads to corruption, civic disharmony, and inattention to collective problems and public goods. Look at the world's megacities: Jakarta, Delhi, Manila, Karachi, Shanghai, New York, Guangzhou, São Paulo. All are dominated by the financial class—people who can insulate themselves from large-scale problems. (Tokyo and maybe Seoul are possible exceptions.) Most of these places have long had trouble providing basic public goods like clean water, breathable air, and safe streets, especially for women. (Here New York may be added to the list of exceptions.) Dense cities may in theory be the vehicle for humankind to ride into tomorrow, but our knowledge of the past suggests that all too often the people at the wheel care little about their passengers. Plans that do not take this process, long recognized by history, into account may find themselves ambushed from the rear.

A void as big as history in these affairs is geography. As cities get larger, diminishing returns kick in. The benefits of bigness are overcome by congestion, which drives up resource use. As buildings get packed together, for example, they need ever-larger systems to pump in fresh, conditioned air—systems that buildings in less crowded areas may not need at all. Meanwhile, the heating and ventilation systems pour out hot exhaust, creating the "heat islands" that are a familiar urban plague. The heat islands drive up air-conditioning use, which further increases the heat islands—a diseconomy of scale.

Most vexing is the countryside immediately surrounding the city. Because transportation costs into the city are minimal, it is a valuable source of products for city-dwellers: produce and meat, water and wood. But it is also the cheapest land near the city, meaning that it is highly desirable for expansion, especially by poor creatives (a thesis associated with Joel Kotkin). The risk is that fighting sprawl and leaving more room for nature will make life harder for the poor and stifle innovation.

Future cities travel into the future on tracks laid decades or even centuries in the past. And they are always in dialogue with their surroundings, reaching ever outward for resources and amenities—sometimes destructively, sometimes creatively. If climate change is a war, tomorrow's ultra-urban world will not fight it in the perfect, air-brushed metropolises of futurist TED talks. Instead, they will fight it in the cities we have.

The only way to go forward is to take care first to look back and then around.

The Dishrack Syndrome

RAY KINOSHITA MANN

Ladies and gentlemen, I invite you to look at high-end kitchen catalogues. The ones featuring images of gorgeous, streamlined high-tech kitchens from manufacturers like Bulthaup and Snaidero. In these images, the future always looks bright (especially if you are rich). Gleaming and electronically outfitted, the kitchens look like they contain everything the affluent homeowner of the future could possibly want. Now let's play a game, "Where's Waldo" in reverse: What is missing?

The dishrack. Search through every image of high-end designer kitchens in the digital treasure house of Google Images and you will find an extraordinary diversity of design approaches. But every single one of these designs lacks a dishrack. The Dishrack Syndrome is, apparently, a universal design principle, untaught in schools but intuited by everyone with access to Revit.

In one sense, this is purely practical: what designer wants to put such a cluttery thing in a photo shoot? But in another, deeper sense, the Dishrack Syndrome is a synecdoche for a much larger issue—a fundamental imbalance in our responses to the future, especially as we begin to consider reconfiguring the urban fabric to deal with climate change. Dishracks by themselves are not particularly important. But their lack is a telling reflection of the design professions' grasp of human necessities.

Most kitchens address the basic question of where to handle hand-washed stuff very poorly, whether the stuff involved is big pots, plasticware, plastic bags, or delicate china. The typical "solution" is to pile it all up willy-nilly in a tiny rack next to or in the sink. When that fills up, people have to dry the dishes by hand and put them away immediately. This small struggle is a daily fact of life for most middle-class people—that is, for the majority of people in the world. But in these ubiquitous kitchen images that form our ideas of the norm, it's invisible. And if we don't show a problem, we don't see it, and we won't solve it. That goes for the future as well—even if we develop high-tech dish-cleaning devices, or dishes that don't need cleaning, or stop using dishes altogether and just eat tablets—there will always be a series of nagging details in around the operation of feeding ourselves and taking care of our end products that simply won't go away.

Now consider another, equally unpleasant and equally invisible necessity: garbage. Writers since Liebig and Marx have understood the ecological imbalance—Marx called it the "metabolic rift"—caused by funneling organic material from the countryside into the city, which flushes it into sewage-treatment plants. Vast quantities of vital nutrients are lost (Victor Hugo bemoaned this in a famous passage from Les Miserables.) A big part of the solution is domestic composting. The logical place for this to occur is the kitchen. Most people would theoretically like to compost, but winter treks across the yard, freezer space tied up by scraps awaiting warmer weather or weekly pickup, and the general "yuck factor" can defeat even the well-intentioned.

In-home composters exist—I have one of them. A unit about the size of a desktop CPU tower and cost of a garbage disposal (i.e. not inexpensive), it makes impressively earthy compost out of a substantial pile of organic waste in about a week. The compost has had wonderful benefits for our garden, but the machine itself is an exhibit in the museum of Why You Need Designers. It is laid out and constructed to have a decent composting action but, as far as I can tell, without consideration for the actions required of people for composting: dumping in scraps without making a mess, storing and adding the sawdust or wood pellets that provide the carbon component, tipping in the baking soda that reduces acidity and odors. None of these issues should be hard to solve. But they will not if they are never examined by designers because they are not seen (or heard or smelled).

Dishracks and composters are like "tells" in poker—tip-offs to larger, more consequential behavior. They betray a profession-wide reluctance to engage with the "yuck factor": the messy details of our lives. Instead, the design brochures feature gleaming surfaces that seem viewed from a distance, as if through a zoom lens. Their only inhabitants are elegantly posed, digitally rendered figures—and the kitchens look like they were designed for them. None of the unpleasant basics are considered. But precisely because those messy details are how we waste resources, pollute air and water, and dump carbon into the atmosphere, they must be attended to, even loved. The dishracks and composters must be central to our imaginations of tomorrow.

Embrace the yuck, love it, own it, solve it!

Subversive Science

BRUCE LINDSEY

Landscapes. Buildings and Machines

Vitruvius, 1st century Roman Architect and author of the oldest known treatise on architecture, suggests that Architecture with a capital A consists of landscapes, buildings and machines. Timepieces, machines for Vitruvius, were sundials which represented earth and the full spectrum of the planets. Architect Paul Shepheard, in his book *What Is Architecture*, states: "There is a scale of things all to do with the land, at one end of which are the forces of nature, the perception of which, at any given place, I would call landscape. At the other end of the scale are the local difficulties solved, and the opportunities opened, by our use of machines – and somewhere in between are the buildings, which if conceived grandly and accurately enough, can extend outward to embrace each end of the scale." Buildings in the middle, landscapes on one end, and machines on the other.

I am not a scientist, although a person I will talk about once described himself as a "quasi-, pseudo-, crypto-" scientist. I am not a biologist, nor an environmental historian, but an architect—one who is inspired by, among other things, landscapes. This might be described by the following statement that my wife and I have come to believe: "the longer we are away from the landscapes where we grew up, the more we feel we are from them." The landscape is Idaho in our case, and the longing for the sight of the mountains at the edge of the horizon.

In this essay I will talk a little bit about the recent past and describe some ideas about sustainability. It will be more anecdotal than comprehensive, and more

about what inspires me about the current situation, which author Barry Lopez has described as a moment "between stories." I will not talk about doomsday statistics or climate change directly. In fact, I believe that students and faculty that I have the privilege of working with everyday are creating the stories of the future every day.

Prologue

"A design machine must have an artificial intelligence because any design procedure, set of rules, or truism is tenuous, if not subversive, when used out of context..."
–Nicholas Negroponte

In the 1970 book, *Architecture Machine*, Nicholas Negroponte, a professor of architecture at MIT and founder of the Media Lab, outlined ideas for "the intimate association of two dissimilar species (man and machine), two dissimilar processes (design and computation), and two intelligent systems (the architect and the architecture machine)." Written before any such machines existed and patterned after ethical robots (a specific class of machines described by cybernetician Warren McCulloch), Negropontes' Architecture Machine was dependent upon an understanding of the environment as an evolving organism as opposed to a designed artifact. Additionally, the interface of the person and machine was predicated on a desire for self-improvement that ascribed intelligence to the artifact or the artificial and was concerned with "problem worrying," not "problem solving"—problem worrying acknowledging the dynamic relationship between problems and solutions in an evolving context.

Negroponte goes on to describe that this could happen through a *dialogue* between the person and the machine and between the machine and the environment. He states that the dialogue between the machine and the environment must be two-fold: First, "an [architecture] machine must receive direct sensory information from the real world," and second, it must be aware of other designers' procedures such that it can provide both "unsolicited knowledge and unsolicited problems." In this way a designer could "tune into controversy," that could challenge the designer's own assumptions, preventing the machine from simply being a "yes man."

Silent Spring

There is no equivalent to say, Joan Baez in the buildings or words of Venturi...
–John Farmer

2012 marked the 50th anniversary of the publishing of Rachel Carson's book *Silent Spring*. This event is widely understood as marking the beginning of the modern environmental movement in the US. Published in 1962, the book was released in September and by November had risen to number one on non-fiction bestseller lists. The book outlined in poetic, explicit, and meticulously researched and referenced detail, the persistent environmental effects of the pesticide Dichlorodiphenyltrichloroethane. It projected a future world "without birdsong." When DDT first became available for general use in 1945, Carson, a marine biologist, attempted to interest Readers Digest in an article about DDT testing to no avail. Thirteen years later, in 1958, her interest in the subject was renewed by a letter from a friend in Massachusetts attributing the death of large birds on Cape Cod to the widespread use of DDT used to control mosquitoes.

The book, which took Carson took four years to complete, brought strong criticism from the chemical industry, including St. Louis-based Monsanto. Monsanto published 5,000 copies of a parody entitled *The Desolate Year* that described a world where the banning of pesticides resulted in disease and famine from ravaging insects. Despite personal attacks that went so far as to describe Carson as a communist, her book Silent Spring was enormously influential and for the first time revealed the extent to which industrial society had separated itself from the environment. To paraphrase video artist Bill Viola, the degree of surprise we feel when we realize that the chemicals that we have poured into our rivers are now coursing through our veins is a measure of the distance that we have placed between ourselves and our environment. Carson testified several times before Congress on the dangers of pesticides. Keeping her illness, a secret, lest it diminishes the legitimacy of her research, she died of breast cancer in April 1964 at the age of 56. DDT was banned in the United States in 1972 but remained in widespread use throughout the world for nearly ten years. It remains in use today. In 1980 Rachael Carson was posthumously awarded the Presidential Medal of Freedom.

In a CBS interview shortly before her death Carson remarked, "But man is a part of nature, and his war against nature is inevitably a war against himself. [We are] challenged as mankind has never been challenged before to prove our maturity and our mastery, not of nature, but of ourselves." Two years after the publication of *Silent Spring*, ecologist Paul Sears described ecology as a "subversive science" that called into question the cultural and economic premises of Western societies—pointing out the ironic fact that the root word for economics and ecology is the Greek word *oikos* for house, household or family. Political scientist William Ophuls in his dissertation of 1972 writes: "Human ecology is against the conquest of nature; against growth as we think of it; against the isolation of thought and action; against individualism as an ideology; and against moral absolutes like the inalienable rights of man. 'The subversive science' is thus a pitifully weak soubriquet for ecology, which demands only that our current

Design with Life

political, social, economic, and moral order be stood on its head."

On Christmas Eve 1968, six years after Carson's book was published, Apollo 8 astronaut Bill Anders took the first picture from space of Earth rising above the moon, which was published shortly thereafter in Life magazine. Entitled Earthrise, the photograph inspired activist John McConnell to propose the first Earth Day at a UNESCO conference on the environment that next year. Following the signing of a proclamation by Mayor Joseph Alioto of San Francisco, the celebration envisioned by McConnell was held on March 21,1970, the vernal equinox. Parallel to McConnell's vision was the extension of an environmental teach-in led by US Senator Gaylord Nelson of Wisconsin that resulted in an Earth Day celebration on April 22nd, 1970. It involved an estimated 20 million people, including a professor of biology from Washington University in St. Louis named Barry Commoner. In 1980 Senator Nelson became a counselor of the Wilderness Society, and in 1995 he was awarded the Presidential Medal of Freedom in recognition of his environmental work. Earth Day is now celebrated by over 500 million people in over 175 countries and is by some accounts the largest secular celebration in the world.

Time Magazine called Barry Commoner, generally referred to as a "founding father" of modern environmentalism, the "Paul Revere of Ecology." His early book, The Closing Circle: Nature, Man and Technology, published in 1971, outlines his four laws of ecology: everything is connected to everything else, everything must go somewhere, nature knows best, and there is no such thing as a free lunch." In 1976, Commoner's bestselling book The Poverty of Power addressed the three E's: 1. Environmental survival, 2. Energy shortage, 3. Economic decline. Here again he suggested that these things were interconnected and were caused by a corporate capitalist economy that should be replaced. Commoner, who lived in Brooklyn, passed away in 2012. During his 1980 presidential bid as part of the Citizens Party a reporter asked Commoner, "Dr. Commoner, are you a serious candidate or are you just running on the issues?"

In 1966, four years after Carson published Silent Spring, economist, poet, and devout Quaker Kenneth Boulding published "The Economics of the Coming Spaceship Earth," an essay describing the "cowboy economy" implications of the decreasing availability of the world's natural resources, extending the ideas of the influential 19th century English economist Thomas Robert Malthus. Boulding's metaphor of the earth as a spaceship was borrowed from Buckminster Fuller's 1963 book, Operating Manual for Spaceship Earth, wherein Fuller outlined the idea that the earth was a spaceship that requires maintenance, recalling metaphors of nature such as LeCorbusier's "a house is a machine for living." In 1966 biologist John Todd established the New Alchemy Institute based on the principle of the "earth as a living machine," followed by the Gaia Hypothesis, developed in the early 70's by scientist James Locklock and microbiologist Lynn Margulis, which proposed that the complex interactions of the earth could be considered as a single organism.

The same year that Boulding published his influential essay, architect Robert Venturi published his seminal book Complexity and Contradiction in Architecture, described in the introduction by noted architectural historian Vincent Scully as "probably the most important writing on the making of architecture since Le Corbusier's 'Vers Une Architecture', of 1923." Along with Aldo Rossi's The Architecture of the City, published in the same year, Venturi's work would help open the post-modern phase of modern architecture's development. Venturi called for an architecture of "either-or," and "both-and" that was hybrid, messy, and ambiguous. Though his Gentle Manifesto was extremely influential, architect John Farmer noted in his book Green Shift: "given the widespread knowledge that the harm as well as the benefits that machine-age society, in peace as well as in war, had brought to humans, as well as to the planet, it is puzzling that the new architectural debate at that time did not really engage with green issues."

Early Warnings

I am two with Nature.
Woody Allen

In the West, the longer history of environmental awareness in the 19th century paralleled the emergence of biology as a science and, according to environmental historian Donald Worster, may come to be called the "Age of Ecology" for the role it played in the foundations of contemporary environmental thought. In North America, the 19th century view was primarily formed by two fundamental ideas: the first followed the work of Emerson, and the second, Thoreau's, was that man and nature are one. Ralph Waldo Emerson's *Nature* was first published anonymously in 1836. The short book, inspired by a visit to the natural history museum in Paris, outlined the spiritual dimensions of nature where, "therefore, all that is separate from us, all which Philosophy distinguishes as the not me, that is, both nature and art, all other men and my own body, must be ranked under this name, nature."

 On land owned by Emerson, Henry David Thoreau began his experiment in walking, living, and recording nature on Walden Pond that resulted in *Walden* or *Life in the Woods* published in 1854. As much a treatise on time as nature, his proposition of "economy" was an American pragmatism that sought transcendence through a nature that precedes and follows us. "Only that day dawns to which we are awake. There is more day to dawn." A lesser known essay by Thoreau titled "Resistance to Civil Government" later re-titled "Civil Disobedience" warned that democracy does not necessarily prevent governments from co-opting citizens as partners of injustice. Seen as the origin of the idea of non-violent resistance, the essay was a great influence on the thinking of Martin Luther King, Mahatma Gandhi, and Nelson Mandela. The essay articulates a citizens' inevitable ethical responsibility and, alongside Walden, prefigures the environmental dimension of justice.

The second main theme from the "Age of Ecology" is the belief that that man is capable of enlightened management. This comes full force in the book *Man and Nature*, published in 1864 by George Perkins Marsh. The book, later subtitled *The Earth as Modified by Human Nature*, describes the interdependence of society and nature. Using historical examples, Marsh described the high likelihood of resource depletion but ultimately believed that nature should be managed for the "benefit of man." He hoped for "a community engaged in agriculture and all the civilized arts, and such a community cannot exist without transforming the landscape." Gifford Pinchot, founder of the U.S Forest Service under President Theodore Roosevelt, was influenced by *Man and Nature* and coined the term "conservation" with reference to natural resources. He went on to describe himself as the "father of conservation." Pinchot worked closely with Roosevelt, helping to create forest reserves, wildlife refuges, and over 17 national monuments, including the Grand Canyon National Monument in 1908. The Sierra Club, founded in 1892 by Pinchot's friend (and later antagonist) John Muir, helped raise awareness about the value of wilderness.

In 1864, while the Civil War raged, Abraham Lincoln signed into law that the 39,000 acres of Yosemite and Mariposa in Southern California should be preserved for public use and recreation. This act was followed by the designation of Yellowstone as the first National Park "for the benefit and enjoyment of the people" in 1872 and the first forest preserve in 1891, eventually leading to the formation of the National Parks Service in 1916. Muir's differences with Pinchot described two sides of a debate that continues today. Pinchot believed that conservation and the protection of nature should be for the common good. Muir, who is credited with the saying "everything is connected to everything else," believed that preservation was an ethical and moral responsibility.

Design with Life

Contributing Authors | Subversive Science | Bruce Lindsey

Aldo Leopold

*We seems a more appropriate description
for ecological relationships.*
Ian McHarg

A Sand County Almanac was published in 1949,
shortly after its author Aldo Leopold's death. While
Leopold's work is generally seen as being a part of
the conservation movement, his ecological conscience
and his idea of a "land ethic" mark the beginning of a
reconciliation of the differences between conservation
and preservation.

The book is organized in three parts. The first part
is a series of "shack sketches," arranged seasonally
as an almanac; the second, a series of "episodes"
outlining his ideas about conservation; and the
third, "The Upshot," presenting his philosophy of the
land. Born in Iowa in 1887, Leopold left the Forest
Service after nineteen years to join the University of
Wisconsin-Madison where he worked in the Forest
Products Research Lab and did wildlife and game
surveys throughout the US. In 1935 he was one of the
eight founding members of the Wilderness Society.
In 1927, due much to his own effort, the Aldo Leopold
Wilderness Area within the Gila National Forest in New
Mexico became the first designated Wilderness Area
in the US.

"Thinking Like a Mountain," an essay in *A Sand County
Almanac*, described a turning point in Leopold's
understanding of nature. While eating lunch with
friends on a high rim rock overlooking a rushing river,
the group saw a she-wolf and pups emerge from
the forest edge. With rifles empty and the mother
wolf down, Leopold knelt over the dying animal and
described seeing "a fierce green fire dying in her
eyes." He sensed that there was something important
that only the mountain and the wolf knew. His initial
youthful view saw fewer wolves as meaning more
deer, "but I realized then, and have known ever
since...he said that neither the Wolf nor the Mountain
agreed with such a view."

Leopold went on to describe the need for a land
ethic. Ethics, "a mode of guidance," deals first with the
relationship between individuals, and second with the
individual and their place within society. He called
for a third ethic, "a kind of community instinct in-the-
making," which included the land, all animals, and the
plants, and was founded on a single premise. Leopold
states: "the individual is a member of a community
of interdependent parts." He described a land ethic
as a basic concept of ecology that demanded an
ecological conscience, placing humans as citizens
within "land as a community." Land as a community
reflected both the diverse and necessarily inclusive
biotic population, and the implication of citizenship
that demonstrated the inherent ethical responsibilities.

Ian McHarg

*The next 100 years will determine whether humans
were a good idea.*
Bill Joy

Ian McHarg, the late Scottish landscape architect,
teacher, and self-styled crypto-pseudo-quasi-
scientist proposed a Theory of One based on the
idea of "creative fitting in health" and its antithesis, a
"reductive non-fit revealed in pathology."

McHarg proposed a "theory of one" with four parts:
Part One: The first requirement for fit is creativity.
McHarg defined creativity abstractly but specifically
as the employment of energy and matter to raise
matter and energy to higher levels of order. He uses
a forest as an example of a high level of order and
suggests that if you burn it, according to the law of
thermodynamics, no matter has been removed or
destroyed but the forest has gone to a lower level
of order. Creativity is the inverse of this. It is the
employment of energy to raise matter to a higher
level of order.

Part Two: The second requirement for this theory
is a criterion for directionality—in other words, an

indication of movement to a higher or lower level of order. Here he suggests that creativity moves from conditions of greater to lesser randomness, from simplicity to complexity, from uniformity to diversity, and from instability to stability or dynamic equilibrium. If we see a process move in this direction it is creative. Put the two together and it must follow that life seeks the most fit environment and adapts it, and itself, to a higher order.

Part Three: This by necessity must be a creative process. Survival is contingent upon finding the minimum work, maximum benefit solution. There is an aesthetic dimension to this that cannot be overlooked. Fit is not just fitting in but creatively adapting and expressing a result that inspires new adaptations.

Part Four is direct: health is the attribute that determines whether a system or process accomplishes creative fitting. McHarg used two definitions of health. The first is that health is the capability to recover from insult, and this is an adaptive criterion. The second is from the World Health Organization, which defines a healthy person as one who not only solves problems but seeks them... "any system is required to find of all environments the most fit, to adapt that environment, and to adapt itself."

In summary, an environment that enables us is creative, and can be identified as creative by its adaptive fit. Creative fitting is required for life, and the result is health.

Ecology and Economics
Economics, *the dismal science*.
Thomas Carlyle

As the 19th century scholar and economist Robert Malthus' warned, the degradation of the environment was the inevitable outcome of a free market society where the need to increase profit results in growth, which equals resource exploitation, which equals resource exhaustion. Influential on the thinking of Charles Darwin, Malthus studied population growth, providing ideas central to the emerging concept of natural selection. Frederick Soddy (1877), a Nobel laureate in chemistry disenchanted by the mass deaths of World War I, gave up chemistry to pursue political economy. Soddy, unsatisfied with the thinking of the day which likened the economy to a machine able to generate perpetual wealth, drew an analogy between economics and physics; to the second law of thermodynamics. Author Annie Dillard illuminates: "According to the second law of thermodynamics, things fall apart. Structures disintegrate. Buckminster Fuller hinted at the reason we are here: By creating things, by thinking up new combinations, we counteract this flow of entropy. We make new structures, new wholeness, so the universe comes out even."

But in current economic practice it has not come out even. Matter must come from energy, wealth from debt, and quoting my friend and political economist Eric Zenscey, wealth is necessarily "limited by the amount of low-entropy energy that it can sustainably suck from its environment and by the amount of high-entropy effluent from an economy that the environment can sustainably absorb." When debt exceeds the capacity of the physical and social environment, as recent events would suggest and as Malthus and Soddy predicted, correction happens through crisis. More recent work by Romanian-born economist Georgescu-Roegen models the economy on a living system, perhaps a more apt metaphor— one that makes explicit the direct relationship between the consequences of a capitalist economy, energy, and entropy, and between ecology and economy. Channeling Aristotle, polymath Noam Chomsky states that when inequality in a democratic society with a capitalist corporate economy becomes too great, there are only two options: get rid of inequality or get rid of democracy. In the meantime, it behooves us to think that we might be better to make less things and more sustainable combinations, so the universe comes out ahead.

Buildings as Nature-Scape

CHARLES MCKINNEY

As the constructed environment supplants the natural one, buildings can:

Welcome the public use of the exterior: sitting on the steps, walking on the roofs, walking under the overhangs, climbing on the walls.

Continue the gestures and efforts started by other buildings: connect in ways that create beneficial microclimates, continue circulation routes, provide habitat.

Consider how they affect the scene: join the chorus, amplify the character of the place, block bad views and sounds, conceal service areas, serve as protectors of the ambiance.

Ennoble life in public: provide special places: to watch a sunset, view the stars, encourage joyful childhood exploration, provide places for celebratory rituals and imaginative courtship.

Incorporate habitat: support generous amounts of soil and water, provide niches that encourage habitation by birds and bugs, include surfaces that support the growth of microorganisms, moss and lichens.

Provide close contact with the fragrances of nature: plants, flowers, soil, wood, damp stone, wet leaves. Provide places of quiet, of sunshine and breeze, of safe repose for a nap, to court with privacy, to lounge or roll in the grass, to watch butterflies, birds, fish and wind ripple water, watch the rain, the snow, the hail, the wind....

Provide places of safe refuge from fire, flood, hurricanes and tornadoes. Accommodate the inevitable ebb and flow of flood and fire.

New York City Parks has a history of structures that serve landscape functions such as Bethesda terrace in Central Park, where stairs and a tunnel under the transverse road evoke a Moorish palace and create a setting for romance.

Bushwick inlet park, designed by Kiss + Cathcart Architects and landscape architects Starr Whitehouse, lives up to the Nature-Scape aspiration. Their design accommodated a soccer field, a maintenance building with vehicle parking, a community room, a playground, public bathrooms, an imaginative landscape, and naturalized shoreline. They made the building a hill. It covered the parking, buffered industrial buildings, provided an overlook for the community room, and turned the park's focus to the River with an elevated loggia that accommodates family celebrations, weddings, and sunset watching.

The Alchemy of Regeneration

JULIE BARGMANN

All land is not created equal. Toxic industries in and on the edge of town degrade the environment and threaten human and wildlife health. Homes and businesses alongside polluting urban corridors become substandard. Contaminants from everyday consumption lurk beneath inner city neighborhoods. This uncomfortable reality remains largely hidden, cordoned off by chain-link fences and buried beneath the inscrutable data of environmental assessments. When hazards are revealed, conventional remediation techniques hide the contamination again. As they say in the trade, "cap and cover" (with a green veneer) or "hog and haul" (to a landfill in someone else's backyard)—anything to camouflage the operations from communities.

An alternative way to address the derelict terrain of noxious legacies calls for building an infrastructure of regeneration. This solution goes beyond unidimensional engineered attempts and introduces dualistic strategies in which science-based remediation technologies are powered by socially driven operations at the scale of civic systems. The biological treatment (bioremediation) of hazardous byproducts becomes part of the continuum of industrial production and—when transparent and participatory—creates a social and cultural landscape of transformation. This form of alchemy shoves entropic demise toward regenerative futures. It doesn't turn lead into gold; it simply renders the heavy metal non-toxic—which, to some kid living on the poisoned soils of New Orleans, is more precious than gold.

Focused on polluted industrialized sites and degraded urban landscapes across the country, D.I.R.T. studio

(DIRT)[1], since its founding in 1992, has experimented with conjoining the science of remediation with the social imperatives of environmental health. By combining the expertise of multiple disciplines, DIRT projects rely on the necessary chemistry to offer more than a stop-gap correction; the goal is always to build a robust system for creating anew. Three projects, described briefly below, explore design propositions that laminate the scientific with the social. The fusion happens via landscape interventions that are as much action plans as they are site plans. Ultimately, regenerative operational systems, implemented at the scale of the city and even the region, are the only match for our industrial past.

Mig Mud: Getting the lead out

In New Orleans, a deadly heavy metal conspired with climate change when hurricane Katrina hit, one disaster on top of another. When the storm landed in 2005, thirty percent of inner-city youth were affected by lead poisoning, the second highest rate in the nation. To address leaded soils citywide, the proposed project Operation: Pay dirt/Big Mud[2] deployed scientific methods and community action in a symbiotic relationship to rebuild New Orleans from below the ground up.

DIRT helped reveal the "geography of lead," spatializing data provided by a local soil-contamination expert. Our team then concocted a treatment recipe, the primary ingredients being phosphate amendments and clean fill. The phosphates (fish-derived apatite compounds or biosolids from waste water treatment) bond with lead to form pyromorphite, which is insoluble in water, neutralizing the toxicity. As the delivery medium and

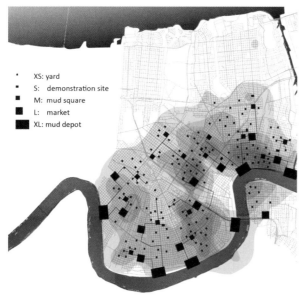

BIG MUD (Action Plan): map showing extent of leaded soils overlaid with the proposed, nested scales of the city-wide landscape regeneration strategy.

Ford River Rouge Plan (Remediation Gardens): montage of the phytoremediation beds with coking operations in the background.

supplement for the lead-locking additive, clean river sediment, which abounds in New Orleans, was added to create an enriched Mississippi River mud. Mixed in-situ with leaded soils, the phosphate amendments work to make a healthy landscape.

The multi-scaled implementation plan calls for the training and employment of residents to collect, deliver, and install the ingredients city-wide at sites that range in size from extra-large distribution hubs, which we called Mud Depots, to smaller Mud Markets, akin to neighborhood garden centers. Properties of many dimensions, freed of the heavy metal over time, claimed as community resources for a lead-safe city, could evolve into a renewed infrastructure of equitably distributed assets.

River Rouge: New Industry Standarts

At the Ford River Rouge Plant, in Dearborn, Michigan, the first integrated automotive manufacturing facility produced Model Ts and Mustangs and a fleet of contaminants. Thousands toured the Rouge not hearing

that lurid last part of the story. Our design team[3] asked Ford to acknowledge and address the pollution, then be transparent about it. In fact, we conceived of the process of remediation as an extension of the industrial legacy they were so proud of.

Here the much-needed attention to the scientific potential and social aspects of the environmental dilemma were complicated by the corporate context. Could clean dirt become, in effect, part of an auto giant's production line? Could the open display of remediation science in action help spawn an operational as well as cultural shift for industry as a whole? DIRT's focus turned to the former coking ovens where soils were poisoned with PAHs (polyaromatic hydrocarbons), contaminants that could be addressed via phytoremediation (treatment with plants). The science had to be force-fed: Ford's environmental department wanted to do business as usual, namely, haul the tainted soil to a landfill. But the idea of "remediation gardens" prevailed, and a specialist in phytoremediation eagerly brought his laboratory out

Design with Life

Vintondale Reclamation Park (AMD Passive Treatment Basins): view of project construction from above, the excavation of the basins for the acid mine drainage passive treatment system.

into the open field. The gardens were an intentional cultural reference, aimed to imbue them with social meaning beyond their scientific purpose. Open to the public, the data-producing phyto-beds juxtaposed with the preserved coke ovens in the background almost begged for another Diego Rivera fresco of our conflicted relationship with industry.

Vintondale: Coal country chemistry

Like hundreds of post-mining towns across coal country, Vintondale, in southwestern Pennyslvania, was surrounded by piles of mine refuse and streams that flowed bright orange with acid-mine drainage (AMD). AMD occurs when rain and ground water inundate and then burst out of mine tunnels; laden with heavy metals, the flow coats streambeds—3400 miles of them in Pennsylvania alone—rendering the waterways lifeless. Addressing this regional environmental disaster, our design team[4] framed the remediation initiative as finishing the work of ancestors. Conceptually and practically, the science of passive AMD treatment would be the next step in

the production of the steel-making ingredient, coke. And constructing these systems could employ the next generation.

The 40-acre floodplain at Vintondale was designed to become a giant ecological washing machine, integrated with a local community park and in full view of visitors traveling along the regional "ghost town" trail. The biological treatment was based on a SAPS (sequential alkaline producing system), a progression of basins constructed of limestone, augmented by mushroom compost, alternating anaerobic and aerobic processes. Metals are captured, the pH is elevated, then the cleansed water is released into the stream, headed toward better health. With the prototype of the Vintondale Reclamation Park built, the hope has been for this approach to multiply into a regional infrastructure of regeneration.

Double Duty

Environmental issues always carry social implications. The two are inseparable. By the same token, design solutions are not singular but rather contain both scientific and human elements. My role reaches far beyond pure form-making. I view myself as a sort of choreographer, attempting to conjoin the scientific with the social. My goal—in fact, my charge—is to create industrial-strength socio-ecological systems to take on the dirty dirt of Earth.

---

1 Based in Charlottesville, Virginia, Founder and Principal of D.I.R.T. studio, Bargmann has collaborated with multi-disciplinary teams of architects, scientists, historians and artists to build regenerative landscapes across the US. www.dirtstudio.com.

2 Operation Paydirt was the brainchild of conceptual artist Mel Chin; collaboration with Dr. Howard Mielke, research scientist with specialization in lead; the Big Mud Action Plan was the implementation arm of the project led by DIRT.

3 Ford River Rouge project led by William McDonough + Partners with DIRT and NelsonByrdWoltz, landscape architects; Cahill, engineers; Dr. Larry Lankton, historian; Dr. Clayton Rugh, phytoremediation specialist.

4 Vintondale Reclamation Park, under the initiative AMD + ART, was spearheaded by Dr. T Alan Comp; team members included DIRT and Robert Deason, hydrogeologist; Stacy Levy, artist; AmeriCorps volunteers.

Resilience

MARGIE RUDDICK

Urban Garden Room,
Steven Yavanian

Resilient landscapes do not exist in a vacuum, but rather engage a dynamic web of life. Resilient design encompasses dramatic spatial scales, from a room to an entire watershed; time frames, from the deep time of geology to the nanosecond of the internet; and activities, from foraging to industrial lumbering operations. Pull on any of these threads, and a ripple will be seen throughout.

Our work as landscape planners spans these scales, yet the general rubric of "sustainable design" by which projects are currently measured, often fails to address the complexities of resiliency. We seek a standard that is more tangible and comprehensive, that can be applied across scales and disciplines: a standard of livability. Aldo Leopold commented on such as standard when he stated: *"A thing is right when it tends to preserve the integrity, stability and beauty of the biotic community.* By that measure, how does a project support life, promote greater health, promote the idea that all landscapes, even interior or hard urban spaces, work on some level as habitat? What follows are brief descriptions of three of our projects, of vastly different physical and temporal scales and complexity. By approaching each project with the common denominator of livability, we are creating finely articulated subsystems within larger systems, orienting us as interconnected organisms within the scale of the planet.

A Room | A Day | A Person

Small spaces are, obviously, limited in their scope and impact but can have a measurable effect on the wellbeing—and thus resiliency—of the people who inhabit and visit them. When the Durst Organization asked us to design the Urban Garden Room, the

signature green space in New York City's first LEED Platinum building, the brief was to make something iconic that felt "natural." Rather than looking to forms that would simply convey an idea of nature, we looked at landscapes in the "natural" world that built on similar constraints: tall and skinny spaces, with low light levels. Drawing on our experience of the Fern Canyons of Humboldt County, California, we decided to design a vertical green space, recognizing that planting at the ground level of the space would be problematic. We designed a series of sculptural forms planted with many different species of ferns, vines, and other herbaceous plants.

Visitors to the Urban Garden Room report changes in the way their bodies feel and respond; their breathing slows, they talk quietly, if at all, and they feel less stressed. We cannot overstate the impact this scale of design can have in way a person feels daily, the way they interact and cohere as a community, and the way they take ownership and assume stewardship of their own environment

A Street | A Lifetime | A Community

At a larger scale, our work includes designing parks and streetscapes which, through mitigating the noxious effects of noise, air, and water pollution, the hazards of poorly planned circulation, and the alienating effects of placelessness, make the environment measurably and qualitatively better. The effect also reorients people to the place they occupy in the natural world, even in the middle of a busy urban boulevard, helping people to grasp that they exist as part of a dynamic process, and not in a static space.

The reinvention of the entry point to Long Island City and the Borough of Queens was, until recently, a prohibitive tangle that was simply not livable: acres of degraded hard surface, a chaotic array of parking, driving lanes for buses, trucks, and cars, all overshadowed by the aging overhead elevated rails and stations serving several subway lines. The multiple and sometimes conflicting modes of transport were not coordinated with the needs of pedestrians to cross the spaces; the frequency of traffic fatalities led to Queens Plaza being dubbed the "Boulevard of Death."

Our redesign of Queens Plaza, leading a team of artists, architects, engineers, and other specialists including Marpillero Pollak Architects and the artist Michael Singer, reinvented Queens Plaza as a green refuge that operates as a network of different distinct spaces, arteries, and veins. Every part of the landscape serves multiple purposes: easing navigation through the site, providing places for rest and gathering, mitigating noise, air and water pollution. The intensively layered native plantings create human-scaled spaces, filter and cleanse storm water on the site (recharging ground water and reducing the volume of piped storm water), scrub the air, and dampen the noise of traffic and overhead trains.

The new landscape made a previously unlivable district of the city more livable for not only the people who live and work there, but also the ecologies that are enhanced by the green infrastructure. The landscape knits together what was adverse—infrastructure, traffic, speed—in a green network that allows each of these to exist without threatening the integrity of the whole; in fact, the aggregation of all of these within a green matrix has created a dynamic environment where there is no hierarchy about better or worse functions—everything has its place.

A Neighborhood | A Century | A Metropolis

Our work with Resilient by Design, a regional project focused on providing preventive solutions to sea level rise for the San Francisco Bay Area, examines what design interventions can affect the sustained livability of areas at risk of flooding. The project asks designers to envision projects that go beyond conventions of "sustainable design," to link equity and economic opportunity to the continued ability of ecological systems to thrive. As Amitav Ghosh frames the problem: "The climate crisis is also a crisis of culture, and thus of imagination." In other words, in order to address climate change, we need to invent a new language of practice.

The San Francisco Bay Delta watershed covers more than 75,000 square miles, from the mouth of the Bay to the Western Slope of the Sierras. Multiple ecosystems, land uses, and cultures vie for this landscape. The Bay sits squarely in the middle of an area at risk for devastation due to sea level rise, earthquake, fires, or drought, accelerated by unchecked anthropogenic environmental degradation. It is easy, from our perspective of human time, to consider the creation of San Francisco Bay a natural process, and to consider human habitation of the region a negative force, but a nuanced examination of the area reveals a complex story.

The San Francisco Bay formed with the melting glaciers at the end of the last ice age, over 10,000 years ago. But that is recent history compared to the story of gold. Over 50 million years ago, rivers containing gold, spewed onto a tropical plain at the

West Oakland, MRL

Queens Plaza, Sam Oberter

edge of the continent. With subduction, this plain eventually tilted up to form the Sierras, bringing the ancient river beds with it. Miners discovered gold in the hills only a few millennia after the formation of the Bay and washed the ancient riverbeds with high pressure hoses which released the gold, as well as sediment, in massive flows. The sediment was flushed into the Bay, forming a new layer of mud. The result greatly expanded the tidal marshes and mudflats and has—paradoxically—helped protect the shoreline from sea level rise by raising the elevation and buffering wave energy and storm surges. Since the 1850's, development pressure transformed much of the tidal marsh into landfill or salt ponds, all but eliminating the native salt marsh vegetation. The massive destruction of the Bay drove environmentalists to fight for new legislation protecting the bay from more artificial fill as well as fine sediments.

Today we find ourselves in a quandary of government regulations around sedimentation and restoration. The marshes are drowning because of the lack of sediment flows into the bay but adding sediment to help with accretion faces complex regulatory hurdles. Reading the evolution of the Bay ecology as an intersection of tectonic shifts, watercourses, migrations of wildlife and humans, economies, and culture can

help set up a non-binary framework for envisioning the future, in which all of the above are considered agents in creating livable environments.

Our design approach addresses these complex systems by creating a layered landscape, proposing an interconnected system of infrastructure, development, and ecology that overlaps stratums of activity, time, and space. For instance, by undergrounding a highway and creating a new open space—including development, parks, and storm water treatment wetlands—the design addresses the current neighborhood issue of air pollution, the regional issue of housing, and the future issue of the Bay Bridge flooding due to sea level rise. By removing a barrier between the neighborhood and water, the design also creates new connections from the neighborhood to the waterfront, strengthening the relationship between people and the Bay. This approach puts life at the center of design.

Surfaces of Urban Life:
Design opportunities for addressing climate and comfort across scales

FORREST MEGGERS

While we have achieved unprecedented infrastructural feats, technical developments, and increased prosperity, our urbanity has also created the grandest challenges we have ever faced. The societal successes that enabled our massive urban expansion to have simultaneously enabled our intellectual capabilities to recognize these problems. We can now characterize and predict with confidence the very real and dire consequences of unchecked resource consumption and environmental degradation. The urban climate is full of dangerous positive feedback loops that models show are driving conditions to be less and less conducive to life (Meggers et al. 2016; Bruelisauer et al. 2014; Allegrini, Dorer, and Carmeliet 2012; Salata et al. 2016).

But we don't create solutions by developing models or by disseminating the science and statistics of climate change, urban heat islands, and ecosystem contamination. We must design solutions to these problems. With a significant cohort of people disinterested in scientific reason, our solutions must not simply react to those scientifically defined motivations. They must be creative beacons that enable new paradigms on a tangible level that broadly engages the community. We can combine solutions to perceivable goals like beauty and comfort with those derived more abstractly like climate change (Bruelisauer and Berthold 2015). The surfaces of our urban infrastructure and, more importantly, our urban

living ecology must be recognized as an underutilized actor with great potential to affect paradigm changes. Our understanding of the dynamics of the built environment and its impact and interface with the environment has never been more important. Buildings are constantly trapping heat from the sun, utilizing high value generated energy, and rejecting heat into the environment. Dealing with these dynamics leads buildings to be the largest sector of greenhouse gas emissions, but also implicates them as a major source of the urban heat island. In our work at the CHAOS lab at Princeton, we investigate energy exchanges and explore the thermal interfaces that are directly perceptible to the public they face (Teitelbaum and Meggers 2017). These are clearly mediated through the spaces created by the buildings both inside and out. Although the people living inside a building certainly experience space, the perception of comfort and the thermal condition imbued upon those people has far less to do with space than most consider. Surfaces matter.

We recognize buildings primarily by their surfaces, yet we believe we aren't in contact with them without touching them. But building surfaces are actually in constant exchange with their occupants and with the surfaces in and around them. This includes both the dynamic living people inside as well as the ecology surrounding them. Any surface above absolute zero emits radiation in the form of photons—no different than the light we see from the sun—just with a bit less energy. We don't see these photons in the visible spectrum, but we do experience the thermal energy they exchange. The recent rise in thermal imaging has provided unprecedented visualization of a new world of surface emission rather than surface illumination, and a new ability to design sensation and perception of temperature. The infrared radiation that surfaces emit is a loss of energy and the received radiation is a gain. Therefore, any cool surface will be heated by any surface facing it that is warmer. Three design opportunities thereby emerge, from the scale of the human to buildings and to urban environments:

1) considering the warm human surface and its radiant heat losses to the surroundings as a significant portion
2) considering the ability to activate building surfaces to manipulate thermal environments without requiring massive conditioning of air
3) considering the urban scale exchanges the role cooler ecological systems to mitigate excessive radiation load driving UHI and outdoor heat stress.

Humans perceive thermal comfort as relating to "air conditioning." In a typical conditioned building, half of the perceived temperature is caused by radiation from surfaces, and not from air temperature. Temperature is in fact misconceived in its role around the sensation of thermal comfort. Comfort is really just the ability of your body to most easily shed the heat released from living. All the processes in your body, from brain activity to digestion to walking, have thermodynamic energy exchanges that result in the generation of entropy and thus heat. This heat keeps your core temperature at a healthy 98.6°F, but to maintain this stasis all kinds of thermal mechanisms are at play in your body, ranging from capillary dilation to sweating and shivering.

Comfort is really the sensation that no extreme measures are being employed to maintain your nominal thermal state. So, while being "cold" is the state of losing too much heat, being "hot" is in fact not about receiving too much heat, but rather an inability to get rid of heat quickly enough. Your surface temperature varies as capillaries dilate and contract, which changes the heat transfer to the air and also the radiant exchanges to surrounding surfaces.

Temperature is again what designers immediately focus on, but the wittedness of skin and the velocity of air movement can have dramatic influences on the rate of heat loss from a person. Thermal delight is invoked by the ability to achieve drastic shifts in heat loss across a wide range of conditions from saunas to ice water. The scale of variation we can achieve just by being hot and sweaty in front of a fan or air conditioning vent is dramatic. The heat loss from the body can increase more than tenfold through evaporation and convection in normal spaces. These non-linear effects are rarely considered in architecture, and human comfort can be addressed much more effectively in design by considering them. Along with other researchers studying human comfort, we have been developing new sensing methods to better interpret the human thermal

Design with Life

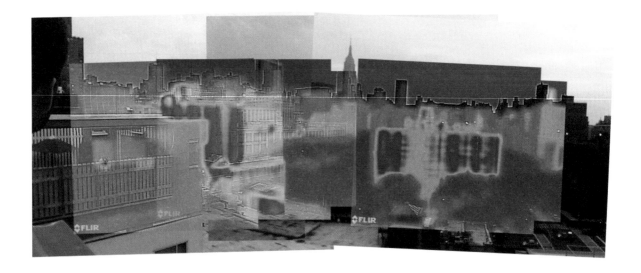

condition in the built environment (Eric Teitelbaum, Jake Read, and Forrest Meggers 2016; Abraham and Li 2016; Arens and Zhang 2006). Our new sensors can detect and interpret radiant heat exchange, and use distributed wireless networks to monitor air conditions more precisely for aspects like humidity along with temperature. These new technologies will shift the current paradigm of comfort models, from the use of empirically derived conditions for room air, to those that respond to the experience of human bodies interacting with not just the air but also the surfaces around them.

Buildings can be designed to leverage their varying temperatures around occupants as well. Interior surfaces can be activated with hydronic conditioning systems, manipulating their temperatures to vary the heat removal from the occupants in a much more precise manner than the highly turbulent mixing ventilation systems that are typically deployed and require the transport of huge quantities of air, which carries 4000 times less energy per unit volume than water. There is a reason our bodies control thermoregulation through our vascular system and not internal airways. Likewise, buildings can operate

more effectively with hydraulic systems, and, like humans, can do more than half of needed thermal exchanges by radiant exchanges, which are much easier to control than air flows. On the exterior, buildings can also learn a lot from living systems. Radiant surfaces can be tuned to absorb and emit radiation strategically to mitigate excess warming of the environment or to leverage passive solar heat. New material science has exposed ways that materials can be engineered to strategically reflect solar heat in visible wavelengths, and to only emit heat in the wavelengths for which the atmosphere is transparent, thereby dumping heat into space and creating free passive cooling (Raman et al. 2014). At the urban scale, the skyrocketing surface temperatures of our built urban fabric come from our failure to use the latent potential of water systems. As sunlight hits our urban structures it is trapped by the geometric form of the city. The sunlight beams in as a direct ray and is absorbed by our built surfaces, causing their temperatures to quickly rise and subsequently radiate out higher temperature photons than their surroundings. But those photons are not emitted in a beam, instead they are diffusely emitted, and therefore the probability that these higher energy

re-emitted photons escape the urban space is low. This causes the radiative trapping effect that drives a large portion of the urban heat island effect.

The urban heat island is often described as having an impact on air temperature, but the radiant emissions from all these very hot surfaces have a much greater impact on the heat transfer to the people in the urban environment than the increase in air temperature of a few degrees. So why does this not happen in deep ecological canyons of our forests? Because plants evaporate water. Evaporating one ounce of water is equivalent to removing the heat equivalent of changing the water temperature by 500 °C. Plants are constantly doing evapotranspiration - pumping water up to their surfaces and evaporating it through their stomata. At Princeton, we have designed and modeled new concepts for making evaporative walls of buildings (Teitelbaum et al. 2015). As part of an NSF Sustainability Research Network called the Urban Water Innovation Network, we have shared those ideas and further explored the dynamics of how access to urban green infrastructure helps mitigate radiant trapping effects, and also can dramatically reduce the heat stress imposed on urban canyon dwellers (Georgescu et al. 2014).

It is not necessary to understand the abstract science that drives these surface mechanisms from the human to building to urban scale in order to invoke the perceptible design interventions they make possible. These interventions can drive a paradigm shift toward acceptance of solutions necessary to address our scientifically characterized grand challenges, without the politics of debating the abstract scientific rationale for doing so.

Good design is implemented because it is accepted as better, not because it is understood as rational. Recognizing the role of human life and ecology as instigators of thermal condition will enable important creative solutions that make people more comfortable in the city by moving away from models that use air temperature as the only meaningful variable in our built environment. This shift will enable architects and designers to engage with surfaces in new thermal ways and, in turn, facilitate meaningful alleviation of the abstract grand challenge of emissions and climate change scenarios with solutions for something everyone can appreciate—being more comfortable.

Design with Life

Abraham, Sherin, and Xinrong Li. 2016. "Design of A Low-Cost Wireless Indoor Air Quality Sensor Network System." *International Journal of Wireless Information Networks* 23 (1):57–65. https://doi.org/10.1007/s10776-016-0299-y.

Allegrini, Jonas, Viktor Dorer, and Jan Carmeliet. 2012. "Influence of the Urban Microclimate in Street Canyons on the Energy Demand for Space Cooling and Heating of Buildings." *Energy and Buildings* 55 (December):823–32. https://doi.org/10.1016/j.enbuild.2012.10.013.

Arens, Edward A., and H. Zhang. 2006. "The Skin's Role in Human Thermoregulation and Comfort." *Center for the Built Environment.* https://escholarship.org/uc/item/3f4599hx.pdf.

Bruelisauer, Marcel, and Sonja Berthold. 2015. *Reclaiming Backlanes: Design Vision for Increasing Building Performance and Reprogramming Common Spaces.*

Bruelisauer, Marcel, Forrest Meggers, Esmail Saber, Cheng Li, and Hansjürg Leibundgut. 2014. "Stuck in a Stack – Temperature Measurements of the Microclimate around Split Type Condensing Units in a High Rise Building in Singapore." *Energy & Buildings* 71 (March):28–37. https://doi.org/10.1016/j.enbuild.2013.11.056.

Eric Teitelbaum, Jake Read, and Forrest Meggers. 2016. "Spherical Motion Average Radiant Temperature Sensor(SMART Sensor)." In . Zurich, Switzerland. https://doi.org/DOI 10.3218/3774-6_115.

Georgescu, Matei, Philip E. Morefield, Britta G. Bierwagen, and Christopher P. Weaver. 2014. "Urban Adaptation Can Roll Back Warming of Emerging Megapolitan Regions." *Proceedings of the National Academy of Sciences* 111 (8):2909–14. https://doi.org/10.1073/pnas.1322280111.

Meggers, Forrest, Gideon Aschwanden, Eric Teitelbaum, Hongshan Guo, Laura Salazar, and Marcel Bruelisauer. 2016. "Urban Cooling Primary Energy Reduction Potential: System Losses Caused by Microclimates." *Sustainable Cities and Society* 27 (November):315–23. https://doi.org/10.1016/j.scs.2016.08.007.

Raman, Aaswath P., Marc Abou Anoma, Linxiao Zhu, Eden Rephaeli, and Shanhui Fan. 2014. "Passive Radiative Cooling below Ambient Air Temperature under Direct Sunlight." *Nature* 515 (7528):540–44. https://doi.org/10.1038/nature13883.

Salata, Ferdinando, Iacopo Golasi, Roberto de Lieto Vollaro, and Andrea de Lieto Vollaro. 2016. "Urban Microclimate and Outdoor Thermal Comfort. A Proper Procedure to Fit ENVI-Met Simulation Outputs to Experimental Data." *Sustainable Cities and Society* 26 (October):318–43. https://doi.org/10.1016/j.scs.2016.07.005.

Teitelbaum, Eric, and Forrest Meggers. 2017. "Expanded Psychrometric Landscapes for Radiant Cooling and Natural Ventilation System Design and Optimization." *Energy Procedia,* CISBAT 2017 International ConferenceFuture Buildings & Districts – Energy Efficiency from Nano to Urban Scale, 122 (September):1129–34. https://doi.org/10.1016/j.egypro.2017.07.436.

Teitelbaum, Eric, Forrest Meggers, George Scherer, Prathap Ramamurthy, Louis Wang, and Elie Bou-Zeid. 2015. "ECCENTRIC Buildings: Evaporative Cooling in Constructed ENvelopes by Transmission and Retention Inside Casings of Buildings." In *6th International Building Physics Conference, IBPC 2015.* Torino, Italy: Elsevier.

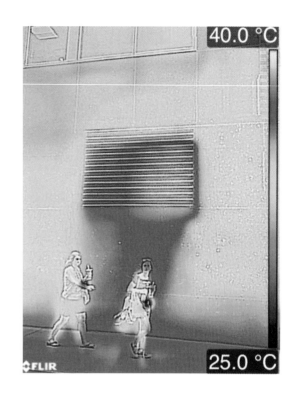

Living in The Autonomous City

DICKSON DESPOMMIER

Cities' origins were coincident with the rise of agriculture, some 10-12,000 year ago. As they grew, these densely occupied areas rapidly evolved into a variety of functional zones (e.g., retail, residential, manufacturing, entertainment). To make room, inner city farms relocated to the surrounding countryside, where they have remained to this day. The built environment morphed from chockablock bazaars and rabbit warren-like commercial centers into today's bustling, mostly well-organized cities, exemplified by the likes of London, Paris, New York, and Beijing. Despite modernization catalyzed by numerous technological advances, including the advent of public health, cities still struggle with the concept of social justice. Big cities are typically stratified, each layer defined by economic status. Essential city services vary both in quality and quantity, with neighborhoods reflecting block to block differences in wealth. In order to even out the distribution of collective resources so that everyone gets their fair share, a more democratic set of organizational principles is required. The fundamental nature of the city begs to be re-imagined, then re-invented.

Even the generally acknowledged best cities (i.e., most habitable) have not yet coordinated all their essential municipal needs—energy, water, food, transportation, commerce, residential, parks and recreation—into a mutually dependent, efficient, pollution-free overarching system of integrated activities. In contrast, the complex mechanisms that unite the many functions of Earth's ecosystems—resulting in nutrient recycling, resource conservation, biodiversity, and

adaptation to a constantly changing environment (i.e., resiliency)—are still hard at work, ensuring continuity of energy flow from one trophic level to the next, year in and year out. If we could somehow translate long-term survival mechanisms employed by ecosystems into technological equivalents, then integrate them into the built environment, our life as urban dwellers would be more balanced, equitable, and greatly enriched. To accomplish this, we have to adopt nature as our guru.

Biomimicry is a relatively new applied science, currently championed by Jenine Benyus, director of the Biomimicry Institute, in Missoula, Montana. Its principals are straightforward and easy to grasp. Closely observe nature and then apply what is learned to our own world. This sounds simple enough but knowing how and what to observe and when to do so is the key to success. The ecological sciences have been around for nearly 100 years, during which time a wealth of data (mostly observational) have been accumulated and systematically analyzed. We now know all the important essentials of ecosystem functions, including how they behave under stress. The time has come to apply this knowledge to the future of the built environment. No new technologies are needed to allow a city to recover all waste streams and recycle them back into the fabric of its infrastructure. No new technologies are needed to allow a city to re-configure municipal services so that they are mutually supportive and robust. What is required is a strong political will with a practical set of plans to go forward with the support of hundreds of millions of urban dwellers.

Energy

The passive capture of energy from wind, solar and geothermal sources is now a common feature of many countries' master plan to become independent of the use of fossil fuels as energy resources. A good example is Costa Rica, powered 100% by a combination of wind, solar, and geothermal energy. Denmark has declared that by 2050 it will be powered only by wind and biofuels and is nearly 80% of the way to achieving this goal as of this writing. Many other countries, including Scotland, Sweden and Finland, have made similar commitments to converting to so-called *green* energy sources. The advent of transparent solar cells for use as windows in domestic and commercial buildings should facilitate the generation of enormous amounts of clean electricity in densely populated regions where sunlight is abundant. Solar farms have also become a viable alternative to traditional sources of energy generation, with the United States, India, China and Germany leading the way. Some small cities are now powered 100% by renewable energy sources—Burlington, Vermont is the largest city in the United States to do so, but it is only a matter of time before the first major city declares itself completely free of the use of fossil fuels. Chicago has set the goal to be 100% free of oil and natural gas for energy generation by 2025. It is probable that sooner rather than later, every major city around the world will do the same and permanently get off the fossil fuel grid. The very air we breathe will rejoice.

Water – use and reuse

Water is essential for all life on earth, but at the municipal level we abuse it and mostly use it only once, then discard it. For example, New York City has an extensive freshwater acquisition system consisting of five reservoirs located some 120 miles northwest of the 8 million citizens who depend on it. Each day, they consume 1.2 billion gallons, and each day they discard nearly an equal amount of treated liquid municipal wastewater into the Hudson River estuary.

Remediation of wastewater into drinking water is a technology that is both safe and easy to integrate into the management of a large metropolis. San Diego, California already does so. Many other large cities get at least a portion of their drinking water from reclaimed wastewater.

Municipal waste streams will always be produced, but carbon-rich solids will be collected and turned into energy by some form of high temperature pyrolysis. Dried sludge harvested from blackwater is an excellent feedstock for plasma arc gasification, for example. Solid wastes will be kept to a minimum, as is already the case for many small to medium-size municipalities (e.g., Linköping, Sweden has implemented and sustained a 1% landfill waste management strategy since 2001). The recycling of manufactured goods will follow rules first outlined in Cradle To Cradle, by McDounough and Braugart (North Point Press, 2002).

Food

Most agricultural economists acknowledge that the current global food system is broken and is solely predicated on profit and national trade agreements rather than human need for a sustainable, safe food supply. Protectionist regulations, designed to enable in-country farm interests to survive, thwart efforts to level the playing field to distribute food more equitably to those who need it most. Urban agriculture is a solution to many of those unfair practices, and if more widely applied, could make the difference regarding access to fresh, safe, healthy food items, and could solve many other problems related to public health as well.

One major example will serve to point up one of the unanticipated advantages of moving a city's food supply closer to its residents. It is estimated that over half of the world depends upon the use of human waste (feces and urine, referred to as night soil) as the sole source of fertilizer. This is because commercial fertilizers are too expensive. The upside is that we get to grow our food with something that we produce every day as the result of our biology. The downside is that using night soil enables pathogenic viruses, bacteria, and parasites to gain access to us in a straightforward fashion: by the fecal/oral via contamination of our food and drinking water. The toll that these infectious diseases exact on those living at the margins of a healthy life in all of the least developed world is staggering. Some 3.5 billion people are affected in one way or another by this insidious agricultural practice, with predictable results – malnutrition and stunting in childhood, followed by a far less productive life than would otherwise be possible. The maintenance of these unacceptable situations via this mechanism is why 47 countries are listed by the World Health Organization as least developed. Eliminating the need for having to use human waste as fertilizer has the potential to reverse this situation without the use of drugs, vaccines or other expensive medical/public health intervention strategies.

It is encouraging to witness the rise in popularity of urban farming and, in particular, farming inside buildings (referred to as controlled environment agriculture, or CEA), including vertical farms. So far, vertical farming has been adopted only by developed countries. As experience with CEA improves, affordable systems will undoubtedly emerge that can be applied to a much wider swath of humanity— those living in extreme poverty, refugees, and people displaced from their homes due to natural disasters. It has always been the case that if something is invented that enhances our ability to live a better life, most people will want to share in that benefit. Industry inevitably finds a way to make that happen; witness the evolution of the telephone, now the cell phone,

mass transit, etc. Undoubtedly, urban farming will also follow a similar pattern, since food that is safe, available 24/7, and healthy is a universal demand, regardless of economic status.

Imagine living in a world in which most of the municipal functions we currently struggle to accomplish (and pay dearly for, as well) are instead carried out by AI-driven autonomous systems. Every building, regardless of purpose, will be a small version of what the city has become: a self-contained ecosystem. Humans, and in fact all other living creatures, already function in this fashion relative to their unique microbiomes. The city will be a place where water is constantly being collected, used, then re-cycled back into the autonomous grid. Excess water will be stored and used in cooling/heating systems, greatly reducing the city's energy footprint. The term wastewater will be dropped from the city planner's dictionary and become relegated to the historical record as an example of collective excessive and insensitive human behavior. Every building will capture energy from sunlight via crystal clear solar windows, or from geothermal sources, and excess electricity stored in long-term batteries that also function as structural supports. In addition, wind power will augment solar power in structures that are taller than 5 stories.

Concrete, steel, and aluminum will become obsolete, being replaced by much cheaper, renewable resources that offer many other advantages over the current limited menu of building materials besides cost. For example, specially engineered woods have been fabricated that are stronger than concrete, fireproof, and easy to shape into forms that today would challenge even the most creative engineering firms. Wood buildings store carbon, in contrast with concrete structures which generate huge amounts of carbon dioxide during the conversion of limestone to cement. Graphene is a pure carbon building material that shows even more promise than engineered

Design with Life

woods, allowing for taller, stronger buildings to emerge into the skyline of future cities, with near inexhaustible quantities of readily available carbon sources to access.

Construction technologies will also undoubtedly become much more advanced over the next 10-30 years, allowing for the emergence and application of sophisticated 3D printing systems fully capable of making a building from scratch. Each edifice may have its own dedicated printer, with the possibility of having a finished project in which the printer is integrated into the top floor. When repairs or technology upgrades are warranted, the printer will descend to the first floor and begin the remodeling process. There will be no need to tear down or abandon anything. A city then assumes the characteristic of a "living entity", capable of evolving using AI as its "genome". Biomimicry becomes synonymous with the built environment.

Buildings that serve as residences will have dedicated CEA food production floors to accommodate its occupants' caloric needs. A few mixed-use buildings that produce edible plants for its occupants already exist (e.g., Pasona 02 in Tokyo) and have attracted the attention of developers around the world. Making sure everything works according to a master plan is the job of the central control board that oversees and manages the day-to-day operations of the city. AI has finally come of age, just in time to save the world from using up every last scrap of natural resource left unexploited by an ever-increasing human population. As the health of the urban dweller increases as the result of all these new approaches to city life, infant mortality rates will surely plummet. There are numerous examples of this happening in the less developed world, as health risks became reduced by employing rudimentary public health measures. When the day finally arrives when all of us benefit equally from living in the autonomous city, the human species will shift its attention to finally assuming a central role as a positive force of nature in our small part of the universe simply by leaving the rest of the natural world alone.

"It is not the strongest of the species that survives, nor the most intelligent that survives. It is the one that is most adaptable to change".
Charles Darwin

Restricted Access: Moving Off the Grid

SUZANNE ANKER

Below: Remote sensing series. Plaster, pigment, resin, glass petri dish, 4 x 4 x 2'' each.

Folloging page:
Remote sensing series. Plaster, pigment and resin, glass petri dish, 4 x 4 x 2''

Today, voguish words such as 'ecology' and 'environment' are so commonly used in public discourse as to seem colloquial, if not downright mundane—almost stripped of both their meaning and import. They summon stereotypical images of pot-smoking, sandal-wearing, under-bathed earthy types engaged in wilderness treks and organic gardening. However, with the benefit of historical perspective, one can look back fairly to 1962 and the publishing of Silent Spring, by Rachel Carson, as a defining and catalytic moment that augured modern environmentalism into more mainstream cognizance.

Ecology, a term coined by Ernst Haeckel in the 19th century, refers to the symbiotic interactions between life forms, their communities, and their interlocking environments. In this sense, nothing goes unnoticed. Although not quite the Butterfly Effect, this supposition considers the synergy of all actions. With the seminal example of *Silent Spring*, Carson shone a light on chemical industries that were peddling their wares during and after WWII. While DDT's ubiquitous applications included the showering upon of children at public swimming pools and Japanese-American citizens interred in repatriation camps, Carson targeted the disastrous effects afflicting the offspring of songbirds—hence the title *Silent Spring*. Carson's influential work introduced a new term into the lexicon: *biocides,* referring to the unchecked proliferation of pesticides into the environment. The publication precipitated a watershed moment and paradigm shift that still ripples throughout society today. Not uncoincidentally, chemical companies have

swollen their profits by acquiring controlling interests in seed companies—at times altering genetic codes while at other times patenting their query.

Is the sum of the parts larger than the whole? How do we account for excess, contamination, and the loss of habitat? What unintended consequences abound for the natural world of which we are a part? Undertakings to dominate and control nature have long been part of the modernist perspective, although counter endeavors along the way have attempted to dismantle such hubris. At this juncture, where rapid ecological change is ubiquitous, efforts are finally being made to review lessons from the past, and to take spirited action in the form of a cultural counter revolution that could, in effect, move off the grid.

For almost every scientific hypothesis, a cultural counterpoint exists. In our age of pixels, bits, and bytes, images have acquired a novel and unique power. Both computational and aesthetic barometers link contemporary culture with laboratory life—in its

Design with Life

liminality and ambiguity. Laboratory life can now be considered within terms of *new representational spaces* accounting for alternating methods of discovery and analysis. While the epistemological underpinnings of the ways in which visual culture and the biosciences form poly-disciplines requiring innovative if not radical perspectives, are alternate geographies underway? At this time of rising ecological distress, novel emergent solutions to ward off toxicity and impending doom require a data bank for developing further ethical perspectives. An essential question: what exactly is the new geography and how can it be mapped?

As an example, remote sensing refers to new digital technologies that can picture locations that are either too toxic or too inaccessible to visit. Utilizing state-of-the-art satellite data, remote sensing apparatuses are being employed to computationally picture such spaces. As an extension of digital photography, these images garner information electronically in order to forego onsite investigation. A further example: the fabrication of my series of sculptures, *Remote Sensing*

(2015-2017), commences with two-dimensional virtual models employing a technique called *displacement mapping*. The resulting files are used to construct physical objects using a 3D printer. The internal software program determines the deposition of variegated color applied to the structure as it is being printed, one layer at a time. Dark areas are extruded less than bright colors, keeping in tone with the ways in which pictorial spaces are generally perceived. These micro-landscapes offer the viewer a top-down topographic effect assembled by streaming zeros and ones. In these rapid, prototype sculptures, numbers become form and forms become numbers. Each configuration of these works takes the geometry of a circle (inspired by Jules Petri's glassware dish) and fuses the divide between the domains of art and science. As geography is digitally remapped into data sets, access to territories merge the urban with the desert—eliciting a worldview without political or tribal borders. Such opportunities are within our purview and provide us the agency with which to observe an expanding picture of the world as governed by the sovereignty of nature and urgent human action.

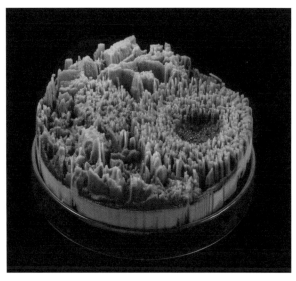 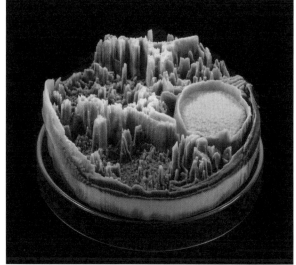

Bodies, Bread, and their Architecture

ORKAN TELHAN

From agriculture to farming, animal husbandry to GMOs, humans have been manipulating living organisms for thousands of years. What we grow, domesticate, and consume has driven the proliferation of many species over time and pushed thousands of others to extinction. Since the second half of the 20th century, on the other hand, thanks to the advancement in biotechnologies, the manipulation of the living has reached unprecedented levels. Today, we edit the genes of mosquitos so that they can wipe out their own ecosystems; program artificial cells to give them agency so they can travel inside our bodies to deliver vaccines or cancer drugs. We use cells like mini factories to grow anything from insulin to milk and silk proteins for making novel materials. Advances in biotechnologies, genetic engineering, and synthetic research are taking us beyond scientific discovery of or curiosity about how and what nature has evolved over millennia. They become the measures of ambition and capacity to design organisms, plants, animals—including ourselves—at every scale, showing what else is possible outsides the confines of evolution.

The ability to design biology—whether it is engineering a single celled organism or transforming entire ecosystems like the human gut—is also not reserved to life sciences, bioengineering, or medical fields. This new space is becoming increasingly accessible to all kinds of design fields from architecture to product design, fashion, and culinary arts. The means and ends of designing living bodies is gaining diversity in terms of meanings, applications, and questions as the

Microbial simid diet.

tools and knowledge become more widely acceptable (Telhan 2017).

In this essay, I will outline a design framework to approach the space and body of the living and provide examples of how biological design can integrate a diverse set of methodologies from different design disciplines and be practiced by non-specialists.

Microbial simid diet.

The Body of the Living

The body of an organism is space governed by interiority. This is an unfamiliar world for traditional design disciplines that are used to the ocular, static, solid, and visual means of representation. It is rather a dark, fluidic, constantly moving space that demands a different type of visibility. This is the place for molecules, cells, microorganisms, and many other types of chemical constructs that work with different logics of assembly, agency, tectonics, and program.

This interiority defies geometry, form, and more familiar measures of abstraction. It is rather calculated stoichiometrically—through ratios of chemical reactions—based on how compounds interact with each other. Thus, the images of this interior body are often rendered out of large data sets by algorithms. The tools of the trade are gene sequencers, microfluidic chips, real-time PCRs, flow cytometers, spectrophotometers, and so on. Instead of imaging individual cells or microorganisms, these tools tend to capture and enable dynamic interactions between enzymes, metabolites, and different forms of chemical energy. They register molecular events, trace microbial signatures and DNA fragments, and calculate chemical differentials over time.

What it means to design in this interiority may mean many different things at different scales. An example will help us to illustrate.

The Body of the Bread: Dough

Few human artifacts capture the complex interaction across agriculture, microorganisms, environment, and culinary culture like bread. It embodies a relationship with soil, air, fire, and water. And over thousands of years it is designed into many different forms, with different ingredients, across vast geographies (Myhrvold and Migoya, 2017).

Bread can be made by everyone, everywhere. At its most basic form, the bread dough is made by mixing flour with water and by adding a leavening agent (like yeast or baking soda), which can produce gas (CO_2) to raise its volume. The final batter is then baked to turn the raw matter into food.

The body of the bread is a type of foam. It is a protein matrix made mostly out of two types of protein *gliadin* and *glutenin* that come from wheat. Both proteins dissolve when the flour meets water. During the kneading process, when the baker stretches the dough, the proteins extend and form a matrix that will eventually trap the gas bubbles that create the frothy structure of the foam.

Giedion, in *Mechanization Takes Command,* writes extensively about the efforts of industrialization in bread making starting from the late 18th Century (Giedion 1948). Being a staple food in almost every diet and culture, bread making has gone through many innovations, from automated kneading instruments and oven designs to the design of its biological matter, the yeast. The desire to make faster rising dough inspired significant effort towards exploring bread's relationship with various gas making agents, which not only increase its volume but also make it soft and chewy. As noted by Giedion, industrialists quickly realized that faster bread production with processes that inflated the dough with the use of carbonic acid, for instance, did not necessarily yield tastier or most desirable bread. Bread made with yeast, on the other hand, offered additional flavors and nutritional benefits. So, in the1900s, the desire for mechanization shifted towards optimizing the biological matter, using faster rising and more durable yeast. Inventing ways to package and deliver live yeast cultures and the ability to ship instant yeast in powder form for mass consumption have been significant milestones in bread making. They allowed fresh bread to be readily accessible in war zones and solved major nutritional challenges in battlefields. But most importantly, they turned everyone into a potential bread maker, as yeast can now be sold to everyone, everywhere.

The Body of the Organism: Yeast

Today, our capacity to transform the biological matter of bread has advanced beyond instant yeast. *Saccharomyces cerevisiae,* commonly known as baker's yeast, can be designed (transformed) by introducing foreign DNA through its cell walls with electricity or heat shock. The DNA can introduce new genes which can program the organism to synthesize new compounds from antioxidants to neurotransmitters, vitamins, or vanilla flavor. Each yeast cell can work like small factory. It can ferment

MDS yeast design process.

the sugars in the dough and produce carbon dioxide, water, ethanol, and other desired chemicals.

Yeast is typically mixed into the dough in powder (where it is dormant) or liquid form through seed cultures. Genetically designed yeast can be cultured in liquid and mixed directly into the flour before the kneading process, so they can be evenly dispersed inside new dough. When the dough is left for rest, the yeast can grow, double up their quantity every hour, and produce the gas that will create the foam. One can also mix yeast that will make custom compounds with unmodified strains that are more effective for gas production.

Baking usually kills all of the active yeast inside the dough. So, whether it is genetically modified or not, no live cultures remain alive at the end, making the bread rather safe for consumption. However, if the desire is to introduce the yeast to the human body alive, the organisms can be encapsulated in special capsules to withstand the high temperatures of baking or the stomach acid. This is how specially designed yeast can be introduced to the human gut similar to a probiotic and become part of its gut flora.

The Body of the Human: The Gut & its Diet
Our guts host billions of live organisms at a given moment. This colonization starts while we are in the wombs of our moms and ends when we decay in soil. Depending on where we are born, what we eat, and our exposure to pharmaceuticals, we host tens of different types of species in our gut, which regulate our body by making chemicals that alter our mental states, immune system, and digestion. These microorganisms are not only essential to maintain health but also key for introducing new capabilities to our bodies.

We explored the potential of creating new interactions with our gut by creating a novel microbiome diet, which shows the potential of how far we can transform our own bodies starting from the bodies of the organisms that inhabit us. For the 3rd Istanbul Design Biennial (theme: "Are We Human?"), we took a type of traditional Turkish bread, simit, and designed its dough using the Microbial Design Studio (MDS) (Telhan 2016).

Simits are sesame encrusted dough rings similar to bagels. Similar to bread dough, simit dough typically consists of flour, water, salt, yeast, with the addition of sesame and molasses. Simits have been part of the Turkish urban food culture since the 17th century, with slight variations in form, flavor, texture, sweetness, and hardness based on location. Simits from Rize, a city on the northern east coast, are known for their dryness and exceptional hardness. They do not have any sesame on them. Ankara simits, on the other hand, have a dark brown color and a much-roasted taste compared to those from Istanbul.

We interrogated what it means to design new simits and a simit diet in light of recent research in life sciences and microbiome research. We used combinatorial and parametric design methods to design a microbial diet based on protocols described in scientific literature. The diet included thirty simits with five different types of ingredients. These ranged from simple ingredients (prebiotics) to feed the existing gut microorganisms and increase their life span, to the addition of novel genetically modified organisms (live GMOs) encapsulated in heat-resistant capsules to withstand baking.

For instance, one simit included microorganisms obtained from the fecal matter of a transgender person who would be considered "skinny." As research in mice and humans show, a continuous exposure to the organisms of a foreign gut flora can potentially transform one's own gut microbiota and therefore result in transferring the same characteristics. We used the opportunity to bring together the promise of the scientific research with a moral dilemma and asked the audiences if they would like to become "skinny" like that LGBT person. In Turkey, the perception of the LGBT population is highly challenged by conservative and nationalist sentiments. The desire to become "skinny" went beyond desiring a typical body image. The idea of the microbial transfer opened up a series of other questions about the nature of queer identity and whether the audience is receptive to queerness on the microbial level.

Other simits raised questions about the extent to which we are willing to transform our bodies by consuming live GMOs and lesser known probiotics which can synthesize compounds to give us sharper focus, mental stability, or better memory retention. As the research beyond the synthesis of these compounds are still in their early stages, we presented the simit designs mostly for their potential and focused on communicating how one can design the dough and the baking process of the simit at home, once the scientific knowledge is verified and approved for human consumption.

Throughout the design process of the diet, we used MDS as our design and prototyping tool to carry out experiments in an automated way. We designed the microbial contents of the dough first in software by specifying different types of DNA to be inserted into yeast to give them additional capabilities (i.e., making vitamins or flavors). MDS inserted the DNA into the yeasts and incubated them inside disposable syringes under specific culturing conditions to provide the organisms with specific temperature, media, and PH settings. MDS was also used to culture yeast and different species of bacteria with each other to create novel symbiotic relations. We could grow eight designs with different parameters in parallel and let the system pick the best outcome based on preferred selection criteria. When the organisms arrive to a desired quantity, the platform post-processed the designs so that they could be mixed in with the remaining ingredients of the dough.

MDS uses algorithms and microorganisms within a feedback loop. Set design criteria based, for example, on taste and nutrition preferences, and let the platform propose a number of candidate solutions. The process is similar to nature's evolutionary mechanisms except here it is directed by human preferences. This directed evolution is computationally programmed and simulated in software and then realized in hardware. Designs that fail inside the microorganisms are detected by the platform and reported back to the software.

Multiple MDSs can be networked with each other to distribute the design tasks across more machines to try more combinations or reproduce the same design across different locations just by exchanging the list of ingredients and a digital recipe. We did not utilize this feature deliberately in our designs. However, this feature allows anyone to be able to try existing simit recipes at home or design their own new recipes with other collaborators using a network. MDS standardizes the process by standardizing how the organisms, media, and DNA are used and how biological information is collected and exchanged during the design process.

For us, Microbial Design Studio and the "Microbial Simit Diet" intend to advance the technologies as well as the socio-political, cultural, and ethical parameters around biological design by exploring design's relation to three living bodies (of bread, yeast, and the human).

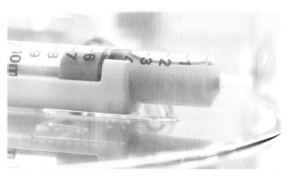
MDS syringe incubation.

In the bigger picture, they demonstrate the application of a biological design framework that opens up the interiority of the living body to other design disciplines. Today, anyone should be able to work with living organisms to design novel biochemistries, at their home and design studio, whether it is for food, biomaterials, or new types of sensors for environmental pollution.

The means of designing living bodies will always be an important endeavor for design disciplines. We advocate for the dissemination of MDS-like technologies to lower the barriers of access and adoption by different disciplines. Ultimately, we need alternative approaches to and diversity in biological design. This will be important to fully explore the potential of biotechnologies and drive both scientific inquiry and design into new horizons.

Giedion, Siegfried. Mechanization Takes Command: A Contribution to Anonymous History. Oxford UP. New York. 1948

Myhrvold Nathan, Francisco Migoya. Modernist Bread. The Cooking Lab. Bellevue. 2017

Telhan Orkan, The Microbial Design Studio: 30-day Simit Diet, 3rd Istanbul Design Biennial Reader, IKSV, Istanbul, 2016.

Telhan, Orkan. From Growing Tools to Designing Organisms: Changing the

Literacies of Design in Michael Filimowicz and Veronika Tzankova, eds: Deepening Teaching for Computational Media and Generalist Design. Cambridge: Cambridge University Press, 2017.

In Vitro Ecology

NURIT BAR-SHAI

10,000 years ago humans started to domesticate plants and animals, now its time to domesticate molecules.
Susan Lindquist

Rethinking biological materials, systems, forms, structures and methodologies, new biotech materials are likely to be used exponentially in our everyday life beyond medical applications. The idea of growing materials in the laboratory—in vitro—revolts under acknowledged concepts such as life & death, artificial & natural. It raises our awareness of future modifications to our bodies, of identity, anatomical architecture, soft and wet structures, as well as to sustainable, ethical, social and environmental responsibility, and the use of living systems as the building blocks for novel materials.

Growing and sculpting materials using living systems, The Passing applies tissue culture engineering, bone cells and 3D printers to grow buttons from biological matter. Turning bone into a material that could be formed and designed, from an inner-body to an outer-body material, is an allegory to prehistoric domestic design tools, crafted while awaiting the return of hunters, and the transformation of materials extracted from their origins to become practical objects. Bar-Shai rethinks Cells: in their differentiation and classification drawing on the direct relationship between form and function, and Bone: a biological material that contains time from our deep past. A time capsule that captures human history within biological matter as a metaphor for archiving and the passaging of genetic information over time. A library containing LIFE's narratives—imagined, real, or engineered.

Inspired by EpiBone, a NYC based startup that grows human bone tissue for skeletal reconstruction, Bar-Shai studied various scaffold models for extracellular matrix environments to grow her artwork. She tested how cells guided by designed support life systems create buttons made out of biological material, and how the impact of various materials and structures, from natural biopolymers to custom-made synthetic 3D printed polymers, could affect cell growth and cell behavior.

In recent years we have developed and mastered artificial environments in an attempt to imitate nature. Manifesting engineering complexities, architectural and behavioral models. Yet we are still far from designing what's so natural for nature to do. Our ability to hack molecules and reassemble them, access the genetic code and the periodic table, allow us to create in collaboration with nature—a "new one". But life doesn't come with an instruction manual, and as we explore and reveal its wonders, we ought to remember to do it with great care. In her work, Bar-Shai is fascinated by the direct impact of the environment on the biological system's behavior and morphology—the study of the form and structure of organisms' appearance, external and internal—and considers In Vitro Ecology to be as important as the impact of its genetic information and modifications of its features.

Taking inspiration from the work and research of Prof. Eshel Ben Jacob, "The Social Life of Bacteria," Bar-Shai's work Objectivity [tentative] is a series of experiments and interventions exploring "smart" microorganisms, linking between microbial morphogenesis and designed ecosystems.

Bar-Shai synthesizes traditional lab techniques as used by scientists together with artistic inquiries, from sound and computational interventions to 3D interfaces. She visualizes the "chemical tweets" of Paenibacillus vortex, soil bacteria known for its high morphological capabilities and sophisticated social behavior. The bacteria has the ability to self-organize and collectively cooperate as a colony, which allows it to survive in a variety of environmental conditions and requires sophisticated communication systems expressed in the development of colonies with complex architecture structures.

This body of work includes the Soundscapes Series, which uses pure sound waves and a range of frequencies to initiate sound-generated topographies for bacterial growth; Sound to Shape, part of the Soundscapes series, which takes biology out of the lab, creating access to experiments that are often done behind closed lab doors and invites sound-artists to collaborate and perform live in a gallery space, using sound-base compositional structures to initiate unique bacterial growth-forms; Morphoecology, a series of experiments that looks into the forms and shapes of bacterial habitats. Bar-Shai utilizes petri plates custom-made in size and form—designed outline—forms that guide bacterial growth or 3D spatial interfaces, which utilize the nutrient agar surfaces to initiate behavior that more closely resembles that found in nature or inside our bodies—as opposed to the standard flat circular surfaces used in labs for measurable control settings objectives. Bar-Shai draws attention to biological systems with interconnected components, and causal processes at multiple levels of abstractions, with requirements and desires that are often external to hers. Adding nature to square the triangle of art-artist-viewer, she attributes ecological context to what defines individual components in this vast system of arbitrary outcomes, binding structures, system organization's and controlled environments.

The passing, process

Biotech Without Borders

ELLEN JORGENSEN

Your life is already genetically modified. Deal with it. DNA manipulation is responsible for the production of food, medicine, industrial enzymes, rubber, plastic and other materials to help minimize human suffering. You are wearing clothes made with engineered cotton, eating cheese made with rennet from a bioreactor, and being treated with medicines made from genetically modified cells. Using this technology has allowed us to avoid starvation through catastrophic crop failure, to live longer and healthier lives through modern medical breakthroughs, and to raise the standard of living for more citizens of the earth. The idea that we can somehow return to a utopian, natural world where people live in harmony with everything else on the planet is a tempting vision. But we would have to kill off most of the human population to realize it. There are simply too many of us not to disrupt other living creatures, and not enough resources to go around unless we are very, very smart about it.

Biomanufacturing is the most earth-friendly technology in our suite of solutions. We have been genetically modifying organisms for the past 40 years, yet there have been no credible instances of harmful genetic environmental pollution. The economic and political story is more worrisome.

In May of 2017 I was asked to speak at the UN during the second annual Multi-stakeholder Forum on Science, Technology and Innovation for the Sustainable Development Goals (SDGs). The UN's ambitious SDGs for 2030 include several that could directly benefit from technologies such as genetic engineering, synthetic biology, and genome editing. Zero hunger, good health and wellbeing for all, affordable and clean energy, responsible consumption and production, and sustainable cities and communities are goals which are all addressable in part via biological science. However, it was clear from the conversations during the conference that the greatly uneven distribution of biotechnological capabilities could very easily fuel political and social instability. What is the most efficient way to spread capacity in the biosciences?

The answer may lie in offering public access to distributed facilities, and the community lab movement is pioneering this concept. At Biotech Without Borders, we aim to remove barriers to access for underserved populations in urban areas by providing a fully-equipped biotechnology lab in the heart of Brooklyn, housed in an unconventional building filled with artists, designers, social entrepreneurs and green technology. The idea that science can be performed in unexpected places was demonstrated in the garage biotech movement of the 1980s when professional scientists founded companies in their backyards. The current iteration relies on unused industrial space in cities, which is reclaimed as community lab space for the purpose of opening access to hands-on engagement with the technology and promoting innovation at the grassroots level. Used equipment from auction sites, cheap DNA synthesis and small biotech consumables companies challenging the large monoliths of the past all contribute to the success of the movement. A free flow of ideas between scientists and the community is also facilitated in these spaces through public events and lectures.

Physical facilities are as diverse as the founders in each community, evolving organically to suit the needs of the particular users as space and equipment are accumulated, modified and adapted. We are now seeing the first real innovations come out of these communities, which at the moment are mainly found in developed countries. A recent summit at the MIT Media Lab highlighted how more of the world is embracing this trend. Sub-Saharan Africa is an area particularly ripe for this. The reliance on found space, the reverse engineering of equipment, and the drive to make complicated science cheaper and easier in order to remove entry barriers resonates with the developing world. Since many participants in the movement are motivated by a desire to see

biotechnology used for good, collegial relationships have formed between labs with a free exchange of information, equipment and materials.

Community labs have facilitated innovation and exploration, but how far can they go? If home 3D printers are a hallmark of the distributed manufacturing of the future, then are home labs far behind? The recent egregious behavior of drug industry players that resulted in overpricing vital medicines spurred a backlash in the form of projects such as the Four Thieves Vinegar Collective's 3D printed EpiPen and the Bay Area Biohackers' Open Insulin Project. If sufficient quality control measures can be put in place, distributed bio manufacturing of medicines may not be that far into the future.

DNA manipulation.

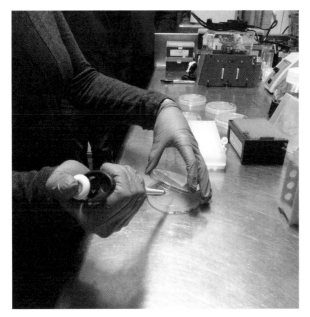

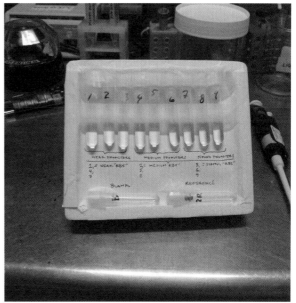

Green The Parking!

WILLIAM MYERS

The resilient city of the future will be dotted with spaces bursting with life, in the literal sense. These plots will enliven city blocks with color, making the immediate area cooler and quieter while cleaning the air and sequestering carbon. Plantings of trees and gardens will alternate between raised beds growing food and containers of compost. Still others will include small ponds, benches, and a variety of hearty grasses like Emerald Zoysia. These spaces will be publicly owned and locally managed by neighborhood associations that will determine their precise use and system for maintenance. The contemporary urban form will at last include recurring and easily accessible green spaces where the din of traffic fades and the continuous, aggressive choreography of parking shifts only to memory. All of this is plausible, but not likely without a fight – or several.

The history of zoning and development in almost every urban center in the world is marked by power wielding and rent-seeking by a wealthy and well-connected few. They represent interests that are currently eyeing millions of parking spaces in cities around the world for potential monetization. The total area in each city varies but is as much as 20% of the urban surface in cities in America. In Los Angeles, for example, car parking takes up 17,020,594 square meters of land. Over the next twenty years there is an overwhelming likelihood that most of this space will become available as autonomous vehicles, hired from time to time for transportation service and not owned, replace private cars and trucks, which currently sit parked 95% of the time on average.

The sheer madness of how public space is occupied in the contemporary city by whoever happens to turn their car off on it is hard to overstate, especially when considering the skyrocketing value of land in many dense cities coupled with a dearth in affordable housing. We must therefore guard against one kind of misappropriation of space simply being replaced by another, in which the interests of a few are advanced at everyone's expense. Cities will be tempted to sell off these spaces, and that must be resisted. Consider the attempt to privatize parking meters in Chicago with Morgan Stanley as the municipal partner. Following a closed-door process, the city agreed to a 75-year deal that allows the bank to earn money from the meters, in exchange for a large one-time payment, one worth much less than future revenues. Under the terms of the deal the bank holds veto power over the meters' removal, obstructing road redesign options. It is reasonable to expect that cities looking to close budget deficits will be tempted by such schemes. But the long-term livability of the city is at stake and only a vigilant, well-informed, and alert metropolitan citizenry will prevail. But why add plants and trees, small-scale farming, and composts? Wouldn't the interests of most people be better served by housing, maybe a few food truck spots, or a bike lane? Why is biology so much better?

The Case for Bio-Space
The new surfeit of space once used for parking can best serve the residents of a city if it is dedicated to supporting and enhancing biodiversity, growing food, and generating soil by processing household

food waste. There are a multitude of reasons why cities would benefit from prioritizing such use, but the most potent effect is advancing the paradigm shift toward regarding nature and biology as integral to our built environments, of seeing how biology and design can co-exist and benefit one another. For it is from that point of view that the approach of biodesign, of incorporating living systems into the making and everyday functioning of the built environment, becomes normalized.

The more immediate, practical effects of bio-space are also powerful. Everyday access including casual contact with plants and dirt have been definitively shown to enhance human health, especially among children who have developing immune systems thirsting for the kind of alien microbes that flourish in soil. Adults also benefit from exposure to the varied microbiome supported by the presence of foliage which, through photosynthesis, also acts as a carbon sink that helps to scrub the air of tiny, volatile organic compounds that are both harmful to our health and abundant in urban centers, as they abrade from paint, tires, plastics, and other species common in our cityscapes. Thoughtfully planted spaces can also act like coral reefs do on the sea floor, providing a foothold for numerous other forms of life, from microbes and insects to birds and bees, that enhance biodiversity and livability. The porous surfaces of green spaces also add the advantage of rain capture, a desperately needed feature in several cities that are becoming wetter.

Bringing food production into cities may seem inefficient on its surface, as agricultural costs tend to fall with scale. But this accounting fails to capture the embodied energy and carbon emissions with which most food is burdened. Hyper local food production provides relatively low-skilled work at high visibility, helping to educate the citizenry about the origins and consequences of their consumption.

Just as visits to national parks tend to correlate with community support and funding for them, proximity to food production can help reinstate our collective understanding of how we rely on clean air, soil, and water as well as the toil of our fellow citizens, to enjoy nutritional abundance. Networked resilience in the food system, including increased knowledge of agricultural practices, would also be welcomed in the coming decades of uncertainty in weather patterns and the increasing likelihood of disasters as witnessed in San Juan, Puerto Rico in 2017.

In the process of greening the city, bicycle lanes are almost universally regarded as a necessary and urgent addition. It is doubtless they are, but they do not require the spaces now given over to car parking. The introduction of autonomous vehicles will mean continual communication and coordination among them, making the required road space for them significantly smaller. Most two-lane residential roads will be able to revert to a single lane while cars themselves can become narrower and remain safe. The case for bike lanes is air-tight, but it needn't infringe on the bio-spaces that can replace parking; there's simply enough room to go around on the road.

A prioritization of biologically-rich design in our soon-to-be-available plots all around the world will require legions of new designers. They will be motivated to think of biological matter and its attendant needs, like a non-toxic environment, with empathy. Their work will forge partnerships with plants and animals and their success will be measured by the degree to which their ideas fuel biodiversity. Resiliency will be regarded by them as considering the survivability and well-being of the non-human as well as the human. It is from such a nourished empathy that entirely new urban forms, measures of value, and definitions of success might spring. We will do well to enable such ideas, for they just might save us.

Poikilohydric Design, Towards a Bio-integrated Architecture

MARCOS CRUZ

We live in a time of increasing water scarcity due to lacking rainfall and high levels of pollution in many parts of the world. Climate change is now defying the reliability of supplies in many areas.[1] According to the UN, around 20% of the world's population is already living in areas with insufficient access to potable water, as well as adequate water to satisfy the demand of ecosystems to function.[2] With a rising population more and more regions are becoming water stressed, forcing us to search for new design solutions in which we can use rainfall more effectively in urban settings.

Our cities continue having a damaging effect on climate change by employing unsustainable material and construction solutions. As a result we are witnessing increasing temperatures that are triggering rising levels of water vapor in the atmosphere. Even though this is leading to the occurrence of intensified rainfall, there are far more enduring dry spells all over.[3] Sprawling cities, however, instead of being only negative contributors, offer a potentially unique resource to provide more intelligent and efficient systems to retain and make direct use of rainfall in our built environment. All the externally exposed surfaces of buildings and urban infrastructures, including blank walls and facades, roofs, retaining barriers, fences, etc. offer waste quantities of area to absorb and store water.

My argument is therefore to promote a new bio-integrated approach in architecture in which hydrophilic conditions existing in botany become an integral part of our designs. This will allow us to take multiple advantage of plants, and in turn help us improve the storm water management of facades; absorption of CO_2, nitrogen and pollutants; while emitting significant levels of oxygen. But to grow plants on buildings in areas of water shortage is not only challenging in terms of the choice and integration of plants, but also potentially costly when dependent of artificial irrigation and maintenance in areas of difficult access. In this context, poikilohydry of organisms is a primitive, yet intelligent mechanism for plants to deal with dry conditions without affecting their overall survival. It is a less advanced defense strategy than that available in higher plants, such as osmotic adjustments, succulent tissue, or longer root systems, to smaller leaves with sunken stomata, smaller lamina, or hairy coverings for evaporative control. But the protoplasm of poikilohydric plants possesses structural and physiological capacities to resist severe and lengthy dehydration periods. They simply turn down their cellular metabolism to become dormant for as long as new water intake enables them to become photosynthetic again. The inability to protect themselves from water deficiency as in other plants is compensated by an aptitude to switch on and off instantaneously depending on moisture readiness.[4]

In recent years, the BiotA Lab at the Bartlett UCL explored the concept of an architectural bark for future building cladding as a means to create a continuous bio-receptive substratum in cities that encourages the growth of microorganisms and small-scale plants on facades without the need for costly maintenance and irrigation.[5] Newly designed façade panel composites with porous cementitious materials were developed as water retaining scaffolds to feed these plants to proliferate.[6] However, such bioreceptive systems were created for climatic regions where rainfall is expected to be abundant, being so far inadequate for dryer places, not the least for xeric habitats that are expanding fast and affecting millions of people. The poikilohydry of plants is in itself a clever response for such conditions, having the benefit of adjusting much more effectively to the environment. 'Poikilohydric plants differ from homoiohydric plants in that they can equilibrate with the relative humidity of the air during drought periods, but then exhibit complete physiological recovery upon rehydration. The poikilohydric habit is found in both the cryptogamic autotrophs such as algae, lichens, mosses, and ferns, and a few vascular plant taxa such as the pteridophytes and lycophytes.'[7]

It is now important to find new design solutions in which we can take advantages of the plant's physiological capabilities, while integrating them more effectively in building structures. To achieve this, novel morphological and material systems need to be investigated. Firstly, there is a need to upgrade current bioreceptive systems to allow for far greater water absorption in the materials than what is possible to date. Such novel materials will have to go beyond the exclusive control of pH level, porosity and surface roughness that has been attempted so far, aiming at a higher and prolonged water retention inside the material matrix to enhance the bio-colonization of roofs and facades when dry conditions are prevalent. These multi-material composites will also rely on the adjacency of smaller and larger poor size aggregates, triggering a selective bioreceptivity

through capillary action that guarantees a continuous growth in specifically designed locations of buildings.[8] Moreover, stratified material gradients are important to help increasing a deliberate level of 'hydropsy'[9] in the inner side of the materials, while having a rough, yet less porous outer surface to decrease the risks of evaporation and thus prolong water availability to feed plants.

In addition to the material design, there is a need to augment the morphological variability and depth of surfaces to diminish water run-offs in a more sophisticated way, and in this manner intensify water catchment on facades. To achieve such surface complexity one has to operate on various scales – micro (material), meso (surface), macro (tectonic) – helping in the succession of plants biofilms to establish in designated areas. While these create an undercoat on which small-scale vegetation will proliferate and hook onto the crevices and nooks of the wall, the textural variance of recesses and protrusions will help resisting falling off of plants when desiccated or blown away by prevailing winds.[10] In addition to common cryptogams, it is worth giving attention to plants categorized as xerophytes, as they are specially adapted to adjust to adverse weather conditions and grow in places where water is scarce.

One of the most significant advances put forward by the BiotA Lab, besides employing new materials and morphological surface complexity, is the use of new computational tools in which hyper-complex geometries can be simulated, leading towards a new bio-ornamental language in architecture. The geometry of nature and the geometry of human artifice are merging into an unprecedented bio-architectural continuum of extraordinary filigree. Following examples in medicine, where the seamless integration of artificially produced apparatuses in the human body, such as pace makers or synthetically grown organs is already mainstream, this novel form of architecture is similarly blending living and inert matter into a new biologically integrated whole.

Design with Life

Design is the result of an intense dialogue between grown and designed tectonics that are shifting architecture towards a new aesthetic paradigm that is hyper-articulated, unpredictable and ever changing. The patchy and fluctuating state in which green and brown/grey/black colorations reflect the conditions of plants being active/photosynthetic or non-active/dormant defines what I considered the emergence of a new 'impure aesthetic'[11]. The main aim for me, however, is the need to develop not only one, but also many different and far more bio-integrated systems than what we have researched so far. If, on the one hand, it is vital to prolong the feeding process of plants via bioreceptive materials that encourage photosynthetic activity on the outer surface of buildings, there is, on the other a need to progress new multifunctional materials that are able to adjust much better to climatic changes, especially in geographic locations and extended periods where water is not obtainable. Beyond the bioreceptivity of walls as mere hosts for growth, I am arguing for a novel para-materiality[12] in which designed materials are becoming literally grown with the help of microorganisms and plants that act as bio-responsive binders for a variety of aggregates. For example, the synthetic bio-silicification and bio-sedimentation of materials offers us the opportunity to move away from the idea of buildings components being mere infrastructures for outer growth. Such designed bio-geological composites will help us creating more sustainable alternatives to current materials such as ordinary Portland concrete (OPC) or clay bricks that contribute so badly to the environment.[13] We are finally able to envision a future that is becoming much more sustainable in material terms. Bio-immersive and bio-responsive systems will make architectural materials behave like plant tissue. The dormancy or vivacity of walls will make them become dynamic and operational, yet different from the utopias in the 60s and 70s where buildings were envisaged to move and act.14 Future buildings will become active in a bio-chemical way with building components designed to prevent the 'architectural tissue' to dehydrate and die, switching it on or off whenever there is rainfall available.

I believe that after many decades of negative impact that our 'civilized' urban societies have inflicted on our health and climate through unsustainable ways of life, it is now time to pay back and turn our cities into active contributors to a better future environment. I argued many years ago about architecture's path towards ecology, with buildings offering the opportunity to create an ever-expanding bio-diverse infrastructure that is responsive and ecologically adaptable. One of the key phenomena is how to manage water more cleverly, which is why I am arguing for the emergence of a new poikilohydric design approach in which architecture is able to calibrate and adjust to the unpredictability of climates. I am here not talking about such systems applied to one or two exceptional buildings; I am envisioning a revolution of architecture in which 20%, 30% or more of our future construction will entail truly biologically embedded and receptive buildings that are fully-grown and integrated. I am foreseeing the advent of a new poikilohydric design in which the desiccation or photosynthetic activity of materials is self-regulated and dependent on the augmented capacity to catch and retain moisture whenever it is accessible. We will finally move towards the design of sustainable bio-integrated architecture.

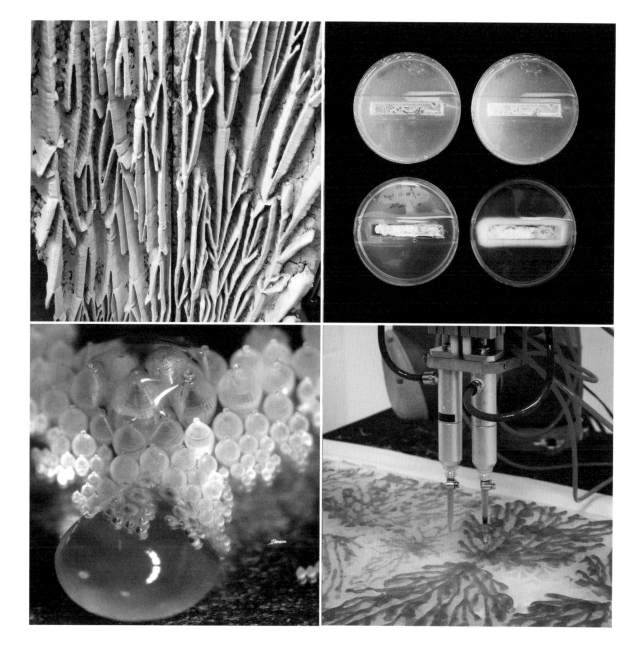

Design with Life

1 Source: National Climate Assessment 2014, USA; and 'Climate change: how Australia's capital cities will be hotter and drier by 2050', article by Sophie Aubrey in News Corp Australia Network, 31st March 2016.

2 Source: *Human Development Report 2006*, UNDP 2006 and *Coping with Water Scarcity, Challenge of the Twenty-first century*, UN-Water, FAO 2007.

3 Source: 'How will climate change affect rainfall?', as part of The Guardian's ultimate climate change FAQ, 12th December 2009, UK

4 Mehltreter, Klaus; Walker, Lawrence R., Sharpe, Joanne M. (eds). *Fern Ecology*, Cambridge University Press. p.155

5 See Cruz, M.; Beckett, R.. 'Biorecepive Design', in *Architectural Research Quarterly Architecture and Biotechnology / Synthetic Biology / Cells as Architects*, Cambridge University Press, UK, p. 51

6 This refers back to the EPSRC-funded research 'Computational Seeding of Bioreceptive Materials', University College London 2015-17. Team: Marcos Cruz (PI), Dr Sandra Manso, Dr Chris Leung, Richard Beckett, Bill Watts.

7 Smith, Stanley D.; Monson, Russell K.; Anderson, Jay E.. 'Poikilohydric Plants', in *Physiological Ecology of North American Desert Plants (Series: Adaptations of Desert Organisms)*, Springer Verlag, 1997, pp. 191-198. The authors paraphrase content from J. Derek Bewley's article 'Physiological Aspects of Desiccation Tolerance', in *Annual Review of Plant physiology*, Vol. 30:195-238, June 1979; and M. Evenari's article 'Adaptations of plants and animals to the desert environment, in M. Evenari; I. Nov- Meir; D.W. Goodall (eds). Ecosystems of the World 12A. Hot Deserts and Arid Shrublands, A. Amsterdam, Elsevier, 1985)

8 The selective bio receptivity of materials defining enhancing and inhibiting areas were already defined in Cruz, M.; Beckett, R.. 'Biorecepive Design', in *Architectural Research Quarterly - Architecture and Biotechnology / Synthetic Biology / Cells as Architects*, Cambridge University Press, UK, p. 61

9 I am extrapolating a medical term to architecture with the aim to illustrate the process of water accumulation inside specific areas of the material.

10 For more detail on this scale differentiation see Cruz, M.; Beckett, R.. 'Biorecepive Design', in *Architectural Research Quarterly - Architecture and Biotechnology / Synthetic Biology / Cells as Architects*, Cambridge University Press, UK, p.56

11 Idem. p.53

12 See full article Cruz, M.. 'Towards a new Para-Materiality', in *Creative Materiality - Architectural Materialism in Post-Human Times* (ed. Maria Voyatzaki), Edinburgh University Press, 2017.

13 The work of Ginger Krieg Dosier / BioMason is a great example of a biologically grown cementitious material, yet it is conceived as an inert once the fabrication process is completed. The materials are dead and do not allow photosynthetic activity. They also lack any design that promoted growth on the surface.

14 I am referring to design predictions by Achigram, Archizoom and other contemporaries who put forward physically moving buildings and infrastructures.

Architecture on Demand
Building Systems with Life-Like Behaviour

PAUL CLEMENS BART and MARVIN BRATKE

Today, not only human but everything manufactured by him - from a pair of scissors to a building - engages in an either active and open or subliminal conversation with us. Design has become a way of communicating. The theoretical foundation of what we call interface and interaction design has been speculated in cybernetics since the 1960s, coming from concepts of Man-Machine relationships and Conversation Theory.[1]

After a period of functionalist reductionism following the industrial revolution we entered what cognitive-scientist Donald Norman proclaimed as the era of "Emotional Design". Buildings, machines, cities began to breathe, walk, plug in and talk.[2]

This self-evidence can be seen in any person born post the digital revolution, instinctively looking for buttons, interactions and ways of communication with designed objects.

Coming from the precedent decades of functionalism and reductionism - an aftermath of the Industrial Revolution - a fabrication related trend to standardization long overshadowed the expressiveness and behavioural capabilities of designed objects. As the Industrial Revolution extended the human body physically, it is - according to Kenzo Tange - our nervous system that is prosthetically extended by the Information Revolution.[3] The children of this revolution are therefore less concerned with issues of physicality but with the relations of communication, emotion and behaviour.

What impact does today's shift in machine behaviour have on us - not only in human-machine and machine-machine but human-human communication? Even though the city itself has become a dynamic entity in our information accelerated society, the paradigm of today's culture of building leave only restrained opportunities for dynamic behaviour and communication with our urban fabric. The rapid transfer of knowledge in an information society demands a new and innovative translation to our building methods as well as towards our perception of built environment. Architecture must be ready to adapt towards autonomous mobility and an on-demand society.

Future building scenarios can be imagined by the introduction of behavioural based building systems that mark a shift from built environment as a finite lifecycle, leading to autonomous, non-finite and real-time solutions that adapt dynamically to the demands of their environments. Tomorrow's construction strategies must address social-architectural issues of integrating automated, self-sustaining and fully mobile solutions into people's daily life – as a system acting at the interface

Design with Life

between architecture, mobility and the citizens of a city. Today's autonomous systems are largely used in logistics and fabrication of industrial goods in fully automated production cycles.[4] There is an opportunity for the building industry to adopt small scale, versatile and autonomous robotic systems to translate a static construct into a dynamic environment.

In a self-assembling fabrication approach of 'negotiated space', architectural building system **noMad** aims to enable architecture with a sensory system, localizing decision making by self-aware unit to unit communication instead of a deterministic, superimposed building plan.[5] Anchored in the world of self-structuring polyhedra, noMad is based on principles of synergetics, the study of geometry in transformation and the impact of a local change on its global systems behaviour: a single unit can autonomously change shape, shifting its state by a simple rotational translation from one polyhedra to the other. Hereby, noMad is operating on distinct

scales of (collective) intelligence and autonomy, each autonomously self-assembling to the next higher order of organisation – from a highly mobile, nomadic state to high population spatial configurations. noMad proposes a system that can self-regulate and adapt, react to outside influences and demands and encourages both interaction and communication.

An amphibious expansion of the noMad product family, **noMad H2O** is a water based assembly system that works in synergy with its land-based base units.[6] Re-activating the ocean as a site for assembly and energy production, a 'breathing' structure actively activates and re-configures itself under the influence of currents and the flow of water using its own internal motor and sensor technology. Originally conceived as a flexible and adaptable solution to extract pollution and prevent more plastic debris from entering ocean water, it could further become a source of low-tech electric energy generation. Its position on the water surface - half hidden

in the cool water and half exposed under direct sunlight - produces thermoelectrically self-sufficient energy. Linear actuators positioned between the unit's framed cushions are contracting at the core of the unit between two opposite sides - enabling soft assemblies, weak connections and intentional breaking points. Developed for a prototypical installation, noMad H2O explores alternative means of low-tech energy production and passive assembly logics.

Showcasing life-like behaviour, such systems can react in real-time to the needs of the social-urban fabric by creating ever transformable architectures, infrastructures and adaptive spaces. Through processing urban big data, utilizing machine learning algorithms, nomadic architectures can have the ability to communicate between each other, delivering towards the city's fast changing demands. These architectural systems should be designed with "prosumer" society in mind - a trend where the consumer equally becomes the producer[7] i.e.

via new and readily available fabrication methods - counteracting the super-imposed top-down approaches of today's urban planning. If the architect is willing to step back in his classic deterministic role in favour of creating open systems of non-finite and ever expanding feedback loops, architecture may move closer to the end user in on-demand solutions: a system that is based on peer-to-peer communication.

1 Interview with Gregory Bateson and Margaret Mead. in Stewart Brand (ed.). CoEvolution Quarterly. June 1973. Page 32pp.

2 Antonelli, Paola. Talk to Me: Design and Communication between People and Objects. New York: The Museum of Modern Art. 2011. Page 6.

3 Tange, Kenzo. Kenzo Tange. in Ekistics 10/66. 1966. Page 275.

4 Mcafee, Andrew & Brynjolfsson, Erik. Machine

Platform Crowd. W W Norton & Company. 2017. Page 103

5 Bart//Bratke. Project noMad. 2014. 22.01.2018 <http://bartbratke.com/portfolio_page/nomad-behavioural-fabrication/>

6 Bart//Bratke. noMad H2O. 2017. 22.01.2018 <http://bartbratke.com/portfolio_page/nomad- H2O/>

7 Kotler, Philip. Prosumers: A New Type of Customer. Futurist. 09-10 1986. Page 24-28.

Living Root Structural Ecosystems of India:
A model for socio-ecological resilience

SANJEEV SHANKAR

Current research and discourse surrounding integration of living systems within infrastructure and buildings is often perceived as speculative, niche and avant garde. While this outlook has many underpinnings, we believe the case study of 'Ficus-based living root structural ecosystems and indigenous tribal communities of Meghalaya' can provide rare real life practical evidence in support of this field, and inspire the global community to re-imagine the 'built' environment as a living nourishing productive life-giving environment.

Living Root Structural Ecosystems are Ficus elastica-based infrastructure solutions within dense subtropical moist broadleaf forests of North Eastern Indian Himalayas (25° 30'N and 91° 00'E). As living plant-based structural ecosystems, these infrastructure solutions are grown and nurtured by indigenous Khasi and Jaintia tribes of Meghalaya over 10 to 30 years and perform as critical rural connectivity and landscape solutions for several centuries in extreme climatic conditions. With 1) low material and maintenance cost, 2) high robustness and longevity, 3) progressive increase in strength and performance, 4) community-led participatory design approach across multiple generations, 5) remedial impact on surrounding soil, water and air, 6) support for other plant and animal systems, 7) keystone role of Ficus plant species in local ecology,

and 8) diverse morphologies including bridges, ladders, towers, viewing platforms and soil erosion/landslide prevention structures, Ficus-based living root structural ecosystems offer a compelling model for long-term socio-ecological resilience and living plant-based sustainable infrastructure solutions.

With more than 100 living structures currently in active use throughout Meghalaya, we have a unique opportunity to study the fundamental principles, which govern these structures and their underlying behaviour/performance. This knowledge can fundamentally shape our approach to 'designing with life' and further inform the vision of nurturing resilient cities. Each living root structural ecosystem is a unique site-specific response, which has emerged through interaction between humans, plants and the environment, offering a living test bed for empirical investigation. In-situ research over an extended time period in collaboration with indigenous tribal communities can help us understand the interactions between various living and non-living agents across different scales and seasons. This will help us comprehend the emergent behaviour and ecosystem services provided by these structures. Such a comprehensive understanding will eventually inspire new improved living plant-based hybrid constructions, which nourish Earth's natural resources and address critical environmental challenges related to biodiversity loss, deforestation, environmental degradation, climate change, food and health.

Ficus genus has more than 850 species globally and testing/applying the knowledge of Living Root Structural Ecosystems to other plant species and geographical contexts can potentially broaden its scope and impact. Exchange between indigenous tribal communities and contemporary scientists will inform a shift in the nature of scientific inquiry and cultivate a balance between ancient intelligence and contemporary thought. As these living structures are revealed to the global community, we believe it will inspire a new sensitivity within society and eventually rejuvenate the relationship between humans and plants. Designing with life is a compelling prospect and to leap into the future we have much to learn from the past.

Regenerative Reliquary

AMY KARLE

When we read or hear the words "architecture" and "resilient cities" most think large scale, envisioning places like New York, Tokyo, Toronto, Paris, London, Chicago or Dubai. I think on a different scale. I think of the body.

We can look to the biotech architecture of the body for models of how to build a resilient city. When the biotech architecture of the body functions properly, it is in physical and mental health and well-being, exceptionally resilient and highly adaptive, the picture of ultimate vitality. The intelligence and design of the body and its' functions, systems and interrelationships – down to the smallest components of cells and DNA – reveal the complex interworking of a profoundly intelligent system designed with multiple highly organized systems including infrastructure, prioritization, electricity, communication, fuel, recycling and waste management, short and long term information storage and retrieval, reproduction, growth, healing life and death. These systems provide an outline for city planning from a holistic standpoint, with all systems working together for the functionality, health and resiliency of the entire system. Models of the body can be applied to scenario planning, adaptability, smart growth, infrastructure, organization, government, economy, cultural and social systems, even to the physical construction of the city and the architecture of buildings and utility systems.

To be resilient, our cities must evolve as we do. Exponential technology and the onset of the 4th industrial revolution provides the opportunity to analyze, heal and enhance our systems, bodies, cities, environment and society in new, exponential ways. Artificial Intelligence, machine learning and neural networking can be used to analyze big data, propose new concepts and designs, find vulnerabilities and propose solutions. These technologies can also be integrated as active tools to continually create, reshape, and offer adaptability and resilience in systems. We can now draft designs (including architecture) and systems generated by inputs, constraints, and forces put upon it in the way that the body makes and heals bones or grows new blood vessels. We can create self-organizing systems that learn and adapt to the environment and utilize new biomaterials and biotech to create no or low waste sustainable products that can be upcycled, recycled or reformed when their use is over. The models, materials, tools and technology are available to create resilient cities and resilient lives, what needs to be established is the vision, organization, and will to do so.

The point we are at in evolution is humans and technology merging. The use of exponential technology including Artificial Intelligence, machine learning, synthetic biology, regenerative medicine, genetic engineering, 3D printing and

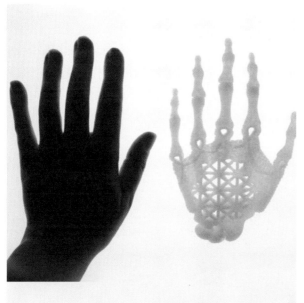

digital manufacturing, autonomous robotics, cloud networking, and supercomputing has the potential to advance us or lead us towards our demise depending on how we use it. As we step into a biotechnologically augmented future, it is of vital importance to research and focus on what is healthy for our bodies, for our cities, and for our world.

The ways in which we design our cities, environments, bodies, and lives requires asking difficult, profound questions about our goals and motivations for the future of humanity and of our world. As our dependence on technology and biotech increases, it requires thoughtful consideration of how we may collaborate with technology to empower us. To be prepared to build or rebuild resilient cities and resilient lives, it is of vital importance to contemplate how and why we should or should not employ exponential technology to do so, and be prepared how to respond to mutations caused by the integration of technology and biotech. The biotech architecture of nature and the body points us towards many intelligent solutions.

As future visions open of how technology and biotechnology can be utilized to support and enhance our cities, our lives, and humanity, we must examine and reflect on what it means to be human from the micro to the macro scale – to inform how we design our lives, our cities, and society to be healthy, resilient and empower and enrich all of humanity. We must also examine and reflect on the intelligence and insights present in the biotech architecture of the natural world to help us get there. There is so much awe and mystery, so much inspiration, and still so much to learn.

Regenerative Reliquary

Leveraging the intelligence of human stem cells, Amy Karle created "Regenerative Reliquary", a bioprinted scaffold in the shape of a human hand design 3D printed in a biodegradable PEGDA hydrogel that disintegrates over time. The sculpture is installed in a bioreactor, with the intention that human Mesenchymal stem cells (hMSCs from an adult donor)

Design with Life

Contributing Authors | Regenerative Reliquary | Amy Carle

seeded onto that design will grow into tissue and mineralize into bone along that scaffold.

Inspired by the generative and parametric design in the body, this piece considers how cells articulate into different forms – what makes a cell become a beating heart, skin, or bone – in naturally occurring "additive manufacturing" created by a multiplier effect. "Regenerative Reliquary" further focuses on the dynamic organ and tissue in our bodies that is constantly remodeling and changing shape to adapt to the daily forces placed upon it: bone.

The ornate aesthetic of the piece was derived from functional design requirements: the overall lattice was created for biomimetic osseointegration; on the microscopic level the scaffold mimics the trabecular structure of bone, the shape that triggers stem cells to become bone cells. The distinct yellow color of the sculpture was required in order to 3D print with such detail in a biodegradable, biocompatible material. Although this specific sculpture is intended to live outside of the body, the design and the manufacturing process suggest that future versions could potentially be implanted and integrated with existing biological features.

In the vision of being able to create a graft out of a donor's own genetic material so that it could be implanted back into the body with low risk of rejection, the ideal scaffold had to be non-toxic and biocompatible, encouraging cell attachment and proliferation, with a highly porous interconnected network that allows for cell growth and movement of nutrients and metabolic waste and the structural properties to encourage stem cell transformation into bone cells. The material also had to be biodegradable with controlled degradation so that the scaffold could be replaced by bone cell mineralization. These required functions and characteristics defined the design and aesthetic.

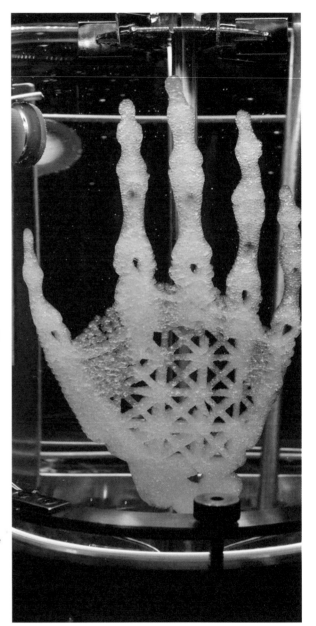

The process Karle employed creating this 3D printed framework that tissue can regenerate on can be used for cell culture and could potentially be applied to design and engineer custom bone grafts or other tissue for medical implant in the future. "I was envisioning a leapfrog technology to design and regenerate anthropomorphic body parts. If this application is developed, the potential healthcare benefit is that a patient's own stem cells could be used for a personalized bone graft".

Although Karle created this piece as artwork for outside of the body – not intended to be implanted, if this application is developed, the potential healthcare benefit of this approach is that a patient's own stem cells could be obtained and used for culture, remodel onto a personalized bone graft designed to be an exact fit out and implanted with low risk of rejection since it is made out of their own DNA, and without complications of foreign implantation. A patient's own cells provide for better integration also because it is living, has the potential to continue growing and remodeling in the body. "I began envisioning a future factory where the same materials – just a few cells, could be used to grow organs, marrow, limbs, and also create art and design objects, even technology for both inside and outside of our bodies... a sustainable factory with low waste, where minute amounts of material can be grown into many different forms, reconfigured and reused for many purposes to enhance and enrich our lives".

A hand design was chosen as a skeletal structure that is uniquely recognizable has human. This relationship to the piece as human-like catalytically raises questions about what it means to be human: how we may potentially grow existing and new human forms, how this concept and approach can be applied to healing and augmenting the body, what we may use human cells to create that is not human, what new forms we could design and grow with cells, and if human cells are used does that mean the new piece is now human?

Leveraging regenerative medicine and bioprinting to create artwork, Karle's work pioneers in the art world and in exponential technology field alike. "Regenerative Reliquary" made artistic, scientific and technological advancements as it required and inspired new innovations to be made in its creation, as well as influences a new way of thinking. In addition to biomedical applications and implications for healing and enhancing the body, Karle considers the future of creating with cells in technological, art and design applications. "We no longer need to turn to inanimate materials like metal, fabric, bricks, or paint to make an object. We can use actual living cells and tissue as materials to build with. The cell, 'nature's building block' can be the basic structural unit for new creations

New Rochelle Echo Bay Waterfront

WINKA DUBBLEDAM

We were asked to redesign the waterfront on Echo Bay, a site directly connected to New Rochelle's Main street. The site was to include the renovation of the Armory, a new hotel, housing and retail, all located in a waterfront park. The site's previous, industrial use inspired the notion of a "smart landscape." Pollution is removed, healthy soil added, storm water filtered, and alternative energy sourced.

Living on the waterfront

To re-connect the waterfront to the surrounding city and the adjacent Five Islands Park, a boardwalk is introduced. The boardwalk connects Main Street, the waterfront on Echo Bay, and Echo Avenue through recreation and green space. The park contains a spacious boardwalk that connects the armory, a hotel, housing and retail developments. New Rochelle is a mere 30 minutes train ride from Manhattan, so this new waterfront development could become a major attractor. To further reunite Main Street and the waterfront, the hotel flanks the street's main axis between the waterfront and city, a path past the renovated Armory. By renovating the armory, New Rochelle gets a flexible event - and exhibition space. The armory's interior is lined with a sail cloth curved structure, that serves as a removable ceiling and continues outside as small pavilion-like shapes. To further diminish the barrier between public and private, large, glass doors are installed.

Residences

Smart prefab housing provides two living styles: Urban Dweller units and Waterfront units. The low rise housing is designed with sustainable materials and insulation, resulting in low energy consumption,

no maintenance, and minimal environmental impact. The Prefab Housing combines high-performance, terra-cotta rain-screens and FSC certified, natural, wood siding. Also, a variety of flexible floor plans are provided. They introduce a new lifestyle with retail and hospitality along Main Street, thus re-invigorating New Rochelle's economy and culture.

Waterfront board walk

Due to its scenic coast, New Rochelle is nicknamed "Queen City of the Sound." However, recent studies indicate the coastline is shrinking. To initiate rehabilitation, wetland vegetation is introduced, and a seawall installed. We designed a Boardwalk as a connector and generator. In addition to providing wetland protection, the boardwalk introduces recreational activities, including water sports, a kayak landing, playgrounds, community gardens, tea house, pop-up event spaces, and visitor parking.

Waterfront Park

The landscape designed by !MELK, is geared towards wetland restoration. In addition to protecting the wetland, the boardwalk and landscape promote recreation. They introduce different levels and textures — grasses, plants, gravel, etc. — in order to differentiate zones, this range also creates beautiful gradients in the landscape. The boardwalk occasionally widens to create platforms — providing viewing-piers, an outdoor theater, and kayak landings. The Boardwalk areas transform the coast into unique, public place, which connects the park, housing, armory, boathouse, and playground, to the city.

Project type:	Mixed-use waterfront design
Scale:	575,000 sf (13 acres)
Status:	Invited oompetition, finalist
Lead designer:	Winka Dubbeldam, Archi-Tectonics
Design team:	Mithila Poojari, Fernando Herrera, Avra Tomara, Takanori Mizutani, Jang Hee Cho, Helena Yun
Landscape designer:	!MELK Urban Design LLC
Structural engineers:	WSP Cantor Seinuck
Mechanical engineer:	AMA Consulting Engineers P.C.
Developer:	Voyager Hotel Group

Design with Life

About the Authors

Terreform ONE (Open Network Ecology) is a nonprofit experimental architecture and urban design research group in New York City. The primary mission is "Design Against Extinction".

Mitchell Joachim, Co-Founder of Terreform ONE and an Associate Professor at NYU. He was formerly an architect at Gehry Partners LLP, and Pei Cobb Freed. He has been awarded a Fulbright Scholarship and fellowships with TED, Moshe Safdie, and Martin Society for Sustainability, MIT. He was chosen by Wired magazine for "The Smart List: 15 People the Next President Should Listen To". Rolling Stone magazine honored Mitchell in "The 100 People Who Are Changing America". Mitchell won many awards including; LafargeHolcim Acknowledgement Award, ARCHITECT R+D Award, AIA New York Urban Design Merit Award, Victor Papanek Social Design Award, Zumtobel Award for Sustainability, Architizer A+ Award, History Channel Infiniti Award for City of the Future, and Time Magazine Best Invention with MIT Smart Cities. Dwell magazine featured him as "The NOW 99" in 2012. He co-authored three books, "XXL-XS: New Directions in Ecological Design," "Super Cells: Building with Biology," and "Global Design: Elsewhere Envisioned". His work has been exhibited at MoMA and the Venice Biennale. He earned a PhD at Massachusetts Institute of Technology, MAUD Harvard University, MArch Columbia University.

Maria Aiolova, Co-Founder of Terreform ONE and Associate Principal at Arup. She leads Arup University in the Americas where she directs learning, research, foresight, and innovation. She worked with the developer of New Lab to create a vibrant community of over 100 companies working in emerging technologies such as urban tech, robotics, artificial intelligence, and connected devices. Maria served as the Academic Director of Global Programs at CIEE, where she created semester-long programs in Berlin, Barcelona, Prague, Shanghai, Cape Town, and New York City. She is an inventor, who holds 18 technology patents.

Most recently, she taught at the University of Applied Arts in Vienna, IAAC, Pratt Institute, and Parsons. She has won a number of honors including; AIA New York Urban Design Merit Award, 1st Place International Architecture Award, Victor Papanek Social Design Award, Zumtobel Group Award for Sustainability, and the Build Boston Award. Her work has been the official selection at the Venice Biennale and has been exhibited at MoMA, The Metropolitan Museum of Art and the New Institute in Rotterdam. Maria received her M.Arch. in Urban Design from Harvard University, B.Arch. from Wentworth IT with Honors, Dipl.-Ing. from the Technical University of Vienna, Austria and Sofia, Bulgaria.

Design with Life

Credits

I. ATMOSPHERE + CLEAN

Monarch Sanctuary
Mitchell Joachim, Vivan Kuan, Nina Edwards Anker, Lisa Richardson, Christian Hubert, Nicholas Gervasi, Maria Aiolova, Anna Bokov, Liana Grobstein, Theo Dimitrasopoulos, Zack Saunders, Xinye Lin, Sabrina Naumovski, Jules Pepitone, Kristina Goncharova, Yucel Guven, Zhan Xu, Larissa Belcic, Shahira Hammad, Deniz Onder, Aleksandr Plotkin, Anouk Wipprecht, Kristian Knorr, Sophie Falkeis, Rita Wang, Michael Brittenham, Mamoun Nukumanu Friedrich-grosvenor, Anastasia MacEwen, Annick Saralegui, Aurela Berila, Daniel S Castano, Aidan Nelson, Dan O'Connor

Anti-Extinction Instrument
Mitchell Joachim, Vivian Kuan, Georine Pierre, Nicholas Gervasi.

Future North
Mitchell Joachim, Jane Marsching, Makoto Okazaki, Maria Aiolova, Melanie Fessel, Dan O'Connor.

II. BIO + TECH

Bio-City World Map
Mitchell Joachim, Nurhan Gokturk, Maria Aiolova, Melanie Fessel, Oliver Medvedik., Chloe Byrne, Keith Comito, Adrian De Silva, Daniel Dewit, Renee Fayzimatova, Alena Field, Nicholas Gervasi, Julien Gonzalez, Lucas Hamren, Patty Kaishian, Ahmad Khan, Laasyapriya Malladi, Karan Maniar, Ricardo Martin Coloma, Puja Patel, Merve Poyraz, Mina Rafiee, Mahsoo Salimi, Manjula Singh, Diego Wu Law.

In-Vitro Meat Habitat
Mitchell Joachim, Eric Tan, Oliver Medvedik, Maria Aiolova.

Gen2Seat
Mitchell Joachim, Oliver Medvedik, Melanie Fessel, Maria Aiolova, Ellen Jorgenson, Dylan Butman, Greg Mulholland, Shruti Grover, James Schwartz, Josue Ledema, Tania Doles, Philip Weller, Greg Pucillo, Shivina Harjani, Jesse Hull, Peter Zhang, Matthew Tarpley, Amanda O'Keefe, Bahar Avanoglu, Ipek Avanoglu, Brent Solomon, Pedro Galindo-Landeira, Yinan Li, Sophie Fabbri.

Liveware
Mitchell Joachim, Vivian Kuan, Matt Mitchell, Taili Zhuang, Nicholas Gervasi, Mat Sokol, Jamal Combs, Chenoe Hart, Seb Fathi, Che Puntes, Molly Ritmiller, Liana Grobstein, Ana Toledano, Shi Zhang, Jade Manbodh, Effie Mbrow, Ezekiel Golan.

Caddisfly Printed Case
Mitchell Joachim, Vivian Kuan, Shi Zhang, Matt Mitchell, Taili Zhuang, Ana Toledano, Molly Ritmiller, Liana Grobstein, Michael Chambers, Jade Manbodh, Effie Mbrow.

Hive of Beehives
Mitchell Joachim, Vivan Kuan, Nina Edwards Anker, Lisa Richardson, Nicholas Gervasi, Liana Grobstein, Theo Dimitrasopoulos, Zack Saunders, Xinye Lin, Sabrina Naumovski, Jules Pepitone, Rita Wang, Michael Brittenham, Daniel S Castano, Aidan Nelson.

III. CIVIC + ECOLOGY

Urbaneering Brooklyn
Mitchell Joachim, Maria Aiolova, Melanie Fessel, Dan O'Connor, Celina Yee, Alpna Gupta, Sishir Varghese, Aaron Lim, Greg Mulholland, Derek Ziemer, Thilani Rajarathna, John Nelson, Natalie DeLuca, Emily VanderVeen, Yu Ping Hsieh.

New York 2106
Mitchell Joachim, Makoto Okazaki, Kent Hikida, Serdar Omer, Andrei Vovk, Noura Al Sayeh, Byron Stigge,

Nathan Leverence, Oliver Medvedik, Lukas Lenherr, Matt Kipilman, Adam Watson, Michael Sorkin, Craig Schwitter.

IV. PUBLIC + ACTION

Urban Tangle
Mitchell Joachim, Vivian Kuan, Maria Aiolova, Matthew Mitchell, Mat Sokol, Shandor Hassan, Molly Ritmiller, Jasmine Hwang, Janghee Lee, Liana Grobstein.

Power of the City
Mitchell Joachim, Maria Aiolova, Melanie Fessel, Adrian De Silva, Laura Goard, Ian Newborn, Caleb Lowery, Kieran Thomas, Viagnehy Fernandez.

V. WATER + RESOURCE

Governors' Hook
Mitchell Joachim, Maria Aiolova, Melanie Fessel, Christian Hubert, Greg Mulholland, Linn Blasberg, Susanna Burrows, Adrian De Silva, Bojana Djukanovic, Shruti Grover, Elizabeth Haid, Jacqueline Hall, Andrew Liang, Pianka Paul, Savina Romanos, Josef Schrock, James Schwartz, Stefan Stanojevic, Ignacio Suqu, Wagdy Moussa.

Super Docking Navy Yard
Mitchell Joachim, Nurhan Gokturk, Maria Aiolova, David Maestres, Jason Vigneri Beane, Carlos Barrios, Alex Felson, Walter Meyer, Melanie Fessel, Zafirah Bacchus, Ivy Chan, Courtney Chin, Adrian De Silva, Julianne Geary, Francisco Gill, Shima Ghafouri, Jacqueline Hall, Kelly Kim, Florian Lorenz, Bart Mangold, Dustin Mattiza, Chema Perez, Alsira Raxhimi, Daniel Russoniello, Melody Song, Allison Shockley, Katherine Sullivan.

VI. WASTE + UPCYCLED

Rapid Re(f)use
Mitchell Joachim, Maria Aiolova, Melanie Fessel, Emily Johnson, Ian Slover, Philip Weller, Zachary Aders, Webb Allen, Niloufar Karimzadegan, Lauren Sarafan.

Babel Waste Capital
Mitchell Joachim, Maria Aiolova, Melanie Fessel, Wagdy Moussa, Spencer Nelson, James Schwartz, Jacqueline Hall, Bart Mangold, Paul Miller AKA DJ Spooky, Oliver Langbein.

VII. HOUSING + RESILIENCE

Homeway
Mitchell Joachim, Maria Aiolova, Melanie Fessel, Philip Weller, Ian Slover, Landon Young, Cecil Howell, Andrea Michalski, Sofie Bamberg, Alex Colard, Zachary Aders, Christian Hubert, Nicholas Gervasi.

Fab Tree Hab
Mitchell Joachim, Lara Greden, Javier Arbona, Landon Young, Ezekiel Golan.

VIII. ENERGY + REGENERATIVE

Post-Carbon City State
Mitchell Joachim, Melanie Fessel, Nurhan Gokturk, Maria Aiolova, Oliver Medvedik, Amanda O'Keefe, Royal Aaron, Kiril Bejoulev, Lafayette Compton, Emmanuelle Emmel, Lila Faria, Daniella Garcia, Dan Gehr, Nicholas Gervasi, Marcos Gonzalez-Bode, Jesslyn Guntur, Hugo Husnu, Michelle Lavin, Jorge Lopez, Estefania Maldonado, Anna Murnane, Dilan Ozka, Michelle Qu, Matt Solomon, Allie Sutherland, Eda Yetim, Peter Zhang, Jennifer Zhao, Rayne Holm, Kristopher Menos, Ivy Feibig, Swati Mamgain, Pablo Berger.

Peristalcity
Mitchell Joachim, Neri Oxman.

School of the Earth
Mitchell Joachim, Peder Anker, Kristina Goncharova, Karim Ahmed, Gary Chung, Nicholas Gervasi, Aleksandr Plotkin, Nunnapat Ratanavanh, Ryan Porter Andrewsen, Aliza Joy Blond, Cash Callaghan, Danielle Margo Domsky, Juan Diego Galvez, Sophia Hampton, Michelle Lee Johnson, Laura Sejin Jung, Devansh Majithia, Annie Pluimer, Cecilia Reid, Arielle Ross, Olivia Catherine Saber, Alejandro Santana, Sabrina Santos, Joshua Shapiro, Cate Stitt Stern, Hanna Stern, Rachel Stern, Celine Sutter, Leland R Sutton, Zoya Teirstein, Jenna Zimmerman.

IX. MOBILITY + ORGANIC

Soft Mobs and Smart Dots
Mitchell Joachim, Aurel von Richthofen, Lydia Kallipoliti, Matt Cunningham, Fred James, Maria Aiolova, William J. Mitchell, Patrik Kunzler, Axel Kilian, Robyn Allen, Louis Basel, Raul-David Poblano, William Lark, Franco Variani, Chee Xu, James Chao-Ming Teng, Peter Schmitt, Yanni Loukissas, Douglas Joachim, Luis Rafael Berrios-Negron, Lorene Gates-Spears, Timocin Pervane, Yu Ping Hsieh.

X. FOOD + WELLNESS

Cricket Shelter
Mitchell Joachim, Maria Aiolova, Melanie Fessel, Vivian Kuan, Felipe Molina, Matthew Tarpley, Oliver Medvedik, Jiachen Xu, Lissette Olivares, Cheto Castellano, Shandor Hassan, Christian Hamrick, Ivan Fuentealba, Sung Moon, Kamila Varela, Yucel Guven, Chloe Byrne, Miguel Lantigua-Inoa, Alex Colard.

Plug-In Ecology
Mitchell Joachim, Maria Aiolova, Melanie Fessel, Christian Hubert, Vivian Kuan, Amanda O'Keefe, Bahar

Avanoglu, Ipek Avanoglu, Pedro Galindo-Landeira, Yinan Li, Brent Solomon, Jiachen Xu, Huy Buy, Regina Flores Mir, Jimmy Tang.

Loudenberg, David Maestres, Kyle McDonald, Dan Paluska, Matt Parker, Andrew Personette, Marc Schwartz, Pablo Souto, Jenna Spevack, Richard The, Matt Tyson, Jason Vigneri-Beane, Bill Washabaugh, Christopher Woebken, Peter Yeadon.

ONE LAB STUDENTS

Ian Paukman, Amy Butchko, Allison Dianne Pienh, Anton M. Savov, Alice Edmonson, Armando Torrepuerto, Becky Alprin, Brian Holland, Carloss Mann, Carcen Nachreiner, Christopher Kieran, Celia Goldsmith, Daisuke Nagamoto, Dan Albert, Derrick Campbell, Dietmar Koering, Dong-Joo Kim, Ed Akins, Ellen Depoorter, Greg Mulholland, Hadley Musselman, Ian Slover, Irene Matteini, Jennifer Linger, Judy T. Kasperovich, Justin Taylor, Larolina Jastrzebska, Karen Kemp, Lesley Roth, Marielle Vargas, Mila Ducheva, Nicholas Pascual, Naomi Rowland, Patrick Candalla, Rashmi Ramaswamy, Ryan Manning, Timothy Brennan, Varun A. Kaushik, Orlando C. Quarless, Sara Newey, Tyler Madden, Vaclav Malek, Nancy Kim, Anthony Stahl, Izabela Karczmarczyk, William Q. Smith, Eva Nemcova, Annabelle Hernandez, Hazem Ahmed, Rebekka Hennig, Alex Sammet, Joanna Pierchala, Annette Williamson, Jennifer Birkeland, Vicki Karlan, Daryl Round, Anne Paillard, Yen Trinh, Tatsui Yuki, Marcus Owens, Monica Hernandez, Lee Youngwhan, Lee Heekyoung, Shim Hoonyong, Kim Minjoo,Choi Songhee, Park Won, Marco Antonio Castro Cosio, Abhijeet Koli, Ahmed Salah-Eldin Abdel-aziz Abou-Elsaad, Anca Matyiku, Ashwini Ashokkumar, Camila A. Morales, Carlos Andres Bolano, Dan Selden, Daniel Russoniello, Gabriel Fuentes, Gabriel Fuentes, Ignacio Diaz-Maroto Rivas, Irene Figueroa Ortiz, Jessy Slim, Khalid Mohammed Hassan El-Mansi, Khalid Mohammed Hassan El-Mansi, Kirsten Ostberg, Michaela Macleod, Neeraj Chatterji, Rena Mande, Susana Eslava, Daniel Olarte, Andrés Carter, Emily Glass, Emily Glass, Brenda Perez, Jacqueline Moldanado, Yasaman Sheri, Zachary Mitchell, Stuart Hyatt, Rayne B. Holm, Henry Wang, Chloe Byrne, Jesslyn Guntur, Jake Madoff, Timothé Husson, Lila Faria,

Matthew Solomon, Annie Liang, Ellen Wood, Bryan Navarro, Mabel Plasencia, Megan Ma, Minkun Kim, Rosa Newman, John Angelo Alonzo, Rawan Alsaffar, Guillaume Bellanger, Pieter Bertheloot, Sean Crowley, Shira Davis, Ella Dorfman, Brandon Ellis, Akshay Goyal, Kevin Hall, Naomi Kaly, Iwanka Kultschyckyj, Sophie Laffont, Whitney Lewis, Zhewei Lin, Jacob Lindsay, Chris Merritt, Hallie Miller, Masha Pekurovsky, Ji Qu, John Rice, Doug Robb, Gina Rodriguez, Giacomo Trentanovi, Caroline Wallis, Hayden White, Elizabeth Anne Williams, Raffaella Zanotti, Xin Zhong, Alexandra Nasar, Thomas John Gooch, Graham Girard, Hikmet Burcin Nalinci, Nicholas Gervasi, Jos Singer, Manjulia Singh, Mel de Jager, Ahmad Khan, Aliya Tejani, Monica Hutton, Tega Brain, Cecil Mariani.

EMERITUS FELLOWS AND COLLABORATORS

Zachary Aders, Noura Al Sayeh, James Allen, Zafirah Bacchus, Sofie Bamberg, Kate Bancks, Linn Blasberg, Anna Bokov, Cory Budischak, Susanna Burrows, Ivy Chan, Courtney Chin, Subhajit Das, Natalie De Luca, Mila Ducheva, Bojana Djukanovic, Viagnehy Fernandez, Melanie Fessel, Contessa Gayles, Julianne Geary, Shima Ghafouri, Francisco Gill, Laura Goard, Nurhan Gokturk, Alpna Gupta, Jacqueline Hall, Shivina Harjani, Kent Hikida, Cecil Howell, Yu Ping Hsieh, Emily Johnson, Kelly Kim, Matt Kipilman, Niloufar Karimzadegan, Lukas Lenherr, Nathan Leverence, Andrew Liang, Aaron Lim, Florian Lorenz, Caleb Lowery, Bart Mangold, Dustin Mattiza, Lesley Merz, Andrea Michalski, Greg Mulholland, John Nelson, Ian Newborn, Makoto Okazaki, Serdar Omer, Alan Paukman, Pianka Paul, Chema Perez, Thilani Rajarathna, Annie Raso, Nishan Ratinam, Alsira Raxhimi, Savina Romanos, Natalia Roumelioti, Daniel Russoniello, Lauren Sarafan, James Schwartz, Craig Schwitter, Allison Shockley, Ian Slover, Melody Song, Michael Sorkin, Stefan Stanojevic, Byron Stigge, Katherine Sullivan, Nacho Suque, Eric Tan, Kieran Thomas, Sishir Varghese, Emily VanderVeen, Andrei Vovk, Adam Watson, Philip Weller, Celina Yee, Derek Ziemer.

Design with Life

We wish to thank our Executive Director, Vivian Kuan for her nonstop heroic leadership and limitless intelligence. Correspondingly, we'd like to recognize all of the remarkable Board of Directors at Terreform ONE over these many years; David Stewart, Heather Lord, John Rudikoff, Scott Pobiner, Christian Hubert, Alex Polier, Dinah Fried, Lisa Richardson, Pat Sapinsley, Eliot Hodges, Marc Neveu, Sanford Kwinter, David Belt, Victoria Stockman, Andrei Vovk, and Jessica Catlow.

The projects included in this book are possible because of the continuous support of our primary collaborators, teammates, and incredible companions; Oliver Medvedik, Nurhan Gokturk, Anna Bokov, Dan O'Connor, Marcel Botha, Ioanna Theocharopoulou, Liana Grobstein, Nicholas Gervasi, Axel Kilian, Nina Edwards Anker, Peder Anker, Louise Harpman, Lukas Kronawitter, and Mike Silver.

Several key grants and resources funded the book. Special thanks for Dean Susanne Wofford and the NYU Gallatin School of Individualized Study. Without Susanne's keen vision and inspiration, this would not be attainable.

Also, the assistance and reassurance of so many colleagues and friends helped push our efforts forward; Al Attara, Christopher J. Glancy, Paul D. Miller aka D.J. Spooky, Kelly Loudenberg, James Patten, Deb Johnson, Jason Vigneri-Beane, Carlos Roberto Barrios, Alex Felson, Walter Meyer, and David Maestres.

We would like to equally thank our network of magnanimous visionaries for encouragement and support; Randy Rosenberg, Lisa Deanne Smith, Matilda McQuaid, Caroline O'Connell, Laura Marie Partynski, Suzanne Marie Musho, Elise Kissling, Betsy Arnone, Michael Fletcher, David Gilmore, Bob Fisher, Jim Cramer, Julie Bargmann, Joe Bargman, Peter Yeadon, Alexandros Washburn, Jonathan Massey, Alex Krieger, Hashim Sarkis, Evan Douglis, Bjarke Ingels, Bruce Lindsey, Richard Sommer, Marc Angelil, Michelle Addington, Alejandro Zaera Polo, Eva Franch, Rachel Armstrong, Philip Beesley, Wellington Duke Reiter, Margie Ruddick, Larry Sass, Winka Dubbeldam, Chris Perry, Mitch McEwen, Natalie Jeremijenko, Paola Antonelli, Raoul Bunschoten, Scott Cohen, Simone Rothman, Mark Chambers, Gerald Bast, Jackie Jangana, and Alyson Griffin.

Furthermore, we'd like to thank the gracious people at Actar; Ricardo Devesa, Ramon Prat, and Marga Gibert for their insight, dedication, and patience.

This book is dedicated to William J. Mitchell and Vito Acconci.

With love to our family members; Mia Carmen Joachim, and Maxxa Eve Joachim, Stephen Mann and Dr. Lubomir Aiolov (1940-2014).

**Design with Life: Biotech Architecture
and Resilient Cities**
Terreform ONE
by Mitchell Joachim
and Maria Aiolova

Published by
Actar Publishers, New York, Barcelona
www.actar.com

Authors
Mitchell Joachim
Maria Aiolova

Edited by
Terreform ONE

Graphic Design
Actar Publishers
and Terreform ONE

Copy editing and proofs:
Irina T. Oryshkevich
Theo Dimitrasopoulos
Tyler Rose Mann

Photographic credits:
Terreform ONE

Printing and binding
Tiger Printing, Hong Kong

Distribution
Actar D, Inc. New York, Barcelona.
New York
440 Park Avenue South, 17th Floor
New York, NY 10016, USA
T +1 2129662207
salesnewyork@actar-d.com
Barcelona
Roca i Batlle 2-4
08023 Barcelona, Spain
T +34 933 282 183
eurosales@actar-d.com

Indexing
ISBN:978-1-948765-20-6
PCN: Library of Congress Control Number:
2019933631

Printed in China

Publication date: July 2019